God and Moral Law

God and Moral Law

On the Theistic Explanation of Morality

Mark C. Murphy

OXFORD
UNIVERSITY PRESS

Great Clarendon Street, Oxford OX2 6DP

Oxford University Press is a department of the University of Oxford.
It furthers the University's objective of excellence in research, scholarship,
and education by publishing worldwide in

Oxford   New York

Auckland Cape Town Dar es Salaam Hong Kong Karachi
Kuala Lumpur Madrid Melbourne Mexico City Nairobi
New Delhi Shanghai Taipei Toronto

With offices in

Argentina Austria Brazil Chile Czech Republic France Greece
Guatemala Hungary Italy Japan Poland Portugal Singapore
South Korea Switzerland Thailand Turkey Ukraine Vietnam

Oxford is a registered trade mark of Oxford University Press
in the UK and in certain other countries

Published in the United States
by Oxford University Press Inc., New York

© Mark C. Murphy 2011

The moral rights of the author have been asserted
Database right Oxford University Press (maker)

First published 2011

All rights reserved. No part of this publication may be reproduced,
stored in a retrieval system, or transmitted, in any form or by any means,
without the prior permission in writing of Oxford University Press,
or as expressly permitted by law, or under terms agreed with the appropriate
reprographics rights organization. Enquiries concerning reproduction
outside the scope of the above should be sent to the Rights Department,
Oxford University Press, at the address above

You must not circulate this book in any other binding or cover
and you must impose the same condition on any acquirer

British Library Cataloguing in Publication Data
Data available

Library of Congress Cataloging in Publication Data
Data available

Typeset by SPI Publisher Services, Pondicherry, India
Printed in Great Britain
on acid-free paper by
MPG Books Group, Bodmin and King's Lynn

ISBN 978-0-19-969366-5

1 3 5 7 9 10 8 6 4 2

for Onora Ann

Acknowledgments

Like many moral philosophers who describe themselves as "natural law theorists," I have often played up the natural law view's image as a moral theory that is not essentially theistic. The defining theses of the natural law view—at least insofar as it is a theory of practical rationality and morality—seem to contain nothing that marks it as a theistic theory, and so it seems that both the theist and the nontheist should be able to sign on. Over the years, though, I have come to wonder whether I, as a Christian theist, should think of this aspect of natural law theory as a merit of the view rather than as an obvious shortcoming. If theism is true, shouldn't the truth of theism penetrate to the core of the correct view of morality? And isn't that above all else the reason for the seemingly continual return by theists to divine command theory—that, despite its explanatory shortcomings, it at least places God at the place in a moral theory where theists should expect to find God?

This book is a reflection on these questions. I am aware of its inadequacies—at least some of them—but I hope that others pursuing these issues will do better than I have, and will be helped to do better by the arguments that they find here.

I owe thanks to a number of good philosophers who took time to offer criticisms and suggestions on various parts of the book: Ron Belgau, Mike Bergmann, Jason Baldwin, Jeff Brower, Paul Draper, John Drummond, Tom Flint, Mark Formichelli, Fred Freddoso, Adam Green, Clint Hall, John Hare, Kelly Heuer, Bill Jaworski, Pat Kain, Nate King, Alasdair MacIntyre, Paddy McShane, Trenton Merricks, Jeremy Neill, Sam Newlands, John O'Callaghan, Nate Olson, Al Plantinga, Alex Pruss, Mike Rea, Jim Sterba, Kevin Vallier, and Christina van Dyke. I owe thanks also to audience members at Notre Dame, Purdue, Calvin College, Colgate, and the 2010 Baylor-sponsored Philosophy of Religion Workshop for discussion of various pieces of the overall argument. I am indebted as well to the Society of Christian Philosophers, the Fordham Natural Law Colloquium, the St. Anselm Institute at the University of Virginia, and the Center for Philosophy of Religion at the University of Notre Dame for lecture invitations that allowed me to present an overview of the book's argument to perceptive (and occasionally wonderfully hostile) listeners, and thus to get a clearer sense of what work needed to be done to make a plausible case for the view of the relationship between God and moral law defended here. I am grateful also for the work of the referees at Oxford University Press for their care in reading and commenting critically upon the manuscript.

I had the good fortune to work out the main lines of the view of moral law presented in Chapters 1 and 2 in a seminar with some of Georgetown's top-flight graduate students: Mark Formichelli, Clint Hall, Kelly Heuer, Alex Kipp, Oren Magid, Tony Manela, Luke Maring, Nate Olson, and Liz Winokur offered helpful suggestions and raised troubling problems for my view of moral law, and I am lucky to get to work with them. I had a chance to think through in a more focused way issues of theistic explanation in ethics with Clint Hall, Kelly Heuer, and Paddy McShane. Georgetown is a wonderful place to work on ethics and it is due in large part to the talented students who come here.

I received support for this work from Notre Dame's Center for Philosophy of Religion, where I was privileged to be the Alvin Plantinga Fellow during the 2009–2010 academic year; during that period, I was also generously supported by Georgetown University through a senior faculty research fellowship. Through most of the writing of the book I was supported by the Fr. Joseph T. Durkin, SJ Chair; shortly before its completion, I was appointed as the Robert L. McDevitt, K.S.G., K.C. H.S. and Catherine H. McDevitt L.C.H.S. Professor of Religious Philosophy. I hope that this book honors the memory of Fr. Durkin and that of Robert and Catherine McDevitt, all of whom are treasured members of the Georgetown community.

I am grateful to the editors of the *Stanford Encyclopedia of Philosophy* for permission to use some of the material from my entries "The Natural Law Tradition in Ethics" and "Theological Voluntarism." I thank also Cambridge University Press for permission to use some of the material from my "Finnis on Nature, Reason, God" (*Legal Theory* 13 (2007), pp. 187–209) and Oxford University Press for permission to use a few paragraphs from my "Morality and Divine Authority" (*Oxford Handbook to Philosophical Theology*, eds. Thomas P. Flint and Michael C. Rea, 2008, pp. 306–31).

My greatest debt is, as always, to my wife, Jeanette. I could not have a better friend.

Mark C. Murphy

Herndon, Virginia
February 11, 2011

Contents

Acknowledgments   vi

Introduction: God and morality   1
0.1 A familiar question pursued in a less familiar way   1
0.2 God as perfect being, and God as explainer   6
0.3 The argument to come   12

1. Moral law   14
   1.1 A sectarian explanandum?   14
   1.2 Moral laws are not merely moral generalizations   18
   1.3 A systems account of moral law rejected   22
   1.4 A universals account of moral law affirmed   30
   1.5 Defeasibility and moral laws   39
   1.6 The ecumenical character of moral law   42

2. Theistic explanation of moral law   45
   2.1 Moral facts, explanation, and theistic explanation   45
   2.2 Moral law and the explanation of moral facts   49
   2.3 Theistic explanation of morality: the obvious strategy   60
   2.4 What sort of theistic explanation?   61

3. Natural law theory   69
   3.1 What is a natural law theory?   69
   3.2 Natural law theory fails to satisfy explanans-centered criteria   74
   3.3 The natural law theorist's first reply: the content of the good   74
   3.4 The natural law theorist's second reply: natural law as law   76
   3.5 The natural law theorist's third reply: God in the explanatory background   80
   3.6 The natural law theorist's fourth reply: divine responsibility for properties   85

3.7 The natural law theorist's fifth reply: natural law as not explanation-eligible 90
3.8 A theistic moral argument against standard natural law theory, partially developed 95
3.9 The explanans-centered argument against natural law theory extended 97

4. Theological voluntarism 100
   4.1 "Divine command theory" and "theological voluntarism" 100
   4.2 Rival versions of theological voluntarism 107
   4.3 Explanandum- and explanans-centered objections to theological voluntarism 116
   4.4 Theological voluntarism and the social character of obligation 124

5. Theistic explanation of the laws of nature 133
   5.1 Bad news and good news 133
   5.2 Mere conservationist and occasionalist accounts of the laws of nature 134
   5.3 Mere conservationism and natural law theory 139
   5.4 Occasionalism and theological voluntarism 140
   5.5 A third way: concurrentism and the laws of nature 142

6. Moral concurrentism 148
   6.1 The basic idea of moral concurrentism 148
   6.2 Concurrentist goodness 150
   6.3 Concurrentist moral necessitation 161
   6.4 A theistic moral argument against standard natural law theory, completed 165
   6.5 Concurrentist moral necessitation and moral obligation 166
   6.6 Concurrentist moral necessitation and the "immoralities of the patriarchs" 172
   6.7 Explanans- and explanandum-centered success 180

References 181
Index 189

Introduction: God and morality

0.1 A familiar question pursued in a less familiar way

This book responds to a familiar question by offering an unfamiliar answer defended in an unfamiliar way. The familiar question is that of the relationship between God and morality: is morality explained by facts about God, and if so, in what way? I will sketch the unfamiliar answer at the end of this chapter (0.3), though it will be unhelpful to present the details of that view until we have seen the inadequacies of the views currently on offer. I begin instead with some remarks about the distinctive character of the methodology I employ, and how this methodology differs from other treatments of the problem.

A common and extremely useful way of approaching the problem of the relationship between God and morality is to proceed in what I call an *explanandum-driven* way. Here is a crude way of describing the explanandum-driven approach, which I think will strike everyone as familiar. When one takes an explanandum-driven approach to a problem, one first tries to get clear on the character of the explanandum; one then asks what are the various explanans-candidates that would, if actual, be sufficient to account for the explanandum; one then asks whether any of these explanans-candidates are actual, or, alternatively, whether any of these explanans-candidates are such that its capacities to explain the explanandum give us good reason to believe that it is actual.

The great bulk of work on the relationship between God and morality has proceeded in this explanandum-driven way. The idea is that morality has a number of fascinating features that either individually or in combination call for explanation, and so it is a task for moral philosophers to ask how morality is to be explained, and, importantly for our purposes, whether such explanations will include facts about God. Consider, say, the *normativity* of morals. Both theists and nontheists have been impressed by the weirdness of normativity, with its very otherness, and have thought that whatever we say about normativity, it will have to be a story not about natural properties but nonnatural ones (Moore 1903, §13). And so Mavrodes argues on this basis that since morality exhibits such normativity, it must be understood in theistic terms; otherwise, the normativity of morality is unintelligible (Mavrodes 1986). Again: consider the *overridingness* of morals. The domain of the moral, it is commonly thought, consists in a range of values that can demand absolute allegiance, in the sense that it is never reasonable to act contrary to what those values finally require. One deep difficulty with this view, formulated in a number of ways but perhaps most memorably by Sidgwick (1907, pp. 497–509), is that it is hard to see how moral value automatically trumps other kinds of value (for example, prudential value) when they conflict. But if the domain of the moral were to be understood in terms of the will of a being who can make it possible that, or even ensure that, the balance of reasons is always in favor of acting in accordance with the moral demand, then the overridingness of morals becomes far easier to explain (Layman 2002). These arguments work by identifying some feature of morality that seems explanation-eligible and arguing that the only, or the best, way to account for these features is by making morality somehow dependent upon God. (I am not endorsing either of these arguments.)

It is important that this explanandum-driven method need not be the province of those who try to maintain some sort of neutrality between theism and nontheism when pursuing investigations in moral philosophy, whether due to substantive agnosticism or methodological scruples.[1] Someone who believes that God exists and is available for use in explanations may pursue this strategy. So might someone who rejects God's existence; such a one might want to give explanandum-driven arguments that morality is better explained on an assumption of atheism (see, for

---

[1] Plantinga (1984) argues that theists ought not to have such methodological scruples; see also Wolterstorff 2009, pp. 162–6. My point here, though, is that even those who take Plantinga's and Wolterstorff's views to heart might nevertheless mistakenly think that the only role that theism plays in philosophical argument is as offering an additional potential explanans for some explanandum.

example, Antony 2008, Hubin 2008, or Maitzen 2009), or might want to allow that moral considerations give some evidence for theism, though it is evidence that is defeated or outweighed by other considerations. It is true, though, that pursuit of this strategy has what we might call "apologetic import": if we would get a better explanation for some feature of morality by way of an explanation that includes God, that gives some evidence for affirming God's existence. (See, for example, Adams 1979b.)

Thinking through the relationship between God and morality cannot be fruitfully pursued, I agree, without allowing explanandum-driven considerations to frame one's investigations.[2] But the distinctive method of this book is that its investigation is also driven by explanans-focused considerations.

In order to make clear how explanans-driven arguments differ from explanandum-driven arguments, it will be useful to begin with a mundane example. Suppose that you leave a bowl of water in a locked room for a week. There is no other source of water in the room. When you return, the bowl looks undisturbed, but now has no water in it. We expect that there is an explanation for this change. One set of considerations to which we will appeal in deciding on the proper explanation arises from the facts to be explained: we can ask, abstractly, what possible causes there might be that would be sufficient to do the job, to transform the bowl from full to empty. We might think that, abstractly considered, given the position of the bowl, it is equally likely that the water simply evaporated and that the water was drunk by some animal. If the considerations upon which we rely in evaluating rival potential explanations in this case are solely explanandum-driven, so that we assess those potential explanations entirely in terms of their sufficiency for explaining the phenomenon to be explained, we might be indifferent between the thirsty animal explanation

---

[2] The question of when explanandum-focused considerations justify theistic explanation is the central issue of Gregory Dawes's *Theism and Explanation* (Dawes 2009). Dawes's focus in that book is entirely on explanandum-focused considerations; whether this is because he does not accept the possibility of what I call "explanans-focused considerations" militating in favor of theistic explanation or because he is in that book interested only in that particular sort of explanation is not clear. At any rate, while I of course accept the centrality of explanandum-focused considerations in theistic ethics, I reject Dawes's position, underargued, that theistic explanation is causal explanation and thus intentional explanation. If there is such a thing as constitutive explanation (cf. Schroeder 2008, pp. 61–79), then theistic explanation need not be causal explanation. As we will see, some sorts of account of God's role in the explanation of moral law make the divine role constitutive, while others make that role causal.

and the evaporation explanation. But when we focus on the fact that *there is a cat still alive in the room*, we will settle on the cat as the explanation for the water's disappearance: for had the cat not drunk the water, there would not still be a living cat in the room; we'd have an ex-cat. Cats are *explainers*: cats' characteristic activities are to explain depletions of oxygen molecules and increases in carbon dioxide molecules, the addition of fur to a sofa-environment, the exchange of relatively pure water in one location with cat piss in another, and so forth. If something is not such as to characteristically explain these things, then it is not a cat. To be more explicit: a being that does not actually do enough such explaining, even if it was once a cat, will cease to be cat—it will become a dead cat. But what we have here in this locked room is a *live* cat; and since live cats *have to* explain the exchange of relatively pure water in one location with cat piss in another, we know what the best explanation for the emptying of the bowl is: the cat drank it. The fixing on this explanation is *explanans*-driven: there is a feature of the situation that *must explain*, and so we incorporate it into our explanation.

The feline explanation of the water's disappearance may fail to be superior to the evaporation explanation on explanandum-driven grounds alone; its superiority is clear only once we take both explanandum- and explanans-driven considerations into account. There was something that called for explanation, and both *it evaporated due to the dry, warm, moving air* and *it was drunk by the cat* may be sufficient to explain the change of the bowl from full to empty. But there was a further set of considerations, explanans-driven considerations, concerning the nature and continuing existence of the cat, which makes the feline explanation superior. To be a cat is to be a being that explains certain phenomena; and so the continuing existence of a cat can make a cat-involved explanation superior to a non-cat-involved explanation.

It is important to see that explanans-driven arguments are not just explanandum-driven arguments in which we have already posited the existence of one of the explanans-candidates. What is interestingly distinctive about explanans-driven explanation is not only that we take to exist an object sufficient to do the explanatory work; what is interestingly distinctive is that we take to exist an object that *necessarily* does that sort of explanatory work, something the *essence* or *nature* of which it is to do that sort of explaining. So we may believe that there is sunlight in the room, and a cat in the room, and both the sunlight and the cat are sufficient to do the job of removing the water from the bowl. What is important from the perspective of explanans-driven explanation is that while the sunlight can exist without evaporating water, the cat cannot exist without taking in water. It is part of what it is to be a cat to do that sort of explanatory work; it is not part of what it is to be sunlight to do that sort of explanatory work.

My point in moving to a discussion of cats and their nature as explainers of the movement of water is to call attention to the road less traveled in thinking through the problem of the relationship between God and morality. This way of approaching the problem does not begin with our focusing on certain puzzling features of morality and asking whether we might sufficiently account for them by nontheistic rather than theistic explanations. It begins, rather, with our focusing on God, and God's role in explanation. God is like the cat in one way: God is an explainer. But, rather obviously, God is not like the cat. For to be a cat is to be the explainer of a feline-specific range of phenomena, in a feline specific way; but God is the first cause, the ultimate explainer of what is the case—to be God is to enter into the explanation of *everything* that is explanation-eligible. (As Aquinas puts it, "God necessarily causes existing in everything that exists" (*Compendium of Theology*, ch. 68).) I will say more about why theism is committed to this view in the next section (0.2). But for the moment let it suffice to say that this view does seem to be part and parcel of mere theism.

Unlike explanandum-driven explanations, explanans-driven explanations lack apologetic value. If one argues, even conclusively, that given God's existence, God's character as essential explainer militates in favor of a certain theistic account of morality, that gives the nontheist no reason to suppose that the best explanation of morality is a theistic explanation (Compare: even if, given a living cat's presence in the room, the cat's character as essential explainer of losses of water militates in favor of a feline explanation for the water's disappearing, that does not give someone who denies that there is or ever was a cat in the room any reason to suppose that the best explanation of the water's disappearance is a feline explanation.) One might draw from this concession the inference that the investigation in this book must be of little interest to those who are skeptical about God's existence, however great the interest may be to those interested in working out the implications of their theistic beliefs.

There is more than one way to respond here, but let me focus on one that I take to be most important. Moral philosophy is often practiced today under an assumption that theism makes no essential difference to ethics (cf. Brink 2007 and Sinnott-Armstrong 2009). If this assumption were true, then we should reach the same basic results in ethics if we assume the truth of theism.[3] And I do assume the truth of theism here. But once we assume the truth of theism, we leave open the possibility that not only explanandum-driven but also explanans-driven considerations will push toward a theistic account of morality. To put it another way, once we assume theism, it may turn out that what ultimately moves us to a theistic account of morality is not so much distinctive features of morality but distinctive features of God. If this turns out to be the case—and this book argues that it is the case—then it is false that theism makes no essential difference to ethics. And that is something that everyone interested in ethics, theist or nontheist, should want to know.

0.2 God as perfect being, and God as explainer

The distinctive method of the book, then, is to bring explanans-centered considerations to the fore in thinking through the relationship between God and morality. This method has merit only if God is plausibly held to be an essential explainer, in the sense characterized in 0.1. What reasons, though, do we have to accept this thesis? I am not asking here for a proof of theism; I will take theism for granted here. What I am asking is whether, *given* theism, we have good reason to think that theism commits one to certain views on God's explanatory role.

I will put to the side what seems plain from the Abrahamic religions' conception of God, which is that one of the central characterizations of God is as creator and sustainer of the whole world. As a matter of revealed theology, it seems plain that God should be understood as having a central explanatory role. But, aside from questions about the propriety of appeal to revelation in this context, it is unclear whether we can get the stronger claim—not just that God is explainer, but God as essential explainer—from revelation. I suggest that instead we argue from perfect being theology—that is, that if we accept the methodology of perfect being theology,

---

[3] Those who deny that theism makes a fundamental difference to ethics may well allow that it could make a difference in the *application* of basic moral norms—perhaps the theist has reason to think that, given a true principle about showing gratitude and theistic claims about the source of good for human beings, we ought to show gratitude to God, while the nontheist has no such reasons.

we will arrive at the conclusion that God has an essential explanatory role with respect to everything that is explanation-eligible.

I understand by "perfect being theology" a technique by which de dicto necessary truths about God are established, employing as its master premise the proposition that God is absolutely perfect and as subsidiary premises propositions regarding the attributes that an absolutely perfect being must exhibit (see, for example, Morris 1987c and Rogers 2000). So the conclusions of perfect being theology are propositions that any being that counts as God must exhibit certain attributes. The substantial burdens borne by a practitioner of perfect being theology are those of making clear both what attributes count as perfections and what reasons we have for thinking them to be perfections. Practitioners of perfect being theology also tend to concern themselves with the further implications that we can draw from God's having these perfections, that is, what are the further (nontrivial) properties that God exhibits that are entailed either by God's having all the relevant perfections or by God's having the relevant perfections along with other necessary or contingent truths.

Does the method of perfect being theology generate the result that God is an essential explainer? Here is a quick argument that it does. The received view is that the divine perfection entails that God is the creator of everything that is not divine. (That is, necessarily, if x is not divine, then God creates x.) Now, if God is the creator of everything that is not divine, then everything that exists is explained by God. Whatever God creates is explained by God's activity. And whatever God does not create is divine, on this view, and so its existence is explained by being somehow related—being identical to, or an aspect of, etc.—the self-existent God.

What I think requires further comment, not just on its own account but as laying the groundwork for later arguments strengthening the thesis of God as essential explainer (2.4), is why we should accept the received view within perfect being theology that God is creator of everything that is distinct from God. Arguments in favor of including this as a divine perfection can proceed either as brute appeals to intuition, or as best capturing a variety of particular judgments we make concerning creation (or bringing-into-existence more generally), or as included within other, better-established divine perfections.[4]

---

[4] The inclusion notion is important; you can't show that some feature is a perfection just by its being entailed by a perfection. *Being omnipotent* is a perfection; *being purple or omnipotent* is

There is little on record from current users of perfect being theology defending the view that creator-of-all-else is a divine perfection, though it is often stated with confidence. Perhaps there is so little written on behalf of this as a divine perfection because its status as such is just obvious. But perhaps we can generate some pressure to give a more perspicuous account. We might note, for example, that being creator-of-all-else does not imply being the creator of anything. We might ask, then, why is being creator-of-all-else-that-exists such a great thing, even when God might have chosen to create nothing at all?

Some users of perfect being theology try to connect God's being omnipotent to God's being creator-of-all-else. So Morris writes that the doctrine that "all things are ontologically dependent on God" is "entailed by the Anselmian conception of God"—that is, God as conceived as absolutely perfect. Morris elaborates:

> It will follow from the Anselmian conception that if any contingent being, or universe of such beings, exists, it must stand in the relation of being created ex nihilo. For the Anselmian God is understood to be omnipotent or almighty. And it is a conceptual truth that an omnipotent or almighty being cannot rely on any independent source for its products. (Morris 1987b, p. 13)

And here is van Inwagen, on the inclusion of *creator-of-all-else-that-exists* in his list of divine perfections:

> If there is a God, then there never was a chaos of prime matter that existed independently of his power and his will, waiting through an eternity of years for him to impress form on it. This could not be, for, if there is a God, nothing does or could exist independently of his will or independently of his creative power. God creates things from the ground up, ontologically speaking. His creation is, as they say, ex nihilo. (van Inwagen 2006, p. 29)

Defending this claim, van Inwagen writes that "A being who is capable of, say, creation ex nihilo is—all other things being equal—greater than a being whose powers do not extend to creation ex nihilo" (van Inwagen

---

not. One might wonder why I am concerned about this issue, since all I need for my purposes is that the divine perfection entails God's status as an essential explainer; if it turns out that being an essential explainer is not a perfection, that would not affect my argument here. But later I am going to go further than the claim that God is an essential explainer, to the view that God's essential explaining is unmediated (2.4). Making this claim is only plausible, I think, if God's being essential explainer is not just implied by the divine perfection but is itself a divine perfection.

2006, p. 32). Like Morris, then, van Inwagen appeals to God's maximal power to explain why God must be creator-of-all-else-that-exists.

But this appeal to omnipotence is pretty clearly inadequate. It will not do to say that *being creator-of-all-else* is a perfection in the same way that omnipotence is, that is, that it is a power that even if not exercised counts as a greatness. That would explain, perhaps, why having the power to create, the power to bring something out of nothing, is a great thing; and it might explain why God's power to create cannot depend on the existence of anything independent of God. It does not at all explain why everything nondivine must be brought into existence by God.

Nor can we plausibly supplement the argument that creator-of-all-else is a divine perfection by some metaphysical thesis about the intrinsic limitations of created being. Suppose that one held some sort of thesis about material objects that they essentially exist in time but essentially cannot persist from moment to moment without being sustained by some conserving power (Kvanvig and McCann 1988). One might hold, then—with the addition of some premises—that God is necessarily sustainer-of-all-material-things-that-endure. But that would not show that being sustainer-of-all-material-things-that-endure is a divine perfection. At most it would show that it is implied by the divine perfection that God is sustainer-of-all-material-things-that-endure. Not every property implied by the divine perfection is itself a divine perfection. *Being perfectly powerful* is a perfection; *being perfectly powerful or particularly purple* is not. In order to show that some property implied by a divine perfection is a divine perfection, it must be that the implied property is somehow an aspect of that divine perfection, somehow included within it. *Being perfectly powerful or particularly purple* is not a way of *being perfectly powerful*; *knowing all about the building of the Eiffel Tower* is an aspect of, is included within, *knowing all about everything*. And so, if we want an argument that creator-of-all-else is a divine perfection from some well-established divine perfection, then we would need to show that being creator-of-all-else is included in rather than merely implied by that divine perfection.

Think about it this way. Suppose, counterpossibly, that a particle comes into existence *ex nihilo* without being created by anyone. What is it about this supposition such that one who accepts it is committed to the view that there is no perfect being? Omniscience need not be threatened; God might well know that a particle, unless prevented, would come into existence. Omnipotence need not be threatened, God might well have had the power to preclude any such particle's coming into existence, but have chosen not to exercise that power, and God might well have the power to annihilate the particle once it has come into existence. What perfection can we appeal to in order to rule out the possibility of this waywardly existing particle in a world in which God exists? Unless we can appeal to some such perfection, we cannot defend the inclusion of *being creator-of-all-else* as itself a divine perfection.

The spontaneously existing particle makes trouble for the idea that God is fundamentally *initiative* rather than *reactive*—for in the story, while God knows of the particle's coming, and can plan around it, God is not the *source* of its coming into existence, and so must simply *react* to its coming. If we take perfection to be more fully realized by beings that are active rather than reactive, that are the source of what comes into being rather than reacting to it, then included in that perfection will be God's status as creator-of-all-else.

The perfection to which I am appealing here is usefully labeled *sovereignty*, and it is both plausible as a perfection and capable of explaining a variety of other attributes that are commonly taken to be divine perfections. Sovereignty involves *sourcehood* and *control*: for some being to be sovereign over a domain is for things in that domain to be dependent on that being for their existence/actuality and to have their character be controlled by facts about that being. (See also Plantinga 1980, pp. 1–2.) Note that sovereignty, involving sourcehood and control, does not on this account entail *discretion*. For a being to be sovereign is to be responsible for other things' existence and character; it need not be possible for these things not to exist or to have a different character. Sovereignty as I am using it is not to be characterized modally;[5] discretion is. Of course, it may belong to the divine perfection to have discretion over certain matters, but alternatively, in certain matters, it may fail to belong to the divine perfection to have discretion, and it may even in certain matters belong to the divine perfection not to have discretion.

---

[5] I take it that analyses of dependence and control in terms of counterfactuals fail; while the truth of certain counterfactuals may be characteristic of relationships of dependence and control, they are not essential to them; and indeed there can be relationships of dependence and control even when the antecedents of the relevant counterfactuals would be necessarily false.

Sovereignty as a divine perfection accounts for creator-of-all-else as a divine perfection—not simply implying it, but including it. For the idea of God as creator is the idea that everything else ultimately depends for its existence and character on God. (See also Leftow 1990, p. 584.) It is common to think that God has discretion over creation—over whether and what to create. But even if this were false—even if God might have failed to create, or even if God could not create a material universe very different in its basic structure from what God in fact created—it would not compromise God's sovereignty, and those who have questioned the extent of God's discretion have not taken themselves to be at all calling into question that creation is dependent on and controlled by God.[6]

It is also worth noting that sovereignty as a perfection, aside from whatever intuitive support it has in our general or specific considered judgments about perfection, has some support from its being fruitful in accounting for other divine perfections. We can see why properties that on their face seem as different as aseity, necessity, omniscience, and omnipotence would be included in, or at least entailed by, the divine perfection. For God to be necessarily sovereign entails divine aseity, on pain of a vicious circle of dependence. For God to be necessarily sovereign entails divine providence, God's control over all else, not just qua individual beings but qua system. For God to be necessarily sovereign entails omnipotence, for whatever possibly exists would have to be brought into existence by God. For God to be necessarily sovereign entails omnipresence, not only understood as divine knowledge but divine activity, for everything everywhere depends on God for its existence. And so forth.

Sovereignty is a perfection, and thus a perfect God will be perfectly sovereign. This makes clear why God must be creator of all that is wholly distinct from God. And it makes clear why theism commits one to the view that God is an essential explainer. To hold that there is something explanation-eligible that is not explained by God, something not dependent on and controlled by God, is to hold that God is not perfectly sovereign. In any inquiry that takes for granted God's existence, then, we can also take for granted the appeal to explanans-focused considerations in theory assessment. For once we take for granted God's existence,

---

[6] The clearest case, to which I return below (2.1), is necessitarianism about creation. The necessitarians about creation have denied that God has discretion about whether to create, though they of course hold that creation's existence and character depend on God.

we know that any phenomenon that is to be explained has a theistic explanation. Given theism, morality must have a theistic explanation. But what *sort* of theistic explanation does morality have?

0.3 The argument to come

Instead of turning directly to the discussion of traditional accounts of the theistic explanation of morality, I begin by considering the concept of moral law and its role in theistic explanation. In Chapters 1 and 2 I argue that moral laws should have a privileged place in the treatment of the question of theistic explanation of morality. For not only is moral law, properly understood, something that can find a place in a wide variety of moral theories (1.1–1.6), any explanation of moral facts must bottom out in moral laws (2.1–2.2), and it would suffice to establish a theistic account of all of morality if we could provide an adequate theistic account of moral law (2.3). An adequate theistic account of moral law, besides meeting standard explanandum-focused constraints, must meet the constraint that everything that is explanation-eligible must be explained by God; I claim that we should understand this requirement in a particularly strong way, such that facts about God must enter immediately into the explanation of moral law (2.4).

In Chapters 3 and 4 I argue against two traditionally dominant theistic accounts of moral law. Natural law theory, a view on which moral law is immediately explained by the natures of the beings whom that law governs (3.1), turns out to entail, in standard formulations, that morality is not theistically explained at all (3.2), and the only emendations of the view compatible with its essentials result in no more than a mediated, and thus unacceptable, theistic explanation of moral law (3.3–3.8). (These points against natural law theory generalize to other broadly realistic moral theories defended by theists, and hold a fortiori against constructivist moral theories; see 3.9.) Theological voluntarism, which makes moral statuses depend immediately on some act of divine will (4.1), can meet the constraint that moral law be immediately theistically explained (4.2). But despite its efforts to avoid absurd implications, it is still open to serious explanandum-centered objections, and indeed the efforts of theological voluntarists to avoid these absurd implications have introduced incoherence into the heart of the theory (4.3); and the recent move by voluntarists to emphasize the social character of obligation fails to offer any help for the view (4.4). Thus the main contenders within theistic ethics show themselves to be unsatisfactory theistic accounts of moral law.

In Chapters 5 and 6 I suggest a way forward on this issue and work out some of the details of a more satisfactory position. I show that there is a close similarity between the issues raised in thinking about God's relationship to the laws of nature and those raised in thinking about God's relationship to the moral law (5.1). And, indeed, extant theories of God's relationship to the laws of nature, mere conservationism and occasionalism, closely correspond to natural law and theological voluntarist accounts of God's relationship to the moral law, sharing both their obvious merits and ultimate unacceptability (5.2–5.4). But there is a third theory of God's relationship to the laws of nature, concurrentism, corresponding to which there is no extant theory of God's relationship to the moral law. Concurrentism claims to provide a view on which God's role in the explanation of the laws of nature is immediate but without precluding a genuine role for creaturely natures; and it is worth asking whether an acceptable version of concurrentism, a *normative* concurrentism, can be worked out for God's role with respect to the moral law (5.5).

The sixth chapter works out this normative concurrentism. The basic idea of the view is that if the human good that morally necessitates an agential response is itself a theistic property, then the moral necessitation that is central to moral laws will be immediately theistically explained (6.1). I work out such a view of the human good by defending a version of Adams's account of the good as resemblance to God, but a version that is recognizably Aristotelian rather than Platonist (6.2): I then show how it can be put to work in the explanation of moral necessities (6.3). Such a view escapes the objections leveled against natural law theory and theological voluntarism (6.3–6.6), and thus can claim explanans- and explanandum-centered success (6.7).

1

Moral law

1.1 A sectarian explanandum?

In the Introduction I raised the familiar question of God's relationship to morality. But the particular moral notion upon which most of this book will focus is that of *moral law*. I will detail the reasons for focusing on moral law in Chapter 2. But in order to make the case there for focusing our inquiry on the theistic explanation of moral law, I need first to explain what moral laws are and to discredit some objections to the very idea of moral law. Some writers think that moral law is a sectarian rather than ecumenical idea—that it has a place only within a very narrow range of moral theories. In this chapter, I will give some reasons for thinking that moral law, properly understood, can have a place in a wide variety of moral views; in the next chapter, I argue for its indispensability in explanations of moral facts and in theistic explanations in particular.

Consider Anscombe's view in "Modern Moral Philosophy" (1958). There she argues that the notion of moral law ought to be jettisoned unless one is working within a theistic framework, for the notion of moral law is unintelligible outside of it. Obviously some work needs to be done to explain the connection between the existence of moral laws and the theistic framework to show that unintelligibility results when one affirms the former but denies the latter. It cannot be, as one might think and as some remarks of Anscombe might be read to suggest, that it is a definitional truth that nothing can be a law unless it is given by some lawgiver. For one thing, it does *not* seem to be a definitional truth—perhaps there are sorts of prescriptive law that require a lawgiver (for example, statutory law) but others that arguably do not (for example, customary law), and that is not to mention non-prescriptive laws (for example, laws of nature)—and even if it were, it would be the most boring and trivial sort of analytical point to make against the idea of moral law that we cannot call them "laws" unless laid down by a lawgiver.

There is a better argument available, though I will argue that this argument also ultimately fails. Anscombe connects the notion of a moral law to what she calls a "law conception of ethics" (Anscombe 1958, p. 30). She does not tell us what she precisely means by a law conception of ethics, but she offers a couple of examples and shows us a few features of this way of conceiving of morality. The Old Testament Jews affirmed a law conception of ethics, on her view, as did the Stoics (Anscombe 1958, p. 30). What seems to be common to both of these views is the way that premises of the form "It is the law that..." function in the standard deliberation of well-disposed moral agents and the way that the facts of the form "It is the law that..." function in correct explanations of what ought to be done and avoided. That is to say, in the standard deliberation of well-disposed adherents of law conceptions of ethics, premises of the form "It is the law that Xs ϕ" have a central place, and the agent's affirming the premises "It is the law that Xs ϕ" and "I am an X" results in the agent's ϕ-ing. And with respect to explanations of its being the case that all those that are Xs ought to ϕ, the ultimate explanation resides in the existence of a law requiring those in some class to perform some action, where to be an X is to be a member of the law-designated class, and where ϕ-ing is necessary to perform the law-required action.

A law conception of ethics is, as Diamond rightly points out, a conception on which the existence of a moral law is a *content-independent* reason for action—what accounts for its being the case that one ought to ϕ is not the merits of the act of ϕ-ing (for example, that it is pleasurable, or noble, or useful) but that it is required, *legally* required (Diamond 1988, p. 165). As Anscombe makes clear, though, it does not follow from this position that the content of the moral law is subject to a contingent divine will (Anscombe 1958, p. 30). It is compatible with the law conception of ethics that the content of the moral law could not be otherwise; indeed, it is compatible with the law conception of ethics that *every* proposition of the form "It is a moral law that Xs ϕ" is either necessarily true or necessarily false. The independence of the content of a moral law in a law conception of ethics consists solely in the reason-giving force of the law—its being such as to make it true that those subject to it ought to perform some action—being in some way independent of the merit of the content.

Given this understanding of Anscombe's view—that is, that the notion of a law conception of ethics is supposed to be the link between moral laws and theism—we can see how the argument is supposed to go. If we hold that moral laws have a place only within a law conception of ethics, then we must hold that moral laws must give content-independent reasons for action. If a moral law gives content-independent reasons for action, then its reason-giving force is not due to its content, what the law requires, but is instead due to something else that gives it the status of law. Anscombe suggests, plausibly enough, that it is the moral law's being laid upon those under its jurisdiction by a superior of the requisite sort that makes the moral law law (Anscombe 1958, p. 27). So she eliminates the Kantian idea of "legislating for oneself" as the potential source for the moral law, on what I take not to be simply a boring definitional point about law but on the basis that one is not authoritative over oneself in the way that moral law is supposed to be authoritative over us (Anscombe 1958, pp. 27, 37). She considers whether society might be the source of moral law, but rejects that possibility due to moral law's having a content that socially-imposed norms might well fail to have (Anscombe 1958, p. 37). To have moral laws that meet both the content-independence constraint and the content constraint we need some being like God, who is good and powerful and in charge, to be the source of the moral law. And so one who attempts to articulate a moral theory that holds that there are moral laws is doomed to failure unless that moral theory includes God's legislating the moral law.

There is more than one point at which one could take issue with Anscombe's argument. Here is one difficulty for her argument, which I will note without pressing. It would be a mistake to think that the only *prima facie* plausible way to secure the content-independence of the moral law—or, better, to secure the only sort of content-independence needed, given the structure of the Anscombean argument just presented—would be through its being imposed by some authority. One might hold, for example, that while the existence of a set of moral laws depends on the merit of the content of that set of moral laws—indeed, it might even be that the existence of that set of moral laws is *entailed* by the merits of its contents—its reason-giving force goes beyond that of its contents. On such a view, moral laws are not content-independent in the sense of "having reason-giving force in a way that is not explained by its merits"; they are content-independent in the sense of "having reason-giving force in a way that goes beyond the reason-giving force of the merits." Since it is only content-independence in the latter sense that is relied upon in Anscombe's argument (that is, those who adhere to a law conception rightly (and ineliminably) make use of "It is the law that..." in their deliberations, and theorists employing the law conception rightly (and ineliminably) make use of "It is the law that..." in their normative explanations), if the existence of reason-giving laws can be entailed by the merits of their contents, rather than by being imposed by a lawgiver, then Anscombe's argument fails.

Is it a real possibility for moral laws to exist in virtue of the merit of their contents while having reason-giving force that goes beyond their contents? Consider, for example, rule-utilitarianism. One might say that the authoritative norms of rule-utilitarianism are themselves reason-giving (they are, in Raz's terminology (1979, p. 18), protected reasons), but they have their status as authoritative not in virtue of being laid down by anybody, but by their having certain merits—being, perhaps, the rules the acceptance of which by all would maximize utility. Some rule-utilitarians talk this way, but I do not know why such rules genuinely are authoritative in virtue of their merits. It is not just me. That the standard objection to rule-utilitarianism is that such utilitarians engage in "rule worship" testifies to the fact that it is a bit of a mystery whence the authority of these rules derives.

Here is the second problem for Anscombe's argument, which is more important for my purposes. She assumes that moral laws have a place only within a law conception of ethics, where a law conception of ethics exhibits the features already remarked upon—that the fact that such-and-such is a law figures both in proper characteristic deliberation and in characteristic correct normative explanations. But this is a mistake. Consider, as a similar case, the appeals to virtue within virtue ethics. It seems plain that one can have an ethical theory in which virtue has an important, theoretically indispensable place without holding that *such-and-such is a virtue* or *such and-such is virtuous conduct* ever plays a role, let alone plays an indispensable role, in the good deliberation of a properly disposed agent (cf. Keller 2007). On the contrary: if one is facing a situation in which one must keep one's promise at some inconvenience to him- or herself, having to form the thought that promise-keeping is what justice calls for is a sign not of being properly disposed but of being, at best, continent. And if one is offering an account of the landscape of the various considerations that are reasons for acting one way or the other, one's account might include the noble, the useful, and the pleasant, and so forth; but it need not include the virtues as reasons for doing anything. But the virtues may have an important place nonetheless: the concept of a virtue may be indispensable for organizing and explaining some of the data regarding reasons for action. This is a real possibility with respect to virtue; and the Anscombean argument does not rule out its also being a real possibility with respect to moral law as well.

These criticisms of Anscombe's view do not give us any reason to think that her view must be false, though. And it is a natural enough worry that the way that I responded to Anscombe's view—that is, to deny that moral law must belong only in a law conception of ethics—should lead us to say that outside of a law conception of ethics the notion of moral law may apply, but only epiphenomenally, itself making no difference from a normative point of view. (If that such-and-such is a moral law need not play a role either in the deliberation of the well-disposed agent or in the explanation of the reasons that one has to perform the required action in some view, isn't the appeal to moral law in that view vain and empty?) But it seems to me that we cannot address this question unless we have a clearer account of what it is to be a moral law. Once we have a tolerably clear analysis in hand, we will be able to see more clearly what its theoretical importance is and why that importance should give moral law a place in a wide variety of moral theories.

1.2 Moral laws are not merely moral generalizations

Promisors ought to keep their promises; speakers ought to assert nothing but the truth; one ought to help the undeservedly suffering. Arguably, each of these is a moral law. But there is a difficulty here. It is obvious that none of these are supposed to have existential import. Speakers ought to assert nothing but the truth does not entail the existence of speakers, and could very well be the case even if no one ever spoke. That one ought to help the undeservedly suffering does not entail the existence of anyone who is undeservedly suffering.

The obvious move to avoid the appearance of existential commitment is to characterize these as universal generalizations. *Speakers ought to assert the truth* is the case if and only if it is true that if one is a speaker, then one ought to assert nothing but the truth. *One ought to help the undeservedly suffering* is the case if and only if it is true that if there are any who are undeservedly suffering, then one ought to help them. (See, for example, Shafer-Landau 2003, p. 268, n. 2.) But it is also plain that to be a universal generalization of the form "if x is an A, then x ought to ϕ" or "if x is an A and y is a B, then x ought to ϕ y" is not sufficient to be a moral law.

Vacuous generalizations. If it were sufficient to be a moral law to be a universal generalization of that form, it follows that if there are no people greater than ten feet tall, then *one ought to kill those over ten feet tall* will turn out to be a moral law. This is absurd.

Perhaps one might say that moral laws are *necessarily true* generalizations of this sort. Thus, it will not be a moral law that one ought to kill those over ten feet tall, for in those worlds in which there is a taller-than-ten-feet human, it is not the case that one ought to kill him or her. This emendation carries the unfortunate commitment—not because it is false, but because it does not belong in an analysis of moral law—that moral laws have their validity as a matter of necessity. But even putting that to the side, the problem remains. It still turns out to be a moral law that one ought to kill all those who successfully disprove Fermat's Last Theorem.

Failure of substitutivity. Moral laws also exhibit failures of substitutivity. It may turn out that we can define a shape S such that, as a matter of fact, all and only human bodies have been S. Nevertheless, it would not be a moral law that those beings that are S are bound not to kill the innocent, even if it is true that if a being is S, then it is bound not to kill the innocent. If something else had been that shape—say, a rock—it would not have been bound not to kill the innocent.

Again, one might retort that moral laws are *necessarily true* generalizations. But there is a still a failure of substitutivity. *Promisors ought to keep their promises* is a moral law. But *promisors who are such that Fermat's Last Theorem is true ought to keep their promises* is not a moral law. But assuming that the former generalization is necessarily true (if x is a promisor, then x is bound to keep x's promises) the latter generalization will be necessarily true as well, and thus both will count as moral laws.[1]

---

[1] Some may think that there is nothing wrong with the idea that *promisors who are such that Fermat's Last Theorem is true ought to keep their promises* is a moral law. I think that this is a

Lack of explanatory power. Moral laws stand, we would think, in an explanatory relationship to their instances. If I ought to help the undeservedly suffering, and it is a moral law that one ought to help the undeservedly suffering, then that moral law should be capable of helping to explain why I ought to help the undeservedly suffering. But understood as a generalization, the moral law that one ought to help the undeservedly suffering is not in itself explanatory—it entails that I am in the class of persons that ought to help the undeservedly suffering without explaining why this should be so.[2] Indeed, the existence of a moral law requiring or forbidding φ-ing would not even entail that there is *any* explanation as to why this is so. So, understood as this sort of generalization, the existence of a moral law neither explains why one ought to perform some action nor even suggests that there is an explanation for why one ought to perform that action.

Insufficient moral commitment. One might suspect that these are merely technical problems in the translation from statements of moral laws to statements of generalizations and that tweaking the technical apparatus will avoid these problems. But there is a problem with the generalization strategy that is, in my view, not merely technical. When one asserts that such and such is a moral law, one is thereby committed to the view that some moral status obtains. Put it this way. To assert that a moral law holds, or is valid, is to commit oneself to the view that one's world is *not morality-free*. But the generalization strategy would turn certain defenders of classically morally nihilistic views into believers in moral law, into believers in a world that is not morality-free. So there must be something wrong with the generalization strategy.

Suppose one says that it is moral law that rational creatures ought to obey God. This means, on the generalization view, that *if x is a rational creature, and if there is a y such that y is God, then x ought to obey y*. But a morally skeptical atheist can assert that *if* there is a potential God-obeyer and a God, *then* potential God-obeyers ought to obey God. But such a one is a moral skeptic—he or she doesn't believe that there exists anything that has a moral status; he or she believes that the world is *in fact* morality-free.

---

monstrosity. Moral laws should be *compact*—they should not include irrelevant features. But the generalizations will contain irrelevant features.

[2] As Dretske remarks, "Subsuming an instance under a universal generalization has exactly as much explanatory power as deriving Q from P&Q. None" (Dretske 1977, pp. 28–9).

But one should not be able to believe that we are under a moral law while holding that the world is morality-free. The generalization strategy must hold that this can be sensibly believed.

An example: J. L. Mackie was an atheist, and a moral skeptic. He thought that certain criteria must be met for certain moral values to obtain, and that they would obtain if there were a being like God. But, says Mackie, there is no being like God (Mackie 1977, p. 48). That Mackie affirms if there were a God, then there would be moral value does not make Mackie less of a moral skeptic. But to affirm a moral law is to be a non-moral-skeptic.

It seems that the identification of moral laws with true generalizations with "ought"-consequents is hopeless. But while this identification is hopeless, it does seem to be a desideratum for a correct account of moral law that it entail[3] the corresponding generalization. There are two ways to proceed from here. We could hold that a moral law is the generalization plus some further factor, an extra constraint that enables us to avoid mislabeling certain vacuously true generalizations as moral laws, and to explain why failure of substitutivity occurs as it does, and to ensure that moral laws will have the explanatory power we expect them to have, and to entail the necessary commitment to the obtaining of moral status. Or we could hold that a moral law is not a generalization-plus-some-further-factor; rather, the holding of a moral law is a distinct state of affairs that is prior to and somehow explains the truth of the relevant generalization.

Where to look for such an account? Perhaps we should take our cue from the following suggestive datum: that by and large the difficulties for the mere generalization account of moral law are the difficulties that beset mere regularity accounts of the laws of nature. To hold, that is, that the laws of nature are merely regularities to be captured by universal generalizations is to fall into the same difficulties regarding vacuous generalizations, substitutivity, and explanatory power with which our mere generalization account of moral laws left us. Perhaps, then, we would do well to look for help to the rival accounts of laws of nature, and to ask how these accounts can be fruitfully adapted into rival accounts of moral laws.

---

[3] This needs some hedging, which I will carry out in more detail below (1.5). It may well be that all moral laws, or some set of them, hold defeasibly. Following Lance and Little (2006), I understand their holding defeasibly at least in part as their entailing the corresponding generalization in standard conditions.

1.3 A systems account of moral law rejected

David Lewis has defended what has been called a *systems* account of the laws of nature. What remains in his view from the mere regularities account is that the laws of nature are true statements of regularities.[4] Lewis adds to this that the laws of nature are those true statements of regularities that form a deductive system, that deductive system that exhibits the best combination of simplicity and strength.

Here is an analogy, though a slightly misleading one. Imagine that one has a bag filled with dice, each of the faces of which is of a different color, and one dumps that bag of dice onto a table. Now, one could describe the situation of the dice on the table—where each die is, and what color is showing—by giving a list. But one could instead look for a pattern among the dice, and use statements of the pattern that enable one to deduce from those statements other facts about how the dice are related to each other and what colors are showing. These statements—though true, and entailing nothing but truths—might fail to be complete; that is, they might fail to tell one everything that there is to know about the position and color of the dice. But a sacrifice of completeness may be acceptable in light of the simplicity of the system.

Defenders of the systems account have argued that the systems view offers us all that we should really want out of a theory of the laws of nature. First of all, it preserves the basic commitment to affirming the existence of a law of nature: that it at least entail the corresponding generalization. But by adding the condition that it is only those generalizations that are part of (that is, are axioms or theorems of) the true system that best combines simplicity and strength, we can avoid the difficulties that beset the mere regularity view.

For the systems view enables us to distinguish between those vacuous generalizations that are laws from those that are not: the ones that are laws are those that fall within the preferred deductive scheme. We preserve the result that one cannot substitute extensionally equivalent expressions into laws because such a substitution may transform a law into a nonlaw, for one generalization may be an axiom or valid theorem of the preferred deductive scheme while the other is not. We can distinguish accidentally

---

[4] I ignore here the emendations Lewis has offered in order to deal with probabilistic laws; see Lewis 1994.

true generalizations from those that are non-accidentally true by how they are related to the preferred deductive scheme.

Explanation is trickier, for the laws of nature, on this view, do not determine—except logically—which physical facts obtain, and one might take it to be a desideratum of explanation that that which explains is metaphysically more basic than that which is explained. One might think, then, that any regularity-plus view of the laws of nature will fail in the way that the mere regularity view fails. But one might argue, as Loewer does, that the status of laws of nature as explanatory is not threatened by the systems view. As he writes,

If laws explain by logically implying an explanandum—as the [deductive-nomological] model claims—then the state of affairs expressed by the law will in part be constituted by the state of affairs expressed by the explanandum. How else could the logical implication obtain? In any case, L-laws [that is, laws as so defined within Lewis's systems account] do explain. They explain by unifying. To say that a regularity is an L-law is to say that it can be derived from the best system of the world. But this entails that it can be unified by connecting it to the other regularities implied by the best system. (Loewer 1996, p. 189)

Loewer's argument, then, attempts to answer a potential challenge to the systems view and returns that challenge in kind. The systems view explains because it is *unifying*: a phenomenon is explained by placing it within the pattern of the natural world expressed by the laws of nature. And if one claims that this is not explanation, because the phenomenon explained is itself part of what it is expressed by the putative law of nature, he asks what other way of explaining might there be that does not have this result. (See also for a recent defense of this view Cohen and Callendar 2009.)

Defenders of Lewis's view have allowed that there is something about this view that seems not to comport with commonsense understandings of laws of nature. Because the laws of nature as portrayed by Lewis remain summaries of their instances, the laws of nature determine their instances only logically, and not in any more robust way. The laws of nature, on this view, do not *govern* their instances. How damaging should we take this to be to the Lewisian account? Helen Beebee says "not very": she takes it to be question-begging for a critic of the Lewisian account to assert that the laws of nature must govern their instances, and so the Lewisian view must count as a failure in that regard. As she rightly notes, "The issue of what question-begging amounts to is a thorny one," but goes on to say that

My use of the term here relies on Frank Jackson's analysis, according to which (roughly) an argument is question-begging if the evidence which is adduced in support of the premises of the argument is such that it would not count as evidence for a sane person who already doubted the truth of the conclusion. In the present case, the evidence adduced... would hardly be accepted as evidence by a (sane) Humean who doubted the truth of [the argument in question]. (Beebee 2000, p. 275)

Assume that Jackson's account of what question-begging amounts to is right, and remember that what is in question is what counts as evidence for or against an analysis of what it is to be a law of nature. Given these two points, Beebee's argument is a failure. The fact that a sane *Humean* would not accept a certain bit of argument as evidence does not show that this bit of argument is question-begging. To be a sane Humean is to have already evaluated the overall merits of the position, and to have settled, sanely, in the Humean's favor. But a person who is uncommitted to either a Humean or an anti-Humean view may well be moved by arguments that are directed toward the fact that Lewis's conception of the laws of nature is non-governing, whereas the commonsense notion is governing. Surely this counts as evidence if we are looking for the best *analysis* of what a law of nature is.

Loewer also seems to think that the governing conception of the laws of nature is a commonsense view, one to which even scientists give lip service, and that Lewis's view does not accommodate it; however, given the other strengths of Lewis's view and the obscurity of the notion that the laws of nature govern, it is a desideratum that bears little weight against Lewis's position. He does suggest that there is an incoherence in the vicinity of the governing view, but when he pauses to construct an argument for it, he stops short of that charge, returning again to the obscurity of this anti-Lewisian position (Loewer 1996, pp. 195–6.) This charge of obscurity can be better assessed when we consider below (1.4) the dominant alternative to Lewis's approach.

I want to note some difficulties for Lewis's view, not so much in order to undercut its credentials as an account of laws of nature, but rather first to provide some motivation for formulating an alternative account of the laws of nature and second to preview the sorts of difficulties that will be in the offing when we attempt to provide a Lewis-style account of moral laws.

Recall that, on Lewis's view, among the conditions that qualify the axioms and theorems of a deductive system as the laws of nature is that the system exhibits the best combination of simplicity and strength. Now, there is an immediate objection to this that writers have attempted to deflect, and that is that the notions of simplicity and strength are determined psychologically rather than logically/scientifically. It would be a peculiarity of Lewis's view if it turned out that when examining various true deductive systems to determine which are the laws of nature of our world, the thing to do would be to turn our attention to our psychologies rather than to the relations among things in the world. Let's be clearer on this: it is *not* troubling that we would need to examine our own psychologies so that we could summarize facts regarding them accurately in a deductive system. Rather, it is troubling that, once these are known and summarized, they would count a *second* time in selecting among the deductive schemes to determine which of these deductive schemes contain the laws of nature.

Lewis and Loewer attempt to soften the blow by arguing that there are standards of simplicity and strength that are independent of the contingent features of inquirers. Perhaps simplicity can be characterized in terms of the naturalness of the properties, and that we can give a more objective measure of the information content of the various competing deductive systems. Even if the most ambitious attempts to objectivize the notions of simplicity and strength were successful, we would be left with the obvious point that there is no obvious way to trade off simplicity with strength in order to realize the *best* combination. The foxes within the community of inquirers will prefer strength to simplicity; the hedgehogs, simplicity to strength. Even if we concede that the scientific community's preferences are authoritative here, a failure of consensus should raise questions about what determines the trade-off levels and so fixes the laws of nature.

It seems to follow—Lewis affirms this, though Loewer denies it—that small differences in the psychologies of scientific inquirers (more fox, or more hedgehog) would entail that there are very different laws of nature in different worlds. Loewer says that we can avoid this result via rigidification, by holding that the extension of "is a law" at some world is given not by the standards of the scientific inquirers in that world but by the standards of the scientists in our world (Loewer 1996, p. 191). Lewis rejects this solution: he says that "this is a cosmetic remedy only. It doesn't make the problem go away, it only makes it harder to state" (Lewis 1994, p. 479).

His hope is that the deductive system that comes out best in terms of simplicity and strength come out first in a robust way: "Maybe some of the exchange rates between aspects of simplicity, etc., are a psychological matter, but not just anything goes. If nature is kind, the best system will be robustly best—so far ahead of its rivals that it will come out first under any standards of simplicity and strength and balance" (Lewis 1994, p. 479). Again, I do not see how we have been given reason to believe that the exchange rate between simplicity and strength is *anything but* a psychological matter. If it is nothing but a psychological matter, then the problem that Lewis hopes will not arise is always with us: on the Lewisian view, when stating what makes something a law of nature we seem to be illicitly double counting psychological facts about inquirers.[5]

The first charge against Lewis's view that I have registered is improper dependence on contingent psychological facts. The second returns to the worry about explanation. There is no doubt that unification can play an important role in explanation. But it seems strange to claim that locating a certain fact within a pattern that is describable via a simple, strong axiom system is any sort of explanation. Think back to the bag of dice that I poured onto the table. If one wishes to explain why a certain die is on the left corner of the table, and showing a green face, it will not do at all to show that the system of axioms that best combines simplicity and strength in summarizing the position and color of all the dice entails that this die will be to the left and green. Now, one might think that this failure of explanation appears so vividly only because we are contrasting it with a better form of explanation: perhaps a commonsense causal explanation of the motion of the dice, which supersedes any explanation via deductive unification, or perhaps the more embracing deductive scheme of the actual Lewisian laws of nature, according to which the position and face color of this die might count as a mere accident. But this strikes me as an implausible reply. If unification makes for explanation, we should want to know why it only makes for explanation globally rather than locally, and why

---

[5] It is also worth pointing out that the structure of Lewis's view exhibits another strange feature: it prioritizes the truth implications of a deductive system over simplicity and strength in such a way as to give absolute priority of truth over simplicity and strength. But surely the extent to which one is willing to tolerate a deductive scheme generating some errors for the sake of achieving greater simplicity or strength is a contingent psychological feature of inquirers.

the existence of a more global explanation cuts off the existence of a more local would-be explanation.

There are difficulties with Lewis's view of the laws of nature. But it is possible that the corresponding conception of moral law—an account of what makes something a moral law that shares structural features with Lewis's—will avoid these difficulties; science is not morals, and what counts as an objection to a theory of the laws of nature may fail to so count with respect to a theory of moral law. But it seems to me that the problems with Lewis's account of laws of nature not only fail to be mitigated, but are indeed aggravated, when transformed into a theory of moral law.

What would a Lewisian account of *moral* law look like? Begin, as Lewis's account of laws of nature begins, with a list of all of the facts to be summarized by the laws. But now we include not only all of the physical facts; we now include all of the normative facts as well. Let's for the moment restrict normative facts to facts of the form "A ought to ϕ." Some facts of the form "A ought to ϕ" will be true of each and every moral agent; others will hold only of a proper subset of moral agents, and indeed some of them will hold only of one such agent. (If we think that the correct moral laws will apply in all possible worlds, we will take into account not only to how these non-moral and moral facts are arrayed in the actual world, but also how they are arrayed in every possible world.) Now, we can attempt to summarize these facts via a deductive system: we will, like Lewis, insist that the deductive system produce no false implications about what one ought to do, but once that desideratum is satisfied, we will count the deductive system that exhibits the best combination of simplicity and strength—where to be strong is to capture the normative landscape—as *the* moral law, and *a* moral law is an axiom or theorem of that system.

This view undoubtedly has some merits. It does capture, as the account of laws of nature captures, the fact that inquirers have an interest in formulating putative laws in a way that exhibits high levels of simplicity and strength. Much moral philosophy can be characterized as an attempt to formulate simple principles that are capable of conveying high levels of information about what one ought to do—the categorical imperative, the principle of utility, and so forth. But it seems to me that this Lewis-style account of moral laws is hopeless.

Consider first Lewis's way of dealing with laws and accidents. We are perfectly happy with the distinction between laws of nature and what is physically accidental; and so it is no objection to Lewis's view that some physical facts, not implied by the best system, turn out to be accidental. (We might wonder whether Lewis's view will count the right facts as accidental, but that is a different objection.) But the difficulty with the account of moral law formulated in the Lewisian style is that it turns out perfectly possible that there will be moral danglers—that the deductive system exhibiting the best combination of simplicity and strength will leave some moral facts unentailed, with the result that they count as merely accidental. But the notion of the morally accidental, unlike that the physically accidental, is anathema. It cannot just happen to be the case that one ought to perform some action.[6]

Consider next the appeal to the best combination of simplicity and strength as the way to fix upon the deductive system that counts as the moral law. There seems to be no mitigation of the worries concerning the issues of the trading off of simplicity and strength in the move from the laws of nature to moral laws. Indeed, appeals to simplicity and strength are typically associated within normative systems with an appeal to *rules of thumb*, which are not the basic norms of a system but rather useful approximations of those norms, more proximate guides to action. It seems then that the Lewisian conception is a better fit as an account of the best rules of thumb rather than as an account of moral law.

Consider next issues regarding the explanatory power of Lewisian moral laws: we have little reason to think that moral laws understood along Lewisian lines are explanatory. Such laws exhibit the patterns that call for explanation, but do not themselves explain the particular moral facts subsumed under them.

As an illustration of this point, suppose that there is a God who necessarily wills the maximal happiness of sentient beings. With respect

---

[6] As Sigwick writes,
There seems... to be this difference between our conceptions of ethical and physical objectivity respectively: that we commonly refuse to admit in the case of the former—what experience compels us to admit as regards the latter—variations for which we can discover no rational explanation. In the variety of coexistent physical facts we find an accidental or arbitrary element in which we have to acquiesce... But within the range of our cognitions of right and wrong, it will be generally agreed that we cannot admit a similar unexplained variation. (Sidgwick 1907, pp. 208–9)

to each moral agent, God wills that that being act in a way that best promote the maximal happiness of sentient beings. And suppose that each moral agent ought to act in a way that best promotes the maximal happiness of sentient beings. Now, we can arrange two true deductive systems that capture the relevant moral facts: one which takes as its single axiom that agents ought to maximize overall happiness; the other which takes as its single axiom that agents ought to do what God wills. It seems plain that we would not be able to find out what the moral law requires merely in virtue of the considerations that a Lewis-style account of moral laws would give us. For it seems consistent with these facts that it is a moral law that one do what God wills, and not a moral law that one ought to maximize overall happiness, though maximizing happiness is what one needs to do in order to do what God wills; it also seems consistent with these facts that it is a moral law that one do what maximizes the overall happiness and not a moral law that one do what God wills, though in maximizing the overall happiness one will (necessarily) be doing what God wills. These two distinct moral worlds are conflated into one by the Lewisian technique of formulating moral laws. A genuine moral law will be something that serves as a basis for an explanation of a variety of particular normative facts; and as the case of God and the maximization of happiness that I just described shows, it seems clear that something can simply and powerfully summarize our moral requirements without explaining them, and so simple and powerful summaries of moral facts are not themselves moral laws.

The trouble with the Lewis-style account of moral law is not hard to identify. It is that the Lewis-style account is, as Beebee calls it, a nongoverning account. All we are given with a Lewis-style account is moral regularity, where what we need is an account of moral governance. In the case of God's will and the maximization of happiness, we would like to know what is it that is calling the tune: the divine will or human well-being? Which of these explains *why* one ought to perform the variety of acts that one ought to perform? Even if it were ultimately acceptable to have an account of laws of nature that are nongoverning, it surely seems unpersuasive to claim that a nongoverning conception of moral laws—what are moral laws about, other than governance?—could be similarly acceptable. (Indeed, Beebee makes her case for a nongoverning conception of the laws of nature by conceding that moral laws must govern and by noting that this constraint on moral law is not obviously a constraint on laws of nature (Beebee 2000, pp. 259–62).)

1.4 A universals account of moral law affirmed

The account of moral laws that I favor is modeled on what can be called the *universals account* of the laws of nature, the view formulated independently by David Armstrong (1983), Fred Dretske (1977), and Michael Tooley (1977). On their view, it is an error to think that a law of nature is a regularity plus some further feature; rather, a law of nature is a relation between universals the presence of which explains the regularity. Rather than being a relationship between the extensions of properties, it is a relationship between the properties themselves.

What is this relationship? Armstrong characterizes it as a relationship of necessitation (F necessitates G; or N(F, G)) (Armstrong 1983); Dretske gives its features logically, so that from this relationship (Nec (Fness, Gness)) and this being F it follows that this must be G (Dretske 1977). Lewis puzzles over this view:

> Whatever N may be, I cannot see how it could be absolutely impossible to have N (F,G) and Fa without Ga. (Unless N just is constant conjunction, or constant conjunction plus something else, in which case Armstrong's theory turns into a form of the regularity theory he rejects.) The mystery is somewhat hidden by Armstrong's terminology. He uses 'necessitates' as a name for the lawmaking universal N; and who would be surprised to hear that if F 'necessitates' G and a has F, then a must have G? But I say that N deserves the name of 'necessitation' only if, somehow, it really can enter into the requisite necessary connections. It can't enter into them just by bearing a name, any more than one can have mighty biceps just by being called 'Armstrong'. (Lewis 1983, p. 366)

Of course Lewis is right that it cannot enter into the requisite necessary connections just by bearing a name. So perhaps we are owed more of a statement of what such necessitation amounts to, though it surely is an open question how much we need to be able to say about that relationship to be justified in embracing this view of laws.

To necessitate is to make necessary. It is not to entail, for more than one reason. First, entailment is in one way too strong; for the notion of necessity here might be weaker than metaphysical necessity. For example: many hold that the laws of nature are contingent, and so when one property necessitates another it is not metaphysical necessity that connects them. Second, entailment is in one way too weak; for something might entail something else without being what makes it necessary. For example: as the notion of necessitation is employed in the literature on truths and truthmakers, truthmakers are supposed to necessitate the truths of which they are truthmakers (Merricks 2007, p. 5). But it is implausible that everything is the truthmaker for all necessary truths, and it is implausible that God's asserting that (some contingent) p is truthmaker for (some contingent) p's being true, even though in both of these pairs the former is related to the latter by entailment. When we characterize necessitation, then, we have to treat it as a relation of determination, of making-it-the-case, and in a way that is sensitive to the sort of necessity at stake.

What the universals account claims is that the universals related in a law of nature are such that some of them stand in a control relation to the others and that this relation of control entails the corresponding generalization. Regardless of whether one thinks that a plausible theory of the laws of nature could satisfy these conditions, it cannot be denied that there are small-scale cases that seem to exhibit this sort of pattern. Suppose that my backyard is frequented by birds, and I do not like the red ones—I don't like their look, I don't like that the red ones tend to be cardinals, which are obnoxious in multiple ways, and so forth. I build a machine to which the birds are irresistibly attracted and which when detecting the presence of a red bird traps said bird. What we have here is a context in which the conjunctive property *being red and avian* necessitates *being trapped*, with the result that it is necessary in that context that if x is a red bird, then x gets trapped. What is primary in the order of explanation are the properties themselves; it is the property *being a red bird* that I aimed to connect to *being trapped* in the constructing of the machine, and in one direction of determination. What happens with respect to red birds being trapped begins with an explanation that is intensionally sensitive; the machine that I produced is a red-bird-catcher, not a catcher-of-anything-the-properties-of-which-are extensionally-equivalent-to-being-a-red-bird. But, if I did a good job of it, it will, at least in standard conditions, ensure the truth of the universal generalization.

Note that it is not just the truth of the universal generalization that it ensures. It ensures it with a certain modal strength: not just as things happen to be, but in any world in which my backyard is equipped with my machine and the standard conditions for my machine obtain. And I think that we should insist on the same condition for the universals account of the laws of nature. It is not enough for the necessitation between universals to generate the truth of the relevant universal generalization; it should ensure it as a matter of physical necessity. (Thus we should not want to define physical necessity in terms of the laws of nature. One might take physical necessity to be a sui generis sort of necessity (see, for example, Fine 2002), or might define it in terms of metaphysical necessity (for example, what is metaphysically necessary so long as no alien universals are introduced and no native universals are exiled).)

What makes this example palatable is that I made explicit the *mechanism* by which the properties are related, and since (plausibly) my designer's intentions can be responsive to the universals as such and can be explanatorily prior to the holding of the relevant generalization, we can see how in a limited context some universals can necessitate—that is, make necessary—others. The example also helps to make the point that we should keep in mind a distinction between what I will call the *text* of the universals account and what I will call the *gloss* that one wishes to put on it. I take the text of the universals account to be that universals in a law of nature stand in a *selection* relation one to another: the selecting property fixes upon the selected property. The consequence of this selection relationship is that a corresponding generalization bearing the relevant modality holds. So if a law of nature is of the form N (F-ness, G-ness), then F-ness selects G-ness, and as a consequence it is physically necessary that if something is F, then it is G.

That is the text; the gloss is exactly how we are to understand this selecting. In advance of examining the merits, the only thing that we can say is that how we understand the selecting of one property by another has to be intensional in character; the selecting property must be relevant to the selection of the selected property; and that the selection must result in the truth of the corresponding physically necessary generalization.[7] Outside of those constraints, which are fixed by the text of the view, which gloss we ought to accept is governed simply by the plausibility of the positions in play. We can imagine views that are closely modeled on my red-bird-catching device described above. Suppose that belief in laws of nature tends to be belief in abstract objects, laws of nature, which strangely nevertheless have the power to see to it that certain generalizations must

---

[7] Again, this physically necessary generalization may itself exhibit defeasibility, so that it holds strictly only in standard conditions; see 1.5.

hold. This view makes the selection extrinsic to the universals involved in the laws, but nevertheless those universals are intensionally relevant in a way that satisfies the text of the view. It seems to me, as it seems to some critics of the universals view, to be an absurd view. But it is only one specification of the universals view. Somewhat less absurdly, suppose that God has decided that certain properties will be linked to other properties, and this divine decision will ensure that what is necessary to ensure that selection occurs. Again, the text is satisfied.[8]

Alternative glosses on the text of the universals view offer accounts of selection that do not rely on some external mechanism. Challenged by Lewis to offer a gloss of the selection mechanism, Armstrong identifies selection as simply causation:

May we not suppose that this [first-order causal] regularity holds *because* something's being F *brings it about* that the same something becomes G? This latter is not a general fact, one expressed by a universally quantified proposition. Rather it is supposed to be an 'atomic fact,' albeit a higher-order fact, a relation between the universals F and G. It is at this point that, I claim, the Identification problem[9] has been solved. The required relation is the causal relation, the very same relation that is actually experienced in the experience of singular causal relations, now hypothesized to relate types not tokens. (Armstrong 1993, p. 422)

Armstrong glosses the text of the universals approach by identifying selecting with causing. There is more than one basis to be skeptical of this solution, but we need not linger on them.[10] One might alternatively hold that selection occurs via dispositional properties: perhaps the selecting property in a law of nature is the trigger condition for some dispositional property, and the selected property is the property thereby manifested.[11]

---

[8] This is how I understand the view of the laws of nature to which an occasionalist is committed. See 5.2 below. For an instance of this sort of view of the selection relationship, see Foster 2004.

[9] Armstrong calls the problem of providing a gloss on the selection mechanism the "Identification problem."

[10] For example, we need to ask how well we can make sense of causation between universals, and how we are going to ensure that this causation ensures the truth of generalizations with the right modality.

[11] It may be surprising that I treat as natural allies views like Armstrong's and views like those of Alexander Bird, who is extremely critical of Armstrong's view and formulates his own dispositionalist account of laws using Armstrong's view as a foil. On my view, Bird's and Armstrong's views are both clear instances of an anti-Humean, governing account of laws of nature; they both accept the text of that view as I describe it. Their disagreement is over how to characterize the selection relation, about what gloss on the text to offer. And, indeed, it is

The claim, then, is that laws of nature explain the regularities because the necessitation relationship that holds among the universals gives rise to those regularities. If the universals, and the selection relationship between them, are more metaphysically basic than the instantiation of those universals exhibiting the to-be-explained pattern, then appeals to the laws of nature involve a very satisfying form of explanation, that is, that in which what explains is metaphysically more fundamental than what is explained.

Further, we can say that a governing conception of the laws of nature is correct. Loewer attempts to foist upon the critic of Lewis's view a dilemma: either the events in the natural world are governed by the laws of nature, or the laws of nature merely summarize those events (Loewer 1996, p. 192). Loewer's own view is that the laws of nature summarize, and are distinguished from other summaries due to their simplicity and strength. To those who complain that this view of the laws of nature casts them as nongoverning, Loewer responds that the alternative governing conception seems absurd: are we to think that the events in the natural order are governed by some abstract object? (Loewer 1996, p. 192) But, while I allow the obscurity of this view of the laws of nature as governing, the response to be made to Loewer is not to give up on the governing conception of the laws of nature but to reject Loewer's view of what the governing relationship commits one to. One can hold that what is crucial is that there be a governing relationship *between the universals*; on Armstrong's view, for example, it is not N(F, G) that governs; it is F that governs G. Of course, on the theistic account I described above, we could hold that there is some further mechanism of selection, say, a divine decision. But neither of these views is entailed by the basic universals account. In order to remain neutral between various glosses here, I will describe the view that laws of nature are governing as the view that laws of nature *express* governing relationships. There is no law of nature without a governance relationship, but that does not mean that it is the law itself that must govern.

I have summarized a case to be made in favor of the universals account. There is no doubt that it carries a higher metaphysical and epistemological burden, both in terms of its commitment to a peculiar necessitation relationship and in terms of providing an account of how we come to

just the character of the selection relationship on which Bird focuses in arguing for the superiority of his view to Armstrong's (Bird 2005).

grasp the presence of this necessitation relationship. I am not going to attempt to evaluate the relative costs of these burdens compared to the benefits gained by fitting more closely with our commonplaces about the explanatory and governing roles of the laws of nature. What I am going to argue is that when we transform the Armstrong/Dretske/Tooley account into a theory of moral laws, we will see that these metaphysical and epistemological worries do not weigh on this theory of moral law any more heavily than they weigh on its rival, the Lewisian conception. The universals conception of moral law will thus bear the comparative benefits of the universals conception of laws of nature without bearing its comparative burdens.

How, then, should we formulate an account of moral laws modeled on the Armstrong/Dretske/Tooley account? Do I want to say that moral laws just are instances of the laws of nature, laws of the form F-ness necessitates G-ness, where a ranges over actions, F is some set of natural properties, and G is the property of *being morally required*?

No. I do not think that moral laws *are* laws of nature; I do not think that the necessitation relation that holds between *being water*, *being salt*, and *dissolving* is the same relation that holds between *being a creature*, *being God*, and *being required to obey*. Physical necessitation is a relationship that holds among physical properties, one would think, and that's not what *being morally required* is. What's more, if I were to conceive of moral laws in precisely this way, there would be two sorts of necessity hanging around: first, whatever necessity is involved in the selection of the moral properties by the nonmoral properties, and second, the necessity that is internal to moral properties like *being morally required*. For to be morally required is *itself* in some way to be necessary; it is to be such that one *must*, one *has to*, one *needs to*, it is *necessary* that one perform some action.

In a law of nature, some universal necessitates another; in this sort of necessitation, one universal selects another, resulting in the truth of a universal generalization that holds with physical necessity. A moral law, on the view that I want to defend, also involves some universal necessitating another, but the central difference (which gives rise to some other important differences) is that the sort of necessitation is different; what we have with laws of nature is (at least) *physical* necessitation, making *physically* necessary, whereas with moral laws we have *moral* necessitation, making *morally* necessary. The central case with which I will be concerned are universals instantiated in actions, where what necessitates are features of an action and what is necessitated is the performing of or the refraining from performance of the action. So, for example, *being the object of one's valid promise* morally necessitates *being performed*; *being an intentional deception* morally necessitates *being refrained from*.[12] But it is not obvious to me that moral laws must always relate to actions. Moral laws might require agents to take certain *attitudes* toward objects or states of affairs; it may be that *being an exploitation of the vulnerable* morally necessitates *being disapproved of*. Moral laws might require that certain states of affairs not obtain; it may be that *being a case of undeserved suffering* morally necessitates *not obtaining*, and whether this sort of putative moral law reduces to moral laws concerned with action is an open question.

For moral laws to involve moral necessitation is for some universals to morally select others, and as a result a certain moral necessity obtains. Let me begin with the latter notion, that of a moral necessity. The first thing to note is that the burden of offering some characterization of *morally necessary* (or of defending the choice to leave as a primitive) is not a burden that falls unequally on defenders of Lewis-style and Armstrong/Dretske/Tooley-style accounts of moral laws. The defender of a Lewis-style account still has that property of *being wrong* hanging around in his or her analysis, and it cannot be denied that this is a modal notion. So if anyone who is tempted to object to my proposed analysis by claiming that this is an extra modal notion being carried by my account that is not carried by the Lewis-style account, that temptation should be resisted. There is no difference here, and thus no metaphysical objections from lack of parsimony and no epistemological objections from lack of access can gain any purchase at this point.

I will not attempt an analysis here of *morally necessary*, though I will state a few commonplaces regarding it, and I will return to it briefly at the end of 1.6. First, I understand *morally necessary* to be a species of *practically necessary*, so that if an action is morally necessary, then it is practically necessary, where to be practically necessary involves there being decisive normative reasons in favor of it.[13] The linking thesis is reasons internalism.

---

[12] "Surely there is no necessitation here, since there are some cases in which promise-breaking and lying are perfectly acceptable?" I will discuss below the issue of defeasibility; see 1.5.

[13] This is not meant to be an analysis, even a partial one, of being practically necessary; it is meant only to make explicit the links between *being morally necessary* and *being backed by reasons to conform one's conduct*.

As Smith states the view, reasons internalism is the view that if an action is such that one morally ought to perform it, then there is normative reason for one to perform it (Smith 1994, p. 62). But there being normative reason to perform it is much weaker than the arguments for reasons internalism warrant; if such arguments succeed, then they succeed not simply in showing that there is some reason to perform the action, but that the action is backed by decisive reasons. (Smith's arguments from rational expectation and from the appropriateness of blame (Smith 1994, pp. 89–91), for example, make sense only if the reasons for acting in accordance with the morally right are decisive reasons; though for an opposing view see Gert 2008. See also Darwall 2006, p. 28.) Second, if A's φ-ing is morally necessary, then if A is morally nondefective and in optimal conditions for action—conscious, aware of relevant circumstances, not drugged, etc., then A φ-s. (I will not attempt to distinguish here practical from moral necessity in any informative way; I will return to the issue briefly in 1.6 when I argue for the ecumenical character of the concept of moral law.)

So taking on an account of moral law modeled on the Armsrong/Dretske/Tooley view of the laws of nature that includes appeal to the notion of moral necessity does not add any burden that would not be present in the Lewis view. What does place an extra burden on the defenders of the universals view of the moral law is that this view includes the idea of an explanatorily prior selection relation between universals—the universals that characterize an action morally select *being performed, being refrained from*, etc. Here the Lewis-style account can claim a lighter commitment: that view is a summarizing, nongoverning view, whereas the commitment to a making relationship expresses the view that certain features morally govern.

In response I want to recall both why the Lewisian conception seems inadequate as a theory of moral law, calling for a view more like the Armstrong/Dretske/Tooley account, and why one might have fewer initial objections to a moral selection relation rather than to a physical selection relation. On the first point: It does seem that the notion that the properties involved in a moral law are right- and wrong-making is part of the commonsense notion of a moral law; moral laws pick out which of the various properties exhibited by an action play a role in making an action have the moral features that it has. We obviously have a strong theoretical interest in distinguishing the *making* features from the *tracking* features, as in the divine command/total utility case described above (1.3). This interest seems to be much stronger in the moral case than in the natural case—brute moral truths are much less theoretically tolerable than brute natural truths.

On the second point: It seems that when we are working with moral necessities, the notion that some properties of an action morally select other properties of an action is less problematic, less prone to the Lewis worry about why the relation between the universals ensures that the relation between particular instances will hold. I have not given an account of the various ways that one property might morally select another. But one obvious way to gloss that notion would be in terms of *rational selection*—put crudely, when some property of an action morally selects a performance property, the former property rationalizes, makes rationally eligible in some way, the performance of the action. (There may be other ways of glossing moral selection, and I will discuss some of these possibilities later in the book (4.2).) But if the selection relation is a rational relation—not, for example, a causal relation—then it would seem that there would be logical relationships between some property morally selecting another property and the corresponding universal generalization holding. If, say, *being the object of a valid promise* morally selects *being performed*, it seems to follow, logically and trivially, that it is morally necessary that if x is the object of a valid promise, then x is performed. Lewis's worry about the universals account of the laws of nature is that there is not going to be such a logical relationship between the necessitation relation and the corresponding generalization, and so he cannot see why it is impossible for the necessitation relationship to hold while the generalization does not. But that objection does not stick in the case of moral laws, which may well appeal to a notion of selection in which such a logical relationship does hold.

This, then, is the view of moral law that I accept and around which this book's argument will be built. A moral law holds when F morally necessitates G; F morally necessitates G when F morally selects G such that it is morally necessary that if x is F, then x is G. If it is, say, a moral law that promises be kept, this is to be understood as *being a promisekeeping's* morally necessitating *being performed*—that is, *being a promisekeeping* morally selects *being performed* such that it is morally necessary that if some action is a case of promisekeeping, then it is performed.

1.5 Defeasibility and moral laws

There may seem to be trouble for this account of moral law from the fact that many hold that moral laws exhibit defeasibility, and this concession may seem to generate puzzles for an account on which moral laws are relationships of moral necessitation between universals.

The puzzles are of more than one sort. Lance and Little have argued, for example, that if one takes a pragmatic rather than a metaphysical approach to questions of laws and lawlikeness, then the view that moral laws exhibit defeasibility will not appear so strange, whereas if one takes the metaphysical approach there would be no motivation to go for defeasibility and some motivation to avoid it. What is the difference between a pragmatic and metaphysical approach, and why does the metaphysical approach rule out ineliminable defeasibility within moral laws?

On the metaphysical approach, the central question about laws is what special aspects of reality they capture: answers have ranged from relations of ideas, to structures of social constraint, to relations between objective universals. On the pragmatist approach, by contrast, one begins with lawful *purport*, as Marc Lange puts it;[14] one begins with what special epistemic function lawlike generalizations serve. While one can then go on to ask of such generalizations what aspects of reality they capture (a question to which there may or may not be a non-trivial answer), the central issue that demarcates something as a law instead of some other theoretical generalization is given in terms of the role the claim plays in the functional structure of epistemology. On the first approach, metaphysics constrains the practice of theory. On the pragmatic approach, the epistemic role played by law-claims places constraints on what answers can defensibly be given to metaphysical claims: reflective epistemology constrains metaphysics. (Lance and Little 2006, p. 155)

But it is unclear whether this distinction genuinely divides two camps. The first, basic point is that metaphysics obviously constrains the practice of both scientific theorizing and philosophical theorizing about the laws of nature: scientific theorizing proceeds naturalistically; and it is obvious that Lance and Little take certain extant metaphysical views to be sufficiently incredible that one need not shape an account of laws of nature in light of their epistemic possibility.[15] Second, it is unclear whether the pragmatic

---

[14] Here Lance and Little are citing Lange 2000.
[15] See the incredulous stare response they offer to the notion that the world calls the shots in determining what are the privileged conditions under which the laws' generalizations hold

approach is at all a distinctive approach. If anyone's approach is paradigmatic of the metaphysical approach, it is Dretske's and Armstrong's. But they surely begin with the role that the laws of nature play in both our commonsense and our scientific practices of predicting and explaining natural events—with what Lance and Little, following Lange, call "lawful purport." But the Dretske/Armstrong view is that the role that the laws of nature play in such inquiry cannot be satisfied unless what one is asserting when one is asserting that there is a law of nature is that there is a certain relation between universals, and so there are no laws of nature (metaphysical claim) unless such relations are present.[16]

Lance and Little's description of the pragmatic approach strikes me not as a sectarian position but as the common, basic methodology by which philosophers have approached the question of what make for laws of nature or moral laws, and the distinction between the views seems to be not in their starting points but in their assessment of how important it is to give the further metaphysical story of what makes statements of the laws true and how successful such accounts are capable of being. A defender of the pragmatic approach seems to be characterized by the view that either it is not particularly important to provide an account of the metaphysics of laws of nature or moral laws, or that even granting the intrinsic interest of the question, such accounts of the metaphysics turn out (or even inevitably turn out) to be uninformative. As for the issue of importance: if it turned out that genuine laws of nature/moral laws could not be distinguished from spurious ones except by appeal to considerations that Lance and Little would label "metaphysical," then the pragmatists could hardly claim victory over the metaphysical approach (both the pragmatists and the metaphysicians would be left with an unsolved problem), and so the question at issue would be simply how successful the metaphysician's account turns out to be.

A first basis to doubt, then, Lance and Little's view that the pragmatist and the metaphysician should take different views on the possibility that

---

universally—this is, as far as I can see, the view that something like an Aristotelian view of biological kinds is just ruled out.

[16] So Dretske gives a catalog of the list of uses to which laws of nature are put in explaining, predicting, etc.; argues that any regularity or regularity-plus account fails to satisfy it; and then argues that there is a view that does satisfy it (Dretske 1977). On the other side, Loewer gives such a catalog as well, and argues that it is best handled by a Lewis-style account (Loewer 1996).

the laws are ineliminably defeasible is that it is unclear whether the pragmatist and metaphysician take methodologically distinct approaches. A second is that they offer no good reason for thinking that there would be a difference. They suggest that one who accepted Armstrong's account of the laws of nature should be wary of defeasibility, because on his view:

Laws are grounded in identities between universals. To accept the ideas that laws could nevertheless be defeasible, one would be forced to adopt a very strange sort of contingent-identity view of universals; and while this might be possible, it is hard to see the motivation for such technical gymnastics. The universals, one would think, being what they are irrespective of contingency and context, are either identical once and for all, or not. Hence the laws that describe such metaphysical relations, one would also think, are themselves either absolute or non-existent. On the metaphysical approach to laws, in short, defeasibility looks suspicious indeed. (Lance and Little 2006, p. 155)

But this is not Armstrong's view and thus the difficulties for defeasible laws that Lance and Little outline are not problems for Armstrong. Armstrong does not hold that the laws of nature are grounded in identity between universals; not only would such a view make trouble for an account of defeasible laws, it would also make trouble for Armstrong's actual view, on which the laws of nature are contingent (Armstrong 1983, p. 158). On Armstrong's view, the relevant relation in cases of laws of nature is not identity but causation, not at the level of individuals but at the level of universals (Armstrong 1993, p. 422; see 1.4). Now, we might well wonder about this posited causal relationship. But there seems to be no reason to think that this relation could not hold defeasibly: *defeasibly, x causes y* is not at all the monstrosity that *defeasibly, x = y* would be. It is, on the other hand, rather a commonplace that causation is a defeasible relation.

This brief response on behalf of Armstrong can help us to see how we ought to respond to Lance and Little's worry in the case of the account of moral law that I have proposed. The account that I have proposed surely counts as metaphysical by Lance and Little's lights, and on their view I should be suspicious of defeasible moral laws. After all, what would it be for something to *defeasibly* necessitate? The key to seeing that this is not at all strange is that necessitation is *making necessary*, and the defeasibility attaches to the *making* rather than to the *necessary*. To follow Lance and Little's lead, to say that defeasibly, *being A* morally necessitates *being performed* means that *in privileged conditions, being A* selects *being performed*, and so in those privileged conditions the corresponding moral necessity holds. There is nothing untoward, I say, in holding that there exist defeasible necessitation relations in some moral laws. So there is no objection simply from defeasibility to the conception of moral laws that I have defended.

A final point. One difference that remains between the view defended here and Lance and Little's view is that the Lance and Little view is carried out at the level of generalizations rather than at the level of properties. The result is that they are going to end up committed to the view that substitutions of necessarily coextensive properties should be allowed into their putative laws of nature. In the case of God and the maximization of utility described above, on their view the credentials of *it is a moral law that one do God's will* and *it is a moral law that one maximize utility* might be identical. But our practice of understanding moral laws is not like this: we want to distinguish between properties that make actions right or wrong, and properties that simply track rightness and wrongness. If the only roles that moral laws played were simply summarizing and predicting ones, then we could see how their view would be perfectly satisfactory. But we use statements of moral laws to characterize what makes actions right or wrong, and so any view that allows (or has no resources to preclude) the free substitution of necessarily coextensive properties into laws of nature will fail to capture adequately the role of moral laws in our practice.

1.6 The ecumenical character of moral law

I have thus far emphasized the points that moral law involves a relation between universals and that this relation is one of moral necessitation. I want to complete the case for the ecumenical character of the idea of moral law within moral philosophy by making further suggestions as to what moral necessitation amounts to.

Moral necessitation is making morally necessary. As I said above (1.4), I do not conceive of *morally necessary* as some sort of necessity wholly distinct from, say, *practically necessary*, the good old practical ought that Anscombe concedes that we cannot do without. Rather, the morally necessary is a species of the practically necessary—it is what is practically necessary on account of, because of, features that are morally relevant. Some norm is a moral law because certain universals, universals that are morally relevant, practically necessitate performance.

I do not hope to be able to characterize precisely what counts as morally relevant features. Let me give the paradigm: the paradigm case of a moral law is that in which the universal that practically necessitates includes no reference to the agent.[17] So *being a killing of an innocent person* practically necessitates *refraining from performing* is a paradigmatic instance of a moral law, because the universal does not include reference to the agent. But it seems false to say, flatly, that ineliminable reference to the agent is sufficient to render even a practical necessity a non-moral-law. While we might hold that *being a leaping before one looks* practically necessitates *refraining from performing* while not constituting a moral law, we might nevertheless also hold that *being a betrayal of one's friend* practically necessitates *refraining from performing* and is thereby a moral law.

As I said, I am not going to attempt a fine set of distinctions. There are various ways to try to distinguish the moral, some of which are so specific to a normative view that they can hardly be held to be analytic features of the concept. The paradigm of the morally relevant is the practically relevant even without essential reference to the agent. When considerations that make essential reference to the agent—considerations regarding the agent's interests, aspirations, relations to others, and so forth—are introduced, it becomes less clear whether the resulting practical necessitation should count as moral law. It also is unclear why we should, prior to our immersion in a particular normative theory, work out the distinction. The distinction between norms the practical force of which is more private and those the force of which is less private is, however, a distinction that is present in *all* normative theories.

If what I have said is on the right track, then we can make an initial case for the importance of the notion of moral law within every normative theory. (I will add to this case in Chapter 2.) For normative theory is concerned not just to categorize what we ought to do, but also to explain it—to give an account of what makes (even if only defeasibly) certain actions practically necessary. And every normative theory is concerned with the question of the extent to which considerations that are

---

[17] To be clearer: I am not saying here that these paradigmatically moral norms must be more practically necessitating than other norms, having more force, normatively speaking. All I am saying is that they are more obviously moral in their character. Even those who doubt that practical relevance can be wholly impersonal do not doubt that if such considerations could necessitate, they would be more clearly *moral* considerations.

paradigmatically moral, or approximate that paradigm, are capable of doing the work of practically necessitating action. If this is so, then the thing to say about the wide range of normative theories is not that they have conceptual space for moral law, or they don't. *All* of these views have conceptual space for moral law. What distinguishes them is whether they in fact affirm the existence of moral laws, what moral laws they affirm, and their grounds for so doing.

2
Theistic explanation of moral law

2.1 Moral facts, explanation, and theistic explanation

The previous chapter provided an account of the concept of moral law and gave reason to think that moral law, thus conceptualized, can play a role in a variety of moral theories. The aim of this chapter is to bring the notion of moral law into contact with the book's overall aim, that is, to show how facts about morality depend on facts about God. The argument of this chapter can be usefully broken into two parts: the first part establishes the privileged role had by moral law in the explanation of moral facts (2.1–2.3); the second part, relying on moral law's privileged explanatory role, asks what sort of theistic explanation of moral law we should expect (2.4).

I begin with some clarifications about *moral facts*, *explanation*, and *theistic explanation*. I of course cannot give an adequate general account of what it is to explain some fact. (By "fact" I mean an obtaining state of affairs.) But when I ask whether there is an explanation of some fact, I am asking whether there is an answer to the question "Why does that state of affairs obtain?" I stipulate that any answer to this "Why" question must appeal to some relationship between facts that is not observer-relative—one that is not dependent on one's mastery or failure of mastery of concept-use and that is not dependent on one's knowledge or ignorance of the relevant facts. One fairly common understanding of "explains" is at least partly epistemic: to explain is, on this understanding, to give new information. But this more epistemic reading of "explains" is parasitic on its metaphysical aspect: the way that explanations give new information is by making one aware of, or calling one's attention to, some relationship between facts that would hold independently of such awareness.

By "moral fact" I am going to mean those obtaining states of affairs that we would typically characterize by saying "A is morally required to ϕ," "morally speaking, A must ϕ," "A's ϕ-ing is the only morally right thing to do," and so forth. What all of these have in common is their appeal to a sort of *necessity*—as I argued in Chapter 1, not logical, metaphysical, or physical necessity, but moral necessity (1.4). I thus will say that all moral facts are of the form *it is morally necessary for A to ϕ*. I allow that the place of A can be taken by a named individual, a definite description, a list of named individuals, a list of definite descriptions, universal quantification over some range of agents, or phrase ("doctors," "parents," etc.) that refers to standard, paradigmatic, nondefective, etc. instances of the kind. (Similarly, the ϕ-ing itself may be described in ways that involve direct or indirect objects picked out by any of those manners of referring.) ϕ-ing of course may refer to an action-type, but as I allowed in 1.4, it might include other states of the agent(s) referred to by "A": having some attitude, exhibiting some practical disposition, and so forth.

So moral facts to be explained include the fact that for each person it is morally necessary that he or she keep his or her promises, that it is morally necessary that Mark Murphy refrain from ignoring his four-year-old's cries for a middle-of-the-night drink of water, that it is morally necessary that Will Clark and Mark Murphy not claim that they are typically called anything other than "Will Clark" or "Mark Murphy," and so forth. It could also include its being morally necessary that Will Clark and I be certain sorts of people, or have certain desires or emotions.

Using this notion of a moral fact has the benefit of specifying a fairly clear explanandum—we want to explain all the obtaining states of affairs that fit this pattern. But it is no doubt, like the notion of explanation described above, somewhat stipulative. I have said nothing to rule out the possibility that there are what one might call "impersonal" moral facts, facts that do not involve a moral necessity bearing on some agent to respond a certain way, but that simply involve an impersonal necessity—for example, *it is morally necessary that there be no innocent suffering*. I have also said nothing to rule out in any substantial way the possibility of moral facts, personal or impersonal, that fall short of necessity. One might think that, say, there is a notion of moral betterness, such that it is morally better that A ϕ than that A ψ, or it is morally better that p than that q, which is not reducible to any notion of moral necessity. I am skeptical about impersonal moral necessity, and less so about irreducible moral betterness. But I put these to the side.

It is worth pointing out that, on the stipulated definition of moral facts provided, moral laws are not moral facts, nor is the fact that a moral law holds itself a moral fact. This is not particularly surprising. Moral facts are *first-order* facts involving act-types' bearing moral necessity. Moral laws are *second-order* facts involving properties morally necessitating other properties. And so no moral law is itself a moral fact, though some moral laws trivially entail moral facts. (If *being a promisekeeping* morally necessitates *being performed*, then it follows trivially that it is morally necessary for everyone to perform what he or she has promised.)

More precisely stated, then, the question with which this book is concerned is whether all moral facts are theistically explained—whether every moral necessity is explained by some fact about God, and if so, what sort of theistic explanation is best from a theistic point of view. I will turn to the very obvious argument that every moral necessity is explained by God in the second half of this chapter; there I will also offer a less obvious argument as to what sort of theistic explanation we should expect (2.4). But it is important at the outset to put to the side an objection based on the alleged necessity of some moral facts and some moral laws. Regardless of whether some moral facts require theistic explanation—perhaps, say, those that involve a requirement to obey some particular divine command—one might object that it is clear that there are many facts about the obtaining of moral necessities for which theistic explanation is in principle unavailable. For a number of such facts are *necessarily* obtaining states of affairs—that is, it is metaphysically necessary that these moral necessities hold. For after all, one might ask, what is the point of trying to explain necessarily obtaining moral states of affairs? When a state of affairs obtains contingently, it might have failed to obtain, and we would want an explanation to account for its obtaining rather than not obtaining. But when a state of affairs obtains necessarily, as some moral states of affairs arguably do, no explanation is called for, or even possible. (See, for example, Wainwright 2005, p. 98 and Wielenberg 2005, pp. 51–3.)

Put to the side for the moment objections to the claim that some moral states of affairs obtain necessarily. For even given the necessary obtaining of those states of affairs, it would not follow that those states of affairs could not be explained. For it is not the case that explanation is only possible, and even called for, when what is to be explained is contingent. For example: on some views of God's nature, God necessarily creates. (This was the view of the Islamic necessitarians, such as Avicenna; it has also been held by some recent Christian philosophers, including Norman Kretzmann (1991).) On this view, *that there is created being* is a necessarily obtaining state of affairs. But it is obvious that the fact that there is created being necessarily holds on this view does not commit a defender of that view to holding that *there is created being* cannot be explained—quite the contrary. There is no reason to believe that this state of affairs obtains necessarily except in virtue of that which would, if true, explain it: that the necessarily existing divine being has a nature that ensures that that being creates.

The mistake is to suppose that it is essential to explanation to show why what need not be nevertheless is. What is essential to explanation is to show why what is, is; this will, in the case of contingently obtaining states of affairs, involve showing why what need not be is, but it may also be that for some necessarily obtaining states of affairs it is possible to show why what must be is, and even must be. If God creates of necessity, then that there is a created world is a necessary truth, but it would also be possible to explain why what must be (that there is a created world), is—it is that God is such as to necessarily aim at actualizing and to necessarily have the ability to actualize a created world. The mere fact, if it is a fact, that the obtaining of certain moral states of affairs is necessary does not, then, give any reason all by itself to suppose that these moral facts are not the sort of thing that can be explained.

Now, one might claim that there is some relevant difference between the creation case and the case of moral facts. But look. The reason that *there is created being* seems to call for explanation, even if one's view has it as a necessary truth, is that there seems to be nothing in the essence of any creature that entails its existence; knowing what the creature is does not tell us why it must exist. We only can know why it (or something like it) must exist by looking to something else—to (on this view) God, whose nature is such as to will to create and to have the power to create. Compare: when we have a moral fact, we have an act-type—an act of the sort to have a certain intention, motive, circumstances, etc.—that is such that if one does not perform it, then one is morally defective. On the face of it—just on the face of it—it is not obvious why an act's bearing a certain moral status would not be explanation-eligible, even one were confident that the act's having that status is a necessary feature of it.

Compare this point to that made by Kit Fine in his argument for the view that normative necessity is a distinct variety of necessity. Now, Fine in my view errs in thinking that normative necessity is a distinct modality that attaches to already fully moral propositions, for example, *it is wrong to break promises* (Fine 2002, p. 249). But it is plausible to hold, as I have argued already (1.4), that normative necessity just is that distinct sort of necessity that we employ in thinking about what it is to be such that one *must not* break promises, that one *cannot do* that sort of thing. And here one of Fine's arguments bears immediately on the issue at stake. It does not seem to be part of what it is *to be pain* that it is morally necessary not to inflict it without further reason to do so (Fine 2002, p. 252), nor is it part of what it is *to be a harmless child* that it is morally necessary that one not aim at that child's death or injury. So even if it is true that, in all possible worlds, it is morally necessary that everyone refrain from indiscriminate infliction of pain and it is morally necessary that everyone refrain from harming children, that is no basis to suppose that we need no explanation of these moral necessities' holding.

Moral facts do not seem to be self-explanatory. Nor again do they seem to be brute: to think that they are necessary and brute generates puzzles rather than solving them. So we should expect that moral facts, all of them, are explanation-eligible.

With these clarifications in place, I can turn to the main arguments of this chapter. They aim to show, first, that explanations of moral facts must appeal to moral laws (2.2). That explanations of moral facts must appeal to moral laws is the basis for thinking that it is necessary and sufficient to establish the theistic explanation for all moral facts that all moral laws are theistically explained (2.3). In particular, the sort of theistic explanation that we should seek is one exhibiting theistic *explanatory immediacy* (2.4). This criterion—that theistic moral theory must provide a theistic explanation of moral law that exhibits theistic explanatory immediacy—will loom large in the attempts in Chapters 3 through 6 to settle on an adequate theistic account of moral law.

2.2 Moral law and the explanation of moral facts

Moral law is not just something that is available in a variety of moral theories; it is something that is indispensable for any moral theory with explanatory ambitions. For every moral fact is explained by at least one moral law, and no moral fact could be explained without appeal to a moral law.

Every moral fact is explained by a moral law. The proof for this was mentioned in Chapter 1. No moral facts are mere "danglers," where the action in question is simply morally necessary. As I noted there, we may have some toleration for physical facts that are brutely physically contingent, not capable of being covered by any law of nature, and so are simply to be accepted as obtaining without explanation. But this cannot be the case in morals. For given the obtaining of some moral necessity, there will be, at some level of detail of description, a point at which the level of description makes morally necessary the performance of the relevant action. If some view as crude and straightforward as hedonic act-utilitarianism were the case, it will be sufficient to give as the characterization of the morally necessary action its being the act that maximizes the total amount of pleasure; if some view as subtle and sophisticated as a mad-dog particularism were the case, then the description may have to be complete, so as to block the possibility of further characterization that would disturb the status of the action as morally necessary.[1] But on both extremes, and on everything in between, there is appeal to a moral law to explain the obtaining of the moral necessity in question. There is always a moral law available to explain any obtaining moral necessity.

Here is another way to put the point. It is a commonplace of moral theory that the moral supervenes on the nonmoral (see, for example, Smith 1994, pp. 21–2 and Jackson 1998, p. 118). Now precisely how to characterize this supervenience relationship is a matter of some dispute, but it seems very plausible that we will not capture all that we want to capture about the supervenience of the moral on the nonmoral if we try to characterize this relationship simply logically, as, say, Kim (1993b) characterizes various sorts of supervenience relationship. Supervenience thus characterized does not rule out symmetry—for example, that *being H_2O* is the supervenience base for, and also supervenes upon, *being water—*

---

[1] Mad-dog particularism, as I understand it, is not committed to the view that there are no moral laws; it is committed to the view that there are no *informative* moral laws, for without a complete characterization of the properties of the act-type in question, it is indeterminate whether *being performed* will be morally necessitated. But there is no reason to think that moral laws must be informative.

whereas we want the relationship between the moral and the nonmoral to be an asymmetric relationship. It is not merely necessary that if an action exhibits these nonmoral properties, then it will exhibit this moral property; it is that *by* exhibiting these nonmoral properties, an action thereby will exhibit this moral property. But such an asymmetric relationship whereby the holding of some set of nonmoral properties sees to it that some moral property holds is just what is involved in a moral law, given the view of moral law on which a moral law consists in some properties' morally necessitating other properties. So we can argue from the thesis of moral supervenience to the conclusion that every moral necessity is explained by some moral law.

So there is always a moral law on the scene available to explain any moral fact. But *need* we appeal to moral laws to explain moral facts? Or might some moral facts be sufficiently explained without appeal to some moral law? The most obvious way to try to work out a strategy like this is to hold that moral facts might be satisfactorily explained by appeal to other moral facts, appealing to some sort of model of subsumption. I want to grant that we sometimes do explain moral facts simply by appeal to other moral facts, but I want to claim that nevertheless such explanations are law-*presupposing*—that we cannot understand how these could be genuine explanations unless we take the explanans moral facts to be themselves entailed in a certain way by moral laws.

We can approach this moral-fact account of explanation by taking under consideration what Mark Schroeder has called the "Standard Model" for explaining normative reasons and moral requirements. Schroeder has argued that there is a single pattern of explanation that has dominated accounts of both reasons for action and moral requirements—indeed, it has so dominated that the possibility of other sorts of explanation has been put into doubt. Here is the Standard Model, formulated specifically in terms of reasons:

Standard Model. The explanation that there is a reason for X to [ϕ] because of P follows the Standard Model just in case it works because there is (1) some further action ψ such that there is reason for X to [ψ] and (2) not just because of P and (3) P explains why [ϕ-ing] is a way to [ψ]. (Schroeder 2008, p. 42, variables changed for uniformity)

The Standard Model functions by citing a reason to perform an act of some type along with a specificatory premise that identifies the action the reason for which is the explanandum as an *instance* of the action the reason for which is the explanans. So we can explain my reason to write on theistic explanation of moral law by appealing to my reason to contribute to ongoing debates in moral philosophy and the fact that writing on theistic explanation of moral law is a way to contribute to ongoing debates in moral philosophy.

Now, we are concerned not with reasons, but with moral requirements; and Schroeder takes it that the Standard Model can be, and has been, used as a central model of explanation in that domain as well. But it is pretty clear that at least one transformation would have to be made in order for this to be a plausible account of the explanation of moral requirements: we would have to move from what is "*a* way" to perform an action that one has antecedent reason to perform to what is, practically speaking, *necessary* to performing an action that one is antecedently required to perform. If I am required to fetch the cabbage for dinner, that going to Wegman's is a way to do so would not explain my being required to go to Wegman's. Nor would going to Wegman's being the easiest, best, most obvious way explain my being required to go to Wegman's. For there is no sense in which I must fail with respect to the requirement to fetch the cabbage for dinner by failing to go to Wegman's, even though it is admittedly a way of fulfilling that requirement. Indeed, I need not fail with respect to that requirement even if going to Wegman's is the best way to fulfill that requirement, all things considered. But if going to Wegman's is the only way to fetch the cabbage, then I am required to go to Wegman's.

Schroeder has much that is illuminating to say about the Standard Model, but his main aim is to move past it—to show that there is a way of explaining obtaining normative states of affairs that is distinct from the Standard Model (it can explain normative states of affairs that the Standard Model cannot explain), is more fruitful than it (it can explain all those normative states of affairs that the Standard Model can explain, and more), and is more fundamental than it (its correctness accounts for whatever success the Standard Model has in explaining reasons). But I want to linger with Standard Model explanations and those in the vicinity in order to raise some difficulties the solution to which will be helpful in our investigation of theistic explanation of morality.

Standard Model explanation seems attractive, even if not the only way to explain facts about reasons or requirements. But it is plain that it is a presupposition of the Standard Model that if there is a reason for X to ψ

and ϕ-ing is a way of ψ-ing, then X has a reason to ϕ. The move from the reason in the explanans to the reason in the explanandum is, given the premise relating one action to the other via the "is a way of" relation, one of entailment. The rationale for this is, I take it, that given the specificatory nonnormative premise, we can see that the reason to perform one action must subsume the other action as well[2]—if I have a reason R to keep my agreements, and showing up for class is a way of keeping my agreements, then surely that reason R must also apply to my showing up for class.

While Schroeder suggests that the Standard Model was treated by some as the exclusive model of explanation of normative facts, it is clear that no one ever took it, as Schroeder formulates it, to be such. That is because, on Schroeder's formulation, when seeking an explanation for A's having a reason to ϕ, we always begin with A's reason to ψ. But if this is correct, then there could never be a reason for action for A that is explained by a reason for action for B, where A$\neq$B. Yet these explanations are ubiquitous. Just as we explain my reason to show up to class by appeal to the fact that I have a reason to keep my agreements, we explain my having a reason to keep my agreements by appeal to the fact that everyone has a reason to keep his or her agreements. Just as we explain my reason to show up to class by appeal to the fact that I have a reason to fulfill my job duties, I have a reason to show up to teach my class in virtue of the fact that professors have a reason to show up to teach their classes. So we explain reasons for action not only by subsuming actions under broader act-types, we explain reasons by subsuming agents under broader agent-types.

Now, Standard Model type explanations might be thought to raise a challenge for my view that all explanations of moral facts must appeal to moral laws. With Standard Model explanations, we have moral facts (or facts about reasons) explained by other moral facts (or facts about other reasons). And we seem to be happy with these explanations, in many cases: they seem to be informative because they appeal to more general explanans facts under which the explanandum facts are subsumed, and one might find to be mere foot-stomping the claim that these are insufficient, incomplete, or otherwise inadequate as explanations. So let me raise a difficulty for Standard Model explanations, one that is not decisive but

---

[2] Schroeder does appeal to subsumption, but he does not attempt anything like a theory of subsumption.

which will require us to make some distinctions that cannot be sustained without appealing to moral laws in offering the explanans.

The Standard Model explanation of reasons works by subsuming a reason to perform some action under another reason. But it is very plain that is not universally true that by subsuming some action-type ϕ within another type ψ that one has a reason to perform we show that one has a reason to ϕ. (This is not a worry about defeasibility, as will be clear from what follows.) If we are appealing merely to subsumption, "is a way of" is to be understood simply as "is an instance of." That gloss is inadequate, though, as it leads to an unwelcome explosion of reasons. Suppose that I have a reason to give aid to this injured person. Now consider any arbitrary action that I might perform while giving aid—say, singing a show tune off-key. *Giving aid to this injured person while singing a show tune off-key*[3] is thus, given the "is an instance of" gloss, an action that I have a reason to perform. But, while I think this is bad, it is not the worst of it. For I have reason to do what is necessary to do in order to do what I have reason to do. I cannot sing a show tune without learning its lyrics. It thus follows that my reason to give aid to this injured person entails that I have a reason to learn the lyrics to a show tune. Indeed, it entails that for every show tune I have a reason to learn the lyrics to that show tune. Indeed, it entails that for every thing that I could do while giving aid, I have reason to prepare myself to do it. RAA.

This problem is easier to overlook when we move from reasons to requirements, given that the relationship in question is altered from "is a way of" to "is necessary for." But I think that we overlook it only by attaching more to the notion of *necessary for* than a purely extensional understanding would provide for us. If we go with a strictly extensional understanding, then we should say that if it is true that there is something that one will necessarily do while performing a certain required action, then one is morally required to perform that required action while exhibiting the necessary concomitant. If I am morally required to fetch the cabbage for dinner, and it is physically necessary that any action that I perform to get the cabbage will be accompanied by my perspiring (at least a little, say), then it follows that I am morally required to fetch the

---

[3] Don't deny that *giving aid to this injured person while singing a show tune off-key* is an action. I obviously could promise you to give aid to this injured person while singing a show tune off-key, and an oppressor could order me to perform that action.

cabbage while perspiring.[4] This means that I will, by the necessity principle, also be under a moral requirement that I see to it that I am in a position to perspire while fetching the cabbage. So not only will I be under a moral requirement to keep myself alive and hydrated in order to go get the cabbage; I will be under a moral requirement to keep myself alive and hydrated in order that I perspire while so doing. RAA.

The worry here cannot be dealt with by Schroeder's favorite way of dealing with unintuitive conclusions about reasons for action, that is, by appealing to the pragmatics rather than the semantics of reason-claims (Schroeder 2008, pp. 92–7). For the problem is not that these entailed reasons and requirements are too trifling; it is that *they have nothing to do* with the reason or requirement that gave birth to them. The "ϕ-ing is a way of ψ-ing" relationship in Standard Model reasons explanations has to be understood more strongly than "ϕ-ing is an instance of ψ-ing"; the "ϕ-ing is necessary for ψ-ing" relationship in Standard Model requirement explanations has to be understood more strongly than "ϕ-ing must be done if ψ-ing is done."

Above I noted as a friendly amendment—surely not denied by Schroeder—that the Standard Model explanations can also subsume agents under a broader class of agents in explaining why an agent has a certain reason or is under a certain requirement. But once we note that we often explain reasons not by subsuming the action under a broader action-type but by subsuming the agent within a broader class, it is immediately obvious that a problem similar to that which arose with respect to the actions that there is a reason/requirement to perform will arise with respect to the agents for whom a consideration is a reason/requirement. The fact that doctors are required to disclose medically relevant information to patients and Gregory House is a doctor *does* explain why Gregory House is required to disclose medically relevant information to patients; the fact that Mark Murphy and Will Clark are required not to affirm that they are not commonly called something other than "Mark Murphy" or "Will Clark"

---

[4] Again, don't say that this can't be a required action. Suppose I am a profuse perspirer; any action I undertake will necessarily, in virtue of my constitution, be accompanied by sweating. You are cool as a cucumber, and sweat only under exertion. Someone to whom we have promised obedience commands us both to go to Wegman's while perspiring. We both are required to do so. Easy for me: I just have to go to Wegman's, and I am assured that I will fulfill the requirement. You will have to take a lap or tote some bales before doing your shopping.

and that Mark Murphy is indeed one of Mark Murphy and Will Clark does not explain why Mark Murphy is required not to affirm that he is commonly called something other than "Mark Murphy" or "Will Clark." The problem here is not as grievous as in the case of subsumption of action-types; I don't think in the case of subsumption of agents into wider classes we get false implications, as I think that we get when we attempt to use subsumption of action-types. But we do get failure of explanation.

What should we say, then, about the power of the Standard Model in normative explanations? Begin with facts about moral requirements, which are our central concern. (I'll comment on facts about reasons briefly below.) I think that the source of the confusions here is the failure to distinguish between two senses of *A is morally required to ϕ*. In one sense, this expresses a moral fact, that it is morally necessary for A to ϕ. In another sense, this expresses, or presupposes, a moral law: *being A's ϕ-ing* morally necessitates *being performed*. Now, I take moral facts to be closed under other necessities, logical, metaphysical, and physical. If it is morally necessary that I go to the store, and it is physically necessary that I sweat while so doing, then it is morally necessary that I go to the store and sweat. After all, if I fail to go to the store while sweating, then I am relevantly morally defective in my action, and that is surely true; because it is morally necessary that I go to the store, and in every accessible world in which I go to the store I sweat while so doing, it is true that I am morally defective in any world in which I fail to go to the store while sweating; and so it is true that I am morally defective in any world in which I fail to sweat (since that would mean I didn't go to the store). By contrast: I do not take moral laws to be closed under these other necessities. For moral laws concern what *makes* actions morally necessary, and my failure to sweat does not make any action here wrong.

I think that this feature of moral facts—that, being closed under necessity, they allow irrelevant features into the actions that are morally necessary—precludes our thinking that the mere fact that a moral fact is subsumed under another moral fact gives us an explanation of the subsumed moral fact. For even if the subsuming moral fact is granted to obtain, it may nevertheless include irrelevant features that should not play any role in an explanation of some other moral fact. Does this show that we may never licitly use Standard Model explanations? I think not; what I think it shows is that when we licitly use Standard Model explanations, it is only because we presuppose that the moral facts we are employing are *law-regulated*—they are moral facts that themselves, if not fundamental moral laws, then entailed, with no irrelevant information added, by fundamental moral laws.

This suggestion should come as no surprise, given the considerations adduced in Chapter 1. Recall that part of the argument against regularity theories of law, whether laws of nature or moral laws, is that subsumption under a generalization by itself never explains—that this salt dissolves in this water is not explained by the generalization if x is salt and y is water, then x dissolves in y. Rather, what bears the explanatory weight is something about the character of that generalization (for example, that it is a theorem of a strong and simple deductive scheme) or about something distinct from the generalization that entails it (for example, that it includes a necessitation relation between universals). So it should be no surprise that mere subsumption of an action into a broader class of actions that there is reason to perform would fail to be explanatory. What we need is an appeal to moral laws. For something counts as a moral law, whether fundamental or derivative, when it exhibits the relation of moral necessitation. Now, if we want to explain an agent's being morally required to perform some action, then we can explain that action via subsumption if we are subsuming the explanandum under a moral law. That is because moral laws are *essentially* apt for use in explanations; we have a moral law only when an action-type's exhibiting a set of properties makes morally necessary that action-type's being performed, and that making relationship is explanatory. When we explain moral facts by subsumption, what we assume is that the features involved in the subsuming moral fact are those that make the action in the subsumed moral fact morally necessary; it would be a failure of explanation if our attention were focused on the explanatorily irrelevant rather than the explanatorily relevant bits.

So: an action-type's *being a doctor's disclosing medically relevant information to a patient* morally necessitates that action's *being performed*. Thus when we subsume this man under the law by noting that he, Gregory House, is a doctor, we have explained why any case of Gregory House's disclosing medically relevant information to a patient will be morally necessary—this man, House, must disclose that information, because his being a doctor contributes to making it so. An action-type's *being someone's keeping an agreement* morally necessitates that action's being performed. Thus when we subsume me (who is someone) and my action of showing up to teach my class (which I have agreed to do), we explain why my showing up to teach class is morally necessary—I must show up, because my showing up's being an instance of keeping an agreement contributes to making it so.

Our concern is with moral requirements rather than with normative reasons generally. But I do want to consider the charge that this account must be in error because it does nothing to help with the problem of normative reasons, yet it seems clear that the sort of account that we offer for the explanation of normative reasons should be the same as the account that we offer for the explanation of moral requirements. I agree to the objection's presupposition, that the solutions should be relevantly the same. But I do think that the solutions are relevantly the same, because reason-statements exhibit the same sort of ambiguity that I identified in statements of moral requirements. Now, reasons as such of course do not *necessitate* any agential response. But it is not far wrong to say that a normative reason *possibilitates* action—it makes it rationally possible to perform it; or again roughly, it makes it possible for a rational agent to perform that action. (Rational possibility is, in this sense, not to be understood as what is open for a fully rational person to perform; it is to be understood as eligibility, as there being some basis for the action such that acting that way is not sheerly irrational.)

So I would identify the same sort of ambiguity in discussion of reasons that I identified in the case of requirements. If you say that I have a reason to ϕ, that may just be a statement that it is rationally possible for me to ϕ, or it may be a statement that *being ϕ-ing* makes rationally possible *performing*, entailing that it is rationally possible for me to perform that action. The former understanding is closed under various operations under which the latter is not. If this being an instance of my ϕ-ing is sufficient for it to be its being possible for me rationally to ϕ, then it does follow from helping an injured person while singing a show tune off-key being an instance of helping an injured person, and its being rationally possible for me to help injured people, that it is rationally possible for me to help someone while singing a show tune off-key. But only reasons in the latter sense are essentially apt for explanation—in the latter sense, reasons are what make it rationally possible to perform some action, and singing a show-tune is not what makes this action something that it is rationally possible to do. So even if we use the Standard Model to explain reasons, it is only when we assume that the arguments that we are offering are law-guided that we can take the arguments to explain the rationality of the actions in question.

I have argued that every moral fact is explained by some moral law, and that moral facts can be explained only by adverting to the presence of moral laws. I should add here that I do not think that we satisfactorily explain any moral fact unless we appeal to *all* of the moral laws that make morally necessary a given agential response. One might well wonder why this would be. For, after all, if we mention one moral law that explains a moral fact, we have shown what makes morally necessary the agential response involved in the moral fact; wouldn't appeal to other moral laws bearing on that moral fact be strictly optional, as they would merely overdetermine the moral necessity of the agent's responding in a certain way?

I say No. Start with an example. Consider the moral fact *it is morally necessary for Mark Murphy not to lie in order to commit adultery*. Now it is sufficient to make this refraining morally necessary that there is a moral law precluding lying. But we would nevertheless think that there is an aspect of the moral fact that remains unaccounted for, its involving adultery; and so we ought to mention that there is also a moral law precluding adultery that makes that refraining morally necessary. Our explanations of the wrongness of actions should not make two actions look morally equivalent when they are not; and an explanation that appeals to the wrongness of lying would not distinguish between a lie and a lie to commit adultery.

I belabor this point for the following reason. In the next section, I will argue that the best way to argue for the theistic explanation of all moral facts is to argue for the theistic explanation of moral law, as the property *being theistically explained* is inherited by moral facts from the moral laws that explain them. One might claim, against this strategy, that we do not need to argue for the theistic explanation of all moral laws in order to explain all moral facts; we need only to argue for the theistic explanation of enough moral laws to cover all of the moral facts. Suppose that there is a moral law that is theistically explained, and that somehow explains all moral facts. On the face of it, this is compatible with there being a slew of moral laws that are not theistically explained and which also explain those moral facts—perhaps even explain them in some ways better, by being more informative. Suppose, for example, that *its being wrong to defy God's will* is theistically explained; that there are other moral laws besides, though these are not theistically explained; and the only thing God wills that we do is just what the moral law requires. So every moral fact would be explained by the moral law that God's will is not to be defied, even if there were a large batch of moral laws that were not theistically explained. I do not count this as full theistic explanation of moral facts, because a satisfactory explanation of moral facts should advert to *all* of the distinct moral laws that bear on those moral facts.

2.3 Theistic explanation of morality: the obvious strategy

Every moral fact is explained by some moral law, and we do not have a full explanation of a moral fact without adverting to all of the moral laws that bear on that moral fact. If one aims to provide a theistic explanation of morality, of all of the moral facts, there is an obvious strategy: to provide a theistic explanation of all moral laws. If all moral laws are theistically explained, then the moral facts explained by those moral laws will be themselves theistically explained. *Being theistically explained* is, I say, inherited by moral facts from the moral laws that explain them.

That *being theistically explained* is inherited by moral facts from the moral laws that explain them is justified not by appeal to some general claim about the transitivity of *explains*, which is dubious, but by appeal to specific features of the relationship between moral facts and the moral laws that explain them.

First, for a moral law to be theistically explained is for facts about God to figure in an account of why some set of properties morally necessitates a kind of agential response. A moral fact is explained by a moral law when it involves a moral necessity that is made to hold because of the moral necessitation present in a moral law. But it seems plain that if something necessitates only because of something else, then what is necessitated is explained both by what necessitates and by what explains the capacity of that thing to necessitate. If the successful spraying of paint is explained by the structure and materials of a spray painting machine, and what explains the spray painting machine's having that structure and those materials is the work of the engineer who designed and built it, then the successful spraying of paint is explained both by facts about the machine and facts about the engineer; the spraying of the paint is engineer-explained just because the facts about the spray-painting machine are engineer-explained. If this contract's being valid is explained by the existence of a statute, and what explains the existence of the statute is explained by the legislative activity of Queen Regina, then the contract's being valid is explained both by facts about the statute and by facts about Queen Regina; this contract's being valid is Regina-explained just because the statute's existence is Regina-explained.

The first point is that theistic explanation of moral law involves facts about God explaining why some properties morally select certain responses; if God explains why properties morally select as they do, then it seems pretty clear that God explains the moral selections themselves. The second point is to note that the relationship between moral selection of responses by some properties seems likely[5] to be related in a particularly intimate way to the moral necessities explained. if moral selection is a rational relationship (as opposed to, say, a causal relationship) (1.4), then the moral necessities explained will be logically (rather than, say, causally) related to the holding of the moral selection relationship between properties that makes for moral law. And when some fact A simply falls logically out of another fact B, then it seems pretty clear that if B is theistically explained, then A counts as theistically explained as well.

2.4 What sort of theistic explanation?

The considerations adduced in 2.2–2.3 justify the remainder of this book's central focus on the theistic explanation of moral law: in providing an account of how we ought to understand theistic explanation of moral law, we can see how theistic explanation of all moral facts (2.1) will have to go. Before we turn to the task of building a theistic explanation of moral law, I want to argue for a desideratum that theistic explanations of moral law should meet. My view is that satisfactory theistic explanations of moral law must exhibit what I will call *theistic immediacy*: the way in which moral law's holding depends on facts about God must be immediate rather than fully mediated by some other set of nontheistic facts.

Let me be a bit clearer on what I mean by theistic immediacy. I take it that we all have an intuitive grasp of what it is to enter immediately or only remotely into an explanation, at least given the sort of explanation at issue. If the cue ball strikes the 8 ball, which in turn strikes the 9 ball, sending it

---

[5] I defend this view in 4.2 below.

into the pocket, we understand that the 9 ball's falling into the pocket is immediately explained by its being struck by the 8 ball and only remotely explained by the cue ball's striking the 8 ball. The reason that we take it that the cue ball's striking the 8 ball is an explanation of the 9 ball's going into the pocket, but only a remote and not an immediate explanation, is that it is only *through* the cue ball's striking the 8 ball's explaining the 8 ball's striking the 9 ball that the cue ball's striking the 8 ball counts as part of the explanation for the 9 ball's falling into the pocket.

The main idea of immediacy in explanation is, then, something like this. Take as basic some explanatorily relevant notion—say, *bringing about*. If we take for granted *bringing about* as the explanatorily relevant notion, we can define explanatory immediacy in terms of it: x's obtaining is immediately explanatorily relevant to y's obtaining if and only if x's obtaining brings about y's obtaining, and there is no set of states of affairs (not including x or y) such that x's obtaining brings about y's obtaining only in virtue of bringing about the obtaining of some member of that set.[6] This notion of immediacy yields the notion of theistic immediacy that I want to defend here as a desideratum for any adequate theistic explanation of moral law: theistic immediacy requires that for the obtaining of every moral law, there is some fact about God that brings about its obtaining, and it is not true that God's bringing about the obtaining of any moral law is exhausted by God's bringing about the obtaining of some distinct state(s) of affairs that bring about the obtaining of that moral law.

I accept theistic immediacy not just as a claim about the way that we ought to theistically explain moral law but more generally as a claim about how to theistically explain anything that is explanation-eligible. It is a very strong thesis, but it is should not be construed more strongly than it is. It is, importantly, not a theory about theistic *completeness* of explanation. (x's obtaining completely explains y's obtaining when x's obtaining brings about y's obtaining and there is no state of affairs wholly distinct from x the obtaining of which brings about y's obtaining.) To hold to theistic completeness would be to hold that facts about God are the immediate *and sole* explanation of whatever is explanation-eligible—that everything that can be explained depends entirely and without qualification on facts about God. But immediacy obviously does not entail completeness; it is

---

[6] I draw on Freddoso (1991, p. 559) for this account of immediacy.

compatible with immediacy that while God enters into the immediate explanation of everything that is explanation-eligible, there are some explanation-eligible facts into the explanations of which nontheistic facts nonredundantly enter.

If we understand theistic immediacy as a general thesis about how facts about God enter into the explanation of everything that is explanation-eligible, how is that thesis is to be defended? Here is one way, which one finds in some concurrentist writings on God's involvement in the natural order,[7] which I think is suggestive but less than fully illuminating. One might say: We ought to exalt God as much as possible, as God is absolutely perfect; on the other hand, we ought not to deny what seems to be plainly true. It is more exalting of the divine nature to have God enter as fully into the explanation of all that exists and obtains as possible. But it seems plainly true that some nontheistic facts enter into the immediate explanation of some phenomena, so we cannot exalt the divine nature by affirming theistic completeness of explanation. But we can nevertheless affirm theistic immediacy: to affirm theistic immediacy is warranted, at least in part, because to do so is to exalt the divine nature as far as possible without denying what seems plainly true.

Now, there seems something right about this strategy: it does seem that even though God is absolutely perfect and thus we should ascribe to God the most perfect role with respect to the way that other things depend on God, we should also allow our understanding of the implications of perfection to be modified by judgments about nondivine matters—for example, the operations of nature. But the strategy is unilluminating in an important way, and its being unilluminating in this way limits the conviction that the argument can carry. Suppose we ask. Why isn't it the case that divine perfection requires not merely immediacy but also completeness? It will not do to be told that, as a matter of fact, our present commitments require that we deny completeness. For one thing, that is no answer at all to the "Why?" question; and what's more, it is always open to us to revise those commitments.[8] And it is not clear that the revision should be in the direction of greater completeness; we might reasonably respond by giving up the view that the divine perfection militates in any general way toward

---

[7] More on concurrentism below (5.5). The argument in the text derives from Suarez, *Disputationes Metaphysicae* 22, 1, 13.

[8] This is, after all, what the occasionalist recommends; see 5.2.

divine involvement in explanation. So this seems to be, on its own, an unsatisfactory account of why theistic immediacy ought to be endorsed.

I do not think that I can show why completeness does not follow from the divine perfection, while immediacy does. My best answer with respect to completeness is that we do in fact hold views on reflection that are incompatible with completeness and we lack any successful argument from the divine perfection to the view that theistic explanation must be complete. But I do think that we have good reasons from considerations regarding the divine perfection to think that immediacy follows from it, and that we do not in fact hold views on reflection that are incompatible with it. The views that we hold on reflection that might seem to conflict with immediacy in fact conflict not with immediacy but with completeness.

What are the considerations regarding the divine perfection that militate in favor of taking some view on the way that theistic facts enter into explanations? In 0.2, I made the argument that the divine perfection that seems to bear on this matter is divine sovereignty, where sovereignty involves *dependence* and *control* (though not necessarily *discretion*). I think that it is plain that dependence and control do not entail completeness of explanation: every explanandum's depending on facts about God and being controlled by those facts does not suggest at all that the explanandum is dependent upon/controlled by nothing but facts about God. As Aquinas points out, there does not seem to be anything untoward about God using instruments in the bringing about of certain effects in the natural order, even if there are some effects that cannot be brought about by use of instruments.[9] And this is what does seem to fit with our considered judgments about explanations in the natural order, that is, that nontheistic facts can be difference-makers, things that immediately enter into explanations of facts in that order.

My view, though, is that the best understanding of sovereignty understood as dependence/control would not permit God to enter into explanations in a fully mediated way, and so while the immediate explanation of some explananda may include more than just theistic facts, the immediate explanation of every explanandum must include theistic facts. For suppose

---

[9] Aquinas, for example, holds that there is nothing unfitting about God's using creatures as instruments in divine causation, although there are some divine actions—creation, say—that preclude use of creatures as secondary causes; see *Summa Theologiae*, Ia 45, 5.

that we distinguish between a substance's coming to exist, a substance's continuing to exist, and a substance's operating in its characteristic way. Now one might claim that our reflections on the object coming into existence out of nothing without divine dependence (o.2) and our commitment to the perfection of divine sovereignty commit us only to the view that God has to enter into the immediate explanation of substance's coming to exist; with respect to substances' continuing to exist or engaging in their operations, God's explanatory role can be fully mediated without detriment to divine sovereignty. Since nothing can continue to exist or engage in its operations without existing, and God explains that, God can be invoked in every explanation of a substance's existing, continuing to exist, or operating.

Now, this picture of God's explanatory role is, in effect, *deism*. And deism is characteristically rejected within orthodox theism. It is worth asking why creation is not enough, why theists tend to go for a stronger view of God's relationship to the natural order than the view that God is responsible for creation. The explanation, I suggest, appeals to the conception of divine sovereignty as dependence/control: that the notion that substances continue to exist and to be able to operate independently of God seems to place them, upon their creation, outside of the scope of divine sovereignty. One might reply: Of course these are not outside of the scope of divine sovereignty; after all, God could decide to eliminate those beings—it is not as if, having created them, God has no choice about whether they continue in existence. But this cannot be an adequate response, if the initial judgment of the object coming into existence without divine dependence (o.2) was correct. For there it seemed insufficient for divine sovereignty that God could have prevented the object from coming into existence, and that God's foreknowledge would have enabled this. So the mere fact that God can act to prevent the object's continued existence does not seem to be sufficient to satisfy the conditions of divine sovereignty.

One might think about it this way. If counterpossible thinking can make sense—if it is the case that some counterpossibles are false and some nontrivially true, or, if not strictly false or nontrivially true, that they point toward some important distinctions regarding metaphysical dependence—we can say that what divine sovereignty requires is that, counterpossibly, if God did not exist, then nothing could come into existence. If it is possible for a particle to pop into existence without theistic involvement, then it would seem that this counterpossible would be false. The fact that God could act so as to prevent particles from popping into existence does not make a difference to the truth of that counterpossible. But, similarly, we should say that, counterpossibly, if God ceased to exist after creating, then nothing could continue in existence; for that it could continue to exist would mean that by creating God has brought something into existence that no longer depends upon God. The fact that God could prevent a thing from continuing in existence should not lead us to reconsider the truth of the counterpossible.

Considerations such as theses—explanans-centered considerations (0.1), considerations regarding the sort of explanatory role that God must have, given God's perfection—explain, I think, why theism seems to militate not just in favor of the sort of explanatory involvement affirmed by deists but also in favor of the sort of explanatory involvement affirmed by those who hold that God not only creates but sustains things in existence. (We will return to this "conservationist" account of God's role in nature in 5.2.) But the same considerations that should lead theists beyond deism also explain why we should take God to be immediately explanatorily involved not only in the creating and sustaining of creatures, but also in their operations. Again, for creatures to be able to operate, bringing about effects in the natural order without immediate theistic involvement, is for those operations to be at most permitted by, rather than dependent upon/ controlled by, God. Again, using the counterpossible test, it is to allow that even if there were no God, these creatures could carry out their operations. This gives them an independence from God that seems incompatible with the divine sovereignty.

My view, then, is that divine sovereignty requires theistic immediacy with respect to the existing, sustaining, and operating of what is not divine. (That theistic facts are immediately involved in the explanation of what is *divine* is of course trivial.) Whenever we are dealing with facts about something's existing, or its engaging in any transactions in the created order, we should expect that those facts have an explanation that includes facts about God.

Another way to buttress this view is to reflect on the way that theism has taken omnipresence on board as a divine perfection. Now, omnipresence is paradigmatically understood with respect to spacetime: the idea is that God is somehow present at every spatiotemporal location. There is no location from which God is absent. Now of course what is needed for presence cannot be literal location. One might appeal to implications of omniscience or omnipotence to provide an account of what constitutes omnipresence, but omniscience and omnipotence do not themselves provide the basis for an adequate account of what omnipresence involves. It seems to me, as it has seemed to many theists, that merely epistemic understandings of omnipresence are far too weak; for God to be omnipresent does not reduce simply to God's knowing what is going on at every point of spacetime. (If, upon glorification, I were to become aware of what is going on at every spacetime point, I would not thereby gain the divine perfection of omnipresence.) It also seems to me that power understandings of omnipresence—for example, that God has the power to act or intervene at any point of spacetime—seem too weak as well; it would be strange to think of God as omnipresent if there were a region of spacetime at which God is entirely inactive, even though God retains the power to act there if God so chooses. The best reading of what omnipresence seems to require is active involvement at each point—that God is present everywhere involves God's being active at every point of spacetime.[10] But for God to be present everywhere via activity is for God to have to have an explanatory role in what is happening at every point of spacetime.

But look. The considerations that lead us to think of omnipresence requiring the exercise of divine control over each point of spacetime do not turn on anything particularly *about spacetime*. One might be driven by explanandum-focused considerations to think that spacetime particularly needs God's active involvement in order to be created and sustained. But on explanans-focused grounds—the idea that God exhibits full control—the considerations pushing toward active control over each point of spacetime push toward God's having an immediate explanatory role with respect to all that exists and all that is done.

Without God, nothing exists, nothing happens. There is no level of counterpossible analysis at which it is true to say that without God, something exists, or that given its existence, it will continue to exist, or

---

[10] Cf. Aquinas on omnipresence: "God is in all things by his power, inasmuch as all things are subject to his power; he is by his presence in all things, inasmuch as all things are bare and open to his eyes; he is in all things by his essence, inasmuch as he is present to all as the cause of their being" (*Summa Theologiae* Ia 8, 3).

that given its continuing existence, it will operate. The best understanding of divine sovereignty requires theistic immediacy. And so the best theistic explanation of moral law will be an explanation that exhibits this immediacy. The search for an adequate theistic explanation begins with the next chapter.

3
Natural law theory

3.1 What is a natural law theory?

For theists, I have argued, an explanation of moral law cannot be properly evaluated solely on the basis of explanandum-centered considerations—that is, considerations regarding whether the distinctive features of moral law can be captured by that explanation. For theists, explanans-centered considerations—considerations regarding God's role as essential explainer of everything that is explanation-eligible—loom large as well (0.2), and God's role as essential explainer cannot be satisfied if the role of theistic facts in the explanation of moral law is anything short of immediate (2.4). We now turn to the task of examining prominent theistic theories of moral law with the aim of seeing whether they can meet these explanandum- and explanans-centered desiderata.

Natural law theory has explanatory ambitions with respect to moral law, and it is one of the theories of moral law that is dominant within theistic moral inquiry. I will describe a version of this view that is based on a standard interpretation of Aquinas's moral theory (I will call this "standard natural law theory"), though in its main theses it is also affirmed by a number of contemporary writers who self-identify as natural law theorists.[1] In spite of the protests of natural law theorists, standard natural law theory has a reputation as a moral theory by theists and for theists. Now, the typical answer to this charge that standard natural law theory is sectarian is to respond that, in essentials, the natural law view can be affirmed by non-theists just as well as by theists, for its central theses are not obviously theistic. My view is that this response is successful as a reply to the charge that

---

[1] I emphasize that this is a *standard* reading of Aquinas's view, not the only plausible or extant reading. As will be clear below (Chapter 6), there are remarks in Aquinas's work that suggest a different account of the way that natural law theory could allow for theistic explanation.

standard natural law theory is essentially theistic. But the success of that response exhibits the weakness of standard natural law theory from a theistic point of view: the fact that standard natural law theory is not essentially theistic shows that it is inadequate as a theistic explanation of moral law. Or so I shall argue.

I begin by characterizing standard natural law theory (3.1) and showing that standard natural law theory is on its face unacceptable as a theistic explanation of moral law (3.2). While natural law theorists have available to them initially plausible maneuvers by which one might try to recapture theistic acceptability for the theory, no such maneuver is successful (3.3–3.7). The failure upon which I want to focus is explanans-centered: natural law theory's account of God's role in the explanation of moral law is either nonexistent or fails with respect to the immediacy criterion (2.4). While I focus on natural law theory, the arguments against natural law theory as a theistic explanation of moral law are not wholly confined to the specifics of this view; rather, Kantian and consequentialist views articulated within a theistic framework are sure to be open to similar objections with similar force (3.9).

Natural law theory aims to explain the moral law, and its way of discharging the explanatory task can be usefully divided into two stages. In one stage of explanation, that which is most proximate to the particular facts about rightness and wrongness of conduct to be explained, the natural law theorist argues from truths about what things are good for persons and truths about how it is appropriate to respond to such goods to conclusions about how it is, or can be, right to act. On Aquinas's view, for example, it is true by nature, and it can be easily known, that things like life, procreation, knowledge, society, and reasonableness in conduct are good for human beings, and worthy of pursuit. (See Aquinas, *Summa Theologiae*, IaIIae 94, 2; 94, 3. Other natural law theories offer somewhat different lists of goods; for a survey, see Murphy 2002c.) So there is always *some* sense to acting for the sake of staying alive, or having/rearing children, or getting along with others, or finding out about the world, or making good choices. But even actions that make sense in some way can be wrong to perform. The problem with lying is not that it does not make sense—we all know that there is a point to telling the lies we tell, and often this point is the realization of a genuine human good—but that the pursuit of the good is inordinate. On the natural law view, there are some ways of pursuing the good that are flawed; and to be a wrong action is just to be an action that is flawed in this way. A right action, by contrast, is just one that is in no way flawed (*Summa Theologiae* IaIIae, 18, 1).

It is obviously, then, an important task to identify the ways in which an act can be intrinsically flawed. Aquinas argues, with enormous plausibility, that the ways that an act can be flawed correspond to the different features that individuate acts: their objects (say, the immediate target, what one proposes to do in acting); their ends (say, the further, distinct goals to be realized through successful performance of the action); and their circumstances (that is, the external conditions in which one acts—the time, manner, alternative actions available, and so forth) (*Summa Theologiae* IaIIae 18, 2–4). The key idea is that *the nature of the goods themselves fixes certain actions as wrong in virtue of their objects, ends, circumstances*. An act might be flawed by virtue of its end: a plan of action might itself propose evil, as on Aquinas's views all lying does, since its object is falsehood, which is opposed to the good of truth. An act might be flawed through an improper ordering of object and end—even if survival and friendship with God are both goods, it is inordinate to seek friendship with God for the sake of bodily survival. An act might be flawed through the circumstances: while one is bound to profess one's belief in God, there are certain circumstances in which it is inappropriate to do so (*Summa Theologiae* IIaIIae 3, 2).

What is apparent from this sketch is that in the immediate explanation of the wrongness of certain sorts of action, it is the goods for persons that call the shots. The wrongness of an act results from a human action's being an inappropriate response to the goods on which that act bears; those goods make it the case that one must, or must not, respond to them in particular ways.[2]

I said that there are two stages in a standard natural law explanation of moral norms. The stage that is more proximate is the account in terms of goods and the action that responds to those goods. But there is a second stage as well. The natural law view includes an account of how goods and the features of human action together fix the moral status of types of actions. But we can also raise questions about why the goods that play this fixing role are goods. And Aquinas's is the common Aristotelian answer: that each being's good is determined by the kind of thing that it is; to be

---

[2] For one recent endorsement of Aquinas's account of the goodness of action, see Foot 2001, pp. 72–7.

human is to be such that certain things are goods for him or her. On Aquinas's view, an agent's happiness is that agent's perfection, where for a thing to be perfected is for its substance or its life (its existence and activity) to be perfected (*Summa Contra Gentiles* I, 37, [2] and *Summa Theologiae* Ia 48, 5); and the specific character of a thing's perfection is fixed by its form (*Summa Theologiae* Ia 5, 5). One might object immediately that this account of the nature of well-being is irritatingly disjunctive—to be an aspect of a thing's well-being is to be something that *either* makes that thing good *or* something that makes that thing's existence/activity good. But this appearance of irritating disjunction can be dispelled. The idea is that a thing's good condition is the completion or fulfillment of its nature, and its good existence is the completion or fulfillment of its good condition. This is what Aquinas refers to as the levels of actuality of a thing—the thing's being actual, or activated; the thing's form is for the sake of its good condition, and its good condition is for the sake of its good existence. So what unifies the nature of well-being is that of completion, or perfection, of a thing's nature.

Now all of these facts about whether something is in good condition, or is engaging in good activity, are, to put it plainly, natural facts. A comparison: that certain states of affairs' obtaining (all the parts are in place, and are able to function properly, and so forth) makes a duck nondefective and that certain states of affairs' obtaining (swimming in clean ponds, hunting for fish where there is plenty to eat, making new ducks, and so forth) makes for a nondefective duck life are matters of natural fact, and what is good for a duck is the maintenance of duckself in good duckly integrity and the performance of the activities, and the participation in the events, of good duckly life. There is, and I am not exaggerating, no interesting structural difference between the basic story about the good for ducks and that of the good for humans, however great the substantive differences between goods for ducks and the goods for humans may be (see also MacIntyre 1999, pp. 78–9). That the obtaining of certain states of affairs (all its parts are in place, and are able to function properly, and so forth) make for a nondefective human and that certain states of affairs (eating enough of the right things to stay healthy, having relationships with other humans, getting to know about the world and about how to move around in it, and so forth) make for nondefective human life are matters of natural fact. What is good for a human is the maintaining of itself in good condition as a human and of carrying out the activities and participating in the events of good human life.

It will be worthwhile to relate this rather abstract characterization of the natural law account of moral law with an illustration of how we connect these points to the explanation of specific moral laws. Recall that on the view of moral laws that was defended in Chapter 1, what makes something a moral law is that it involves some property morally selecting a response property, resulting in the holding of a corresponding moral necessity (1.4). How, then, do we explain in particular a moral law like *it is morally wrong to lie* in natural law terms? (I emphasize that this is illustrative only; natural law theorists might deny this is a moral law, or explain it somewhat differently; what is important is the structure of the explanation.)

To hold that *it is morally wrong to lie* is a moral law is to hold, on the Chapter 1 view, that the property *being lying* morally selects *being refrained from*, so that it is morally necessary to refrain from lying. Now, the property *being lying* is the property *being speaking what one believes to be false with the intention to deceive*. But that an action is characterized by the intention to deceive makes that action defective, as knowledge is a human good, and to intend to deceive is to act against what is good. Thus, it is morally necessary to refrain from lying: there is decisive reason not to lie, and if an agent is morally nondefective and in optimal conditions for action—conscious, aware of the circumstances, not drugged, etc.—then that agent refrains from lying. Note that the property *being lying* bears a certain normative power—the power to morally select *being refrained from*—because it bears this necessary relationship to something that is humanly good by nature. Thus *all* natural law explanations of moral law: they function by showing that an act-type bears on a human good in a certain way; the character of the good does the work of seeing to it that various properties applying to act-types morally select various responses. (For Aquinas's rejection of lying, see *Summa Theologiae* IIaIIae 110; for some recent natural law accounts, see Grisez 1993, pp. 405–12, and Murphy 2001, pp. 234–8.)

The natural law theorist thus explains the moral law and its features ultimately by appealing to facts about human nature and its defective and nondefective realization. The natural law applies to all that share this common nature. Its normativity flows from the goods that fulfill our natures, and its objectivity from the status of these goods as matters of natural fact. And the determinate content of the moral law—that certain kinds of action are ruled out, and others not—is fixed by the particular goods that fulfill us. That one is a human being, for whom life is good, necessitates everyone's refraining from murdering, mutilating, or assaulting him or her—the good of life entails that any action that is opposed to one's good in this way is ruled out, as a defective response, as a bad sort of action. The explanation runs from the nature of the good to the inevitable badness of certain sorts of response to that good, and thus to the necessity of agents' not performing such actions.

3.2 Natural law theory fails to satisfy explanans-centered criteria

Now it goes without saying that natural law theory's strategy for explaining moral laws is open to serious objection at more than one point. One might claim, for example, that it fails on its own terms to capture the normativity, or the content, or the objectivity of moral laws. These would be explanandum-centered objections to the natural law view, objections that the features of moral law that want explanation have not been adequately made intelligible. But I will not press these concerns; defenders of this view have tried to deal with them elsewhere (Finnis 1980, Grisez 1983, Chappell 1995, Lisska 1996, MacIntyre 1999, Murphy 2001, and Gomez-Lobo 2002). My concerns are, rather, with the natural law view's ability to satisfy the *explanans*-centered criteria. For on those grounds the natural law view seems to be a clear failure. It is plain that nothing in the explanation of moral law given in 3.1 is theistic; the natural law explanation of moral law proceeds entirely in nontheistic terms. It seems, on the face of things, that one explains moral law in an entirely Godless way if one explains moral law as the natural law theorist explains it. The desideratum that God is the explainer of all that is explanation-eligible is not satisfied by natural law theory, and *a fortiori* the desideratum that such facts be explained by theistic explanations that exhibit immediacy (2.4) is not met either.

3.3 The natural law theorist's first reply: the content of the good

One might claim that one cannot be entitled to claim that the moral law is explained in an entirely Godless way unless one examines more closely the content of the good as characterized within some natural law theory or other. For suppose that among the goods that fulfill persons is some God-involving good—say, friendship with God, or knowledge of God, or submission to God. It might seem that it would follow from such a view that natural law theory does not involve an entirely nontheistic account of moral law.

The first point to note in response is that even if it were true that the human good's including some God-involving content implies that at least some moral laws will be theistically explained, we would not have achieved what we are seeking—theistic explanation that extends to all moral law—unless all of the human good is God-involving in this sense. But that is what natural law theorists have characteristically denied—they have held, rather, that there is a variety of human goods, some of them God-involving, some of them not. Friendship with God may well be a human good—I would of course affirm this—but so too are life, knowledge, friendship with other humans, and so forth. So on the face of things, it looks as if the existence of other goods that have an independent, and not simply duplicative, role in explanation of moral law would show that this reply is not sufficient to satisfy the demand for full theistic explanation.

But I want to make a second argument, one that suggests that the fact that the content of the good includes God does not at all mean that *any* of the moral law is theistically explained. Think of things this way. In investigating the explanation of moral law, the natural law theorist points us to what *makes it the case* that such-and-such is an aspect of the human good and to what *makes it the case* that such-and-such is a nondefective response to that good. But we have not seen any reason to think that, on the natural law view, any state of affairs involving God's existence helps to explain the truth of any proposition concerning what is an aspect of human well-being and what counts as an appropriate response to it. That it is part of the human good to know God is not, on the natural law view as it has been thus far characterized, made true by any state of affairs involving God's existence. Given the human form, humans are perfected by knowing, and are more perfected by their knowledge to the extent that the knowledge is of the most fundamental explanatory principles; if there is a being that is the most fundamental explanatory principle of all, something that is the source of all being distinct from itself, then of course it will be good for humans to know that being. Again: that it is part of the human good to be in friendship with God is not, on the natural law view as it has been thus far characterized, made true by any state of affairs involving God's existence. Given the human form, humans are perfected by relationships of friendship, and are more perfected by their friendship to the extent that that friendship is of the best sort; if there is a being of perfect knowledge and goodness, and friendship with that being is possible, then of course it will be good for humans to be in friendship with that being. These accounts of the truth of the propositions *it is part of the human good to know God* and *it is part of the human good to be friends with God* do not even entail God's existence, so God's existence can hardly be asserted by those accounts.

One might find dubious the view that it could be part of the human good to know God or be friends with God without God's existing, so God's existing must be part of the explanation of any human goods that involve God. But I think this is just a confusion. *It is humanly good to respond in a certain way to x* does not entail x's existence, or even the possibility of x's existence, for *it is humanly good to respond in a certain way to x* does not entail *there is an x such that it is humanly good to respond to it in certain ways*. The human good might well include aspects that are never in fact realized, and indeed perhaps even impossible to realize. For example: I take it that we know that knowledge of the external world is a human good—it is better to have a clear, warranted picture of the world than to be confused or only accidentally correct. But we might know this to be true even while allowing that some skeptical thesis about the possibility of knowledge of the external world could turn out to be correct. If such a skeptical thesis turned out to be correct, the proper reaction is not to re-think what would perfect us as humans; it is, rather, to regret that some way in which that we could have been made better-off turns out to be impossible for us.

3.4 The natural law theorist's second reply: natural law as law

The basic structure of a natural law account of moral norms makes no appeal to God (3.2); the explanatory burden is borne by an account of fundamental human goods, the status of which as goods is explained by a theory of human nature the perfection of which is the realization of those states of affairs (3.1). The fact that the content of the human good may include God-involving states of affairs does not help matters from the point of view of theistic explanation (3.3). If the theistic natural law theorist is to show that this view can satisfy the explanans-centered desiderata—that God enters into the explanation of moral law, and does so in a way that involves immediacy (2.4)—then he or she will have to appeal either to resources possessed by the natural law view to which I have not called attention or to a further development of the view that is consistent with its main lines as laid out thus far.

One might make an argument of the former sort based on the way that the account of moral norms is presented in the work of Aquinas, the paradigmatic natural law theorist. One might notice that on Aquinas's view, what we are given is an account of the grounding of moral facts in terms of a theory of law—a particular sort of law that Aquinas denominates "natural." And it is part of Aquinas's theory of law that law is laid down by a lawmaker, for on his view law is an ordinance of reason made by one who has care of a community (*Summa Theologiae* IaIIae 90, 3). So one might lodge an objection to my view that God is absent from the explanation of moral law on the natural law account. For Aquinas thought that the fundamental truths of morality that follow upon truths about our human kind are themselves satisfying of the criteria for being genuine law and can satisfy those criteria only because they are ultimately authored by God, who has care of the entire universe (*Summa Theologiae* IaIIae 91, 1–2). On Aquinas's view, then, the moral law is law only because it is made so by God, and this means that moral law is after all theistically explained.

Whether or not Aquinas is right to describe the natural law as he does, this objection is a failure. For it involves an equivocation on the notion of "law." Moral law is, as I have argued in Chapter 1, a relationship of moral necessitation between properties. So the proper question to ask is whether it is the status of the norms of the natural law as laid down by God as lawgiver that explains the relationship of moral necessitation that holds between, say, *being lying* and *being refrained from*. And it is clear that this is not Aquinas's account. On Aquinas's account, the binding power of moral norms—their obligatoriness—is to be understood by reference not to divine commands but to the human good, promotion, protection, and respect for which is dictated by those norms. Not surprisingly, obligation is, for Aquinas, a kind of necessity (*Summa Theologiae* IIaIIae 44, 1, obj. 2, not denied). He identifies two kinds of necessity to consider in regard to human actions: one that results from coercion, which is contrary to the will; and another that results "from the necessity of an end, namely, when one cannot reach the end of virtue without doing a certain thing" (*Summa Theologiae* IaIIae 58, 3, ad 2). Aquinas identifies obligation with the necessity of the latter kind: that one is obligated to adhere to a certain precept means that the following of that precept is required for one to attain the good of the agent, "the end of virtue." The status of the norms of the natural law *as law* requires us to appeal to God, but the status of those norms as *binding precepts* requires, on Aquinas's view, no such appeal. Or, at least, we have not yet seen any reason why it should.

One might deny that I have correctly identified Aquinas's account of obligation, holding that for Aquinas obligation involves either the necessity of an end or the necessity imposed by a command from a superior.[3] But while this might be an acceptable reading of Aquinas's (admittedly few) texts on obligation stripped from their context in Aquinas's overall moral theory, it is clear that read in the context of that theory Aquinas could not hold this sort of disjunctive theory of obligation. For the first principles of the natural law, which provide the basis for *all* rational action on Aquinas's account, are those that specify the sorts of goods that make action intelligible and on which the more specific precepts of the natural law (and the virtues which take their first principles from the natural law) are founded (*Summa Theologiae* IaIIae 94, 2). An additional sense of obligation appealing to the commands of a superior would either float free from considerations of rationality in action (implying that some action could be obligatory but entirely rationally unmotivated) or rely for its rational force on the more basic notion of obligatoriness, that in which the rational necessity is grounded in the good.

We are asking whether God somehow contributes to the explanation of the moral necessitation relationships expressed in the moral law, and the fact that natural law counts as "law" within Aquinas's view only because it is laid down by God does nothing to explain those moral necessitation relationships. Having made that reply, I want to go a bit further and claim that Aquinas is in error when he supposes that the precepts of the natural law do in fact satisfy the conditions for counting as law. For Aquinas's

---

[3] Here is the text that is ambiguous on the relationship between commands and moral necessity: "Necessity is twofold. One arises from constraint, and this removes merit, since it runs counter to the will. The other arises from the obligation of a command, or from the necessity of obtaining an end, when, to wit, a man is unable to achieve the end of virtue without doing some particular thing. The latter necessity does not remove merit, when a man does voluntarily that which is necessary in this way" (*Summa Theologiae* IIaIIae 58, 3 ad 2).

account requires that he equivocate on the notion of *lawmaking* in order to make the case that natural law is law. Aquinas's explanation of how the natural law is law depends on God's having made human beings in such a way that they are able to grasp these necessitation relationships by nature (*Summa Theologiae* IaIIae 90, 4 ad 1), and so Aquinas suggests that because of this divine activity it is true that God *communicates* to human beings the precepts of the natural law and so counts as *having commanded* them to perform the actions required by those precepts. But this is an error: God's role as described by Aquinas is simply causal, and we have no adequate basis for taking God to have performed a speech act of any sort in having made human beings so that they could come to an awareness of the content of the natural law.

It is essential to Aquinas's argument that natural law is law that natural law counts as having been laid upon us by way of some divine speech act (*Summa Theologiae* IaIIae 92, 2). But it is clear that whatever else we want to say about the way that God's having made us a certain way involves our ability to come to know, and easily know, certain propositions, we should not want to say that any of this counts as the performance of a divine speech act. Speech acts have sincerity conditions, so that even when we accept that another has performed a sincere speech act, we can say how certain differences in that speaker's mental states would make that speech act count as insincerely (and thus defectively) performed (Searle and Vanderveken 1985, pp. 17, 18–19; also Alston 1999, pp. 77–8). So my telling you that there is beer in the fridge would be insincere if, rather than believing there is some beer, I instead believed no such thing. But if I simply lead you to believe that there is beer in the fridge, even intentionally, by leaving beer receipts around, there is nothing I am doing that would count as *insincerity*. I can in that case *mislead*, but there is no insincerity present. And, not coincidentally, my leaving beer receipts around is not a case of lying, though we would allow that it deceptive, because all lies are speech acts, and my leaving beer receipts around is no speech act.

So speech acts have sincerity conditions. It is thus a clear test of whether a speech act has been performed whether we can specify how the alleged speaker's mental states could have been different such that the alleged speaker's act would count as insincere. But by this test it is plain that God's actions in creating human beings with the capacity to come to know the norms of the natural law does not count as performing a speech act at all.

God's creating us in such a way that we would by nature come to hold views about how to act that God took to be in error would make God a deceiver, but not a liar. Since natural law cannot be law, on Aquinas's view, without a divine speech act, natural law is not law in the sense that Aquinas characterizes it.

3.5 The natural law theorist's third reply: God in the explanatory background

Though John Finnis (1980) and Anthony Lisska (1996) are deeply in disagreement about how to specify some of the fundamental features of the natural law position—the central question on which the two differ is whether the property *being good* is reducible to some natural property; Finnis denies this reducibility, Lisska affirms it—they would nevertheless both affirm the natural law explanation of the moral law sketched in 3.1. Each would affirm that the starting points for practical reason are fundamental goods, which goods are the basis for principles of right action; and each would affirm that the status of these goods as goods is fixed by the nature of the human being and what constitutes that being's perfection.[4] And both Finnis and Lisska are theists, and affirm that we should embrace a theistic explanation of moral law (Finnis 1980, pp. 371–410 and Lisska 1996, pp. 128–31). On their view, while my characterization of natural law theory is correct so far as it goes, it is incomplete, for I have given only natural law theory's *proximate* account of the moral law. I have not given the *complete* account. The complete account includes facts about God. So my view that the natural law account provides no theistic explanation of moral law is mistaken.

What are these "complete" accounts of the natural law that include facts about God and thus give the lie to my claim that natural law theory provides no theistic explanation of moral law? Begin with Finnis, whose view is developed at length in *Natural Law and Natural Rights*. Finnis is

---

[4] Critics of Finnis's view often claim that he denies the latter thesis. But Finnis has insisted on numerous occasions that his view affirms the grounding of natural law in human nature, and connects his view to a teleological conception of human nature: he describes his view as a teleological theory of well-being in which "the basic forms of good are opportunities of being; the more fully a man participates in them the more he is what he can be. And for this state of being fully what one can be, Aristotle appropriated the word *physis*, which was translated into Latin as *natura*" (Finnis 1980, p. 103).

explicit that part of his aim in that book is to provide an account of moral norms "without needing to advert to the question of God's existence or nature or will" (Finnis 1980, p. 49). But while he thought that one could provide an account of the moral law in natural law terms without in any way appealing to theistic facts—an account presented at the same explanatory level at which rival egoisms, Kantianisms, utilitarianisms, virtue theories are characteristically presented—he also thought that the formulation of such a view raised further questions that a complete theory would have to answer.

> What further explanations are required? After all, the basic forms of human flourishing are obvious to anyone acquainted... with the range of human opportunities. And the general requirements of reasonableness... are, likewise, as obvious as the norms of rationality, principles of logic, and canons of explanation that are presupposed in any explanation... [W]ould it not be a mistake to expect any deeper level of explanation of the practical reasonableness of community, authority, law, rights, justice, and obligation, once their explanation has been pursued from practice to self-interest, and thence to the common good which both friendship and rational impartiality require us to respect and favour?
>
> The answer must be: No, we cannot reasonably rest here. There are further practical questions; and there are also further relevant theoretical questions about both the whole structure of norms and requirements of good that has been identified, and the whole structure of explanations already advanced. (Finnis 1980, p. 371)

As a theoretical matter, that there is an objective, naturally authoritative moral law is itself a remarkable fact calling for further explanation; as a practical matter, we seem able to ask whether there is any further point to our pursuit of our good, both individually and in common. In neither case does it seem vain to seek such further explanations; there seems to be initially neither reason to suppose the existence of a natural law and the absence of any further point to acting on it to be brute facts or simply self-explanatory matters. So in the final chapter of *Natural Law and Natural Rights* Finnis explores these further questions, answering them in theistic terms.

Finnis begins by offering a version of the cosmological argument, holding that reason suggests that we pursue adequate explanations of the obtaining of contingent states of affairs, and that no such explanation could be satisfactory until we reach an uncaused causing, something whose existence is self-sufficient—Finnis calls it "D"—a being the nature of which includes its existing, so that it could not not be (Finnis 1980, p. 386). With respect to the disputed theoretical questions, Finnis holds that the set of obtaining states of affairs whose explanation will ultimately terminate in this uncaused cause includes states of affairs whose obtaining is affirmed within his natural law view.

> By 'D' or 'God' is . . . meant (i) that which explains the existence of the questioning subject; (ii) that which explains the existing of good states of affairs, and the opportunity of making them exist; (iii) that which explains our ability to recognize goods, to grasp values, and their equivalent practical principles; and (iv) that which explains our ability to respond to the attractiveness of those goods, to the rational appeal of the principles. (Finnis 1980, p. 404)[5]

Further explanation can be offered for the existence of the natural law on the basis of D's creative causality being responsible for there being agents with the capacity to know the good, be moved by it, and pursue it effectively.

Practically, Finnis holds that without appealing to D—a being which, we may speculate, has a personal mode of existence (Finnis 1980, p. 389)— the basic goods, with their ineliminable relativity to our interests, whether individually or in common, will "seem, to any thoughtful person, to be weakened, in their attractiveness to reasonableness, by a certain relativity or subjectivity" (Finnis 1980, p. 373). But (and here Finnis allows that he is moving beyond what can be established or defensibly affirmed of D from natural reason) if we were to come to justifiably believe that D's creative causality proceeds from D freely and intelligently, not to serve any one of D's needs (for D is self-sufficient) but as a kind of play, then one could enjoy goods of community with D in freely cooperating in D's activity. Thus one can place one's own, and others', pursuit of the basic goods in a wider context that itself has an intelligible point.

Now it seems to me that the attempt to answer further practical questions about the natural law must be, in the terms set by Finnis's own natural law view, a nonstarter. For what we learn from Finnis's theory of natural law is that in figuring out what is worth doing, the answers that are available to us bottom out in the basic goods. For every craft or line of inquiry, and likewise every action and decision, have point and intelligible

---

[5] I have omitted the first item from this list (which does not appeal specifically to D's capacity to explain states of affairs concerned more immediately with the natural law), and renumbered.

purpose only through their bearing on one or another of these basic goods, and none of these basic goods is reducible to an aspect of or an instrument for the realization of some other good. Practical questions, one might plausibly suppose, ultimately have to be answered by appeal to the basic goods. If there is some further point beyond them, necessary to underwrite their goodness, then the basic goods are not so basic, after all.

Or put it another way. When Finnis describes the relationship with D in terms of which our pursuit and promotion of the basic goods gains a fuller level of intelligibility—practical, not theoretical—it is in terms of explaining how D's activity in creating, conserving, and directing the world is a kind of *play*, and we are cooperating with D in this intrinsically good activity, thus being in *community* with D. These are basic goods, and if there is any trouble about those basic goods being relative to us in some sense, the trouble should reappear here in the explanation.

But the failure of the attempt to provide a further practical account of the goods on which the moral law is based does not so much as suggest that no further theoretical account of the moral law is forthcoming. Again, though, it seems to me that this theoretical account is a failure, for it does not explain the natural law. This is of course not a criticism of theism, or of his argument for theism, or of theistic explanations of morality. My criticism is that Finnis has misidentified what the theistic explanation that he offers takes as its explanandum. The D-explanation that Finnis offers for the natural law does not explain the natural law as such, but rather why human beings are capable of acting successfully on it.

It is plain that the D-explanation does not aim to explain the *goodness* and *morally necessitating* character of the basic goods—it does not explain why knowledge (for example) is good for us, and why it morally necessitates certain sorts of action—so much as to explain what makes our grasp of this goodness, and the modification of our conduct in light of it, possible. After all, the specific states of affairs to which Finnis appeals in laying out the explanatory relationship between D and the natural law are those states of affairs concerning the human capacity to know and act on the natural law which we might take to be necessary for humans to be genuinely bound by it—ought-implies-can type constraints. I suppose that one might claim that, insofar as goods must be the sort of thing that are in principle possible to know and pursue, explaining how we are able to know and pursue the basic goods counts as explaining the natural law. But Finnis does not give us any reason for thinking that we must appeal to D to explain even these facts. For *that humans are capable of knowing the natural law* and *that humans are capable of being motivated by it* are not contingent facts about individual human beings; they are necessary truths about the kind *human being*. By Finnis's lights, *knowledge is humanly fulfilling* and *humans are capable of knowing that knowledge is good* and *humans are capable of being motivated by the goodness of knowledge* are all necessary truths about the human *kind*, and given his criterion for appealing to D as ultimate explainer—that we are to seek out explanations for *contingently* obtaining states of affairs—these states of affairs fall outside of the range of D's explaining.

Now, one might respond that while Finnis begins his discussion of D and the rational pressure toward further explanation by noting that what calls for explanation is *contingently* obtaining states of affairs, nothing precludes our modifying Finnis's view to allow that even necessary states of affairs may well require further explanation. Even if some state of affairs necessarily obtains, it does not follow that this state of affairs requires no explanation. Some necessarily obtaining states of affairs may have their necessity through some other state of affairs (2.1). And even those that have their necessity of themselves nevertheless may need to be explained by analyzing the state of affairs, so that we can see why it must obtain. All of that leaves open the possibility that D could have a role in explaining the necessary states of affairs the obtaining of which constitutes the existence of the natural law. But this does not provide the theistic explanation for moral law that we are looking for; it would provide only reason to think that there is such an explanation; and, what's more, given that any such explanation would be relegated to the explanatory background, it is hard to see how it could satisfy the criterion that theistic explanations of moral law must exhibit immediacy (2.4). Unless the natural law view provides that explanation, and does so in a way that exhibits theistic immediacy, we have reason to think the natural law view defective from a theistic standpoint.

Now, one might note that while the natural law is not contingent, the existence of beings that can be bound by the natural law is contingent, and so *that* can be explained by D. This is, in effect, the tack taken by Lisska. Lisska, as I noted above, holds that the proximate explanation of the natural law makes no mention of God: "The existence of God and the role of the eternal law do not comprise the first set of questions to be considered" in thinking through an account of moral law (Lisska 1996, p. 126). The role of God is in the "ultimate" or "capstone" explanation; it is by appeal to God's role as the explainer of why contingent beings of the kind to be bound by these natural law norms exist at all that we complete the explanation of the moral law in theistic terms (Lisska 1996, p. 130).

But this is pretty clearly not helpful. To explain the existence of beings to whom the natural law applies is not to explain the natural law. The natural law theses that Finnis and Lisska affirm and that call for explanation concern necessary relations between universals, not the existence of any particulars; explaining the contingent existence of those particulars does not explain the necessary relations between universals that constitute the natural law. An analogy: suppose that, while I am childless, wrongheadedly benevolent lawmakers pass a law that holds that any children of Mark Murphy will, upon the age of majority, receive full financial support for the rest of their days. I do not explain the existence of this law, not in the least, by becoming the parent of children to whom this law applies. Without my children's existence, the law would be just as valid; it would simply not be what one might call "operative"—it would not be having any normative effect on legal actors. Similarly, to make God's role in natural law simply that of bringing into existence beings to whom that law applies would not do anything, not in the least, toward giving God a role in explaining the validity of the moral law that binds us; it would explain only why the moral law is operative, having normative effects on moral agents.

3.6 The natural law theorist's fourth reply: divine responsibility for properties

The explanans-centered considerations on which I insisted in 1.2 and 2.4 will not be met simply by appealing to God as moral lawmaker (3.4) or by appealing to God as ensuring the background in which moral law is normatively effective (3.5). For not only do these replies fail to secure theistic immediacy in the explanation of moral law (2.4), they fail to secure *any* sort of theistic explanation. In asking whether one might elaborate the natural law view in ways that secure theistic explanation, and immediately so, one might take a strong hint from the conception of moral law that was defended in Chapter 1, on which moral law is characterized in terms of a relationship of moral necessitation between properties (1.4). If the form of moral law relates properties, then perhaps

God's explanatory role with respect to moral law is that of bringing into existence the relevant properties that will then stand in that relation. After all, if everything distinct from God depends on God (0.2, 2.4), and we are taking ontologically seriously the existence of properties—as one must, if one is going to offer a theory of moral law modeled on the Armstrong/Tooley/Dretske theory of laws of nature—then we must hold that properties' existence is to be theistically explained, and immediately so. So we can appeal to God's role in bringing about these properties in order to explain God's role in the moral law within a natural law theory.

How might one formulate a view of God's role in the existence of properties that would do the necessary work in providing a theistic explanation of moral law? Here is one possibility: On one view of properties, no property exists in any world unless that property is instantiated in that world. So suppose, as the natural law theorist supposes, that the property *being human* is particularly salient in moral laws, playing a central role in determining both the goods to which human beings must respond and the appropriate response to those goods. One might claim, on the conjunction of this view of properties and the salience of the property *being human* in accounting for the moral law, that it is simply God's creative act of bringing some humans into existence that explains why the kind *human* exists and exhibits God's role in explaining moral facts. Note well: this view is not the view discussed previously (3.5), that without God there would be no humans, and so no beings to which moral laws can make a normative difference. On that view, it is consistent with there being no humans that *being a treating of a human as a mere means* morally necessitates *refraining from performance*; there would simply be no beings whose conduct would be properly regulated by the resulting moral necessity. On the view presently under consideration, there is no such property as *being human* without God's having created some humans, and no such moral law as *humans are not to be treated as mere means*, so God's role in explaining the moral law is much more robust.

One could, on the other hand, offer an alternative account of God's role in bringing about the existence of the relevant properties. This alternative account is consistent with both the affirmation that there are no uninstantiated properties or with its denial. On this view, properties exist in virtue of some divine activity—say, some activity of divine thought, in which a creative possibility is represented in some way by the divine mind.

Human is a certain creative possibility; there are no doubt other such possibilities involving created rational material beings. But if the kind is ontologically dependent on the divine mind, then again we have theistic explanation of moral law—for the properties related by moral necessitation would not exist were it not for the divine mind's activity.

It is clear that with the introduction of divine responsibility for the relevant properties, we are finally in the ballpark of theistic explanation of moral law. The previous answers that we considered gave no reason to think that either the properties related by moral necessitation or the relationship of moral necessitation itself is theistically explained; but as all there is to a moral law is properties related by moral necessitation, it is hard to see how these previous answers could be relevant to the explanatory issue with which we are concerned. But the appeal to divine responsibility for properties obviously bears on our explanandum.

I am going to press two sorts of worries about the appeal to divine responsibility for properties, worries that I think can be appreciated without articulating a particular theory of the properties for the existence of which God is responsible. The question is whether the properties for which God is responsible (or the existence of the properties for which God is responsible) are to be identified with God or aspects of God (or facts about God). I take it that for those who hold that God is responsible for the existence of properties there can be distinct views on this question. So Leftow argues for universals as divine concepts, answering Yes (Leftow 2006). I take it that someone friendly to the view that divine responsibility for properties holds only in virtue of God's seeing to it that the universals are instanced would be inclined to a No answer, though this is not an entailment of the position. My view is that if we answer No, holding that the properties relevant in moral laws are not themselves divine, then even if we do get some sort of theistic explanation of moral law here, it is not one that exhibits theistic immediacy, and so fails the test for adequate theistic explanation of moral law defended in 2.4. If we answer Yes, holding that the relevant properties are themselves divine, then there is no issue of immediacy, but we still face an explanatory problem that requires yet a further elaboration of our explanans.

Suppose we answer No: properties are not themselves divine. God's role in bringing them into existence would make it the case that moral laws are theistically explained. But we would not have secured the sort of theistic explanation desired, in which theistic explanations are immediate

(2.4). This seems most obvious with respect to the account of God's responsibility for the existence of properties on which all that is required is that God create a being that exemplifies the property. For all that would be required, on this view, for God to explain the moral law would be for God to bring into existence some human being and then allow that human being instantly to cease to exist. That there was a human being for one moment would be sufficient for the property *being human* to exist in that world and for the moral laws that require the existence of the property *being human* to be vindicated. This is obviously not a case in which we have immediacy of theistic explanation. The role of God's creative act is causal; the immediate explanation of the moral law will refer just to the relevant properties and their intrinsic capacities to morally necessitate certain sorts of being.

While the failure of immediacy may be most intuitively obvious on this view, it is also the case on any theistic activist account of properties on which properties are not themselves divine. For, again, if God's role is simply the causal role of bringing these properties into existence, that is consistent with the moral necessitation being entirely between the properties themselves. The theistic explanation of the moral necessitation will be fully mediated: God brings the properties into existence, but the immediate explanation of why one property morally selects another will refer immediately entirely to those properties and only mediately to God. (Thus we would be inclined, on this view, to say that if, counterpossibly, these properties could exist without God's bringing them into existence, they would be related in all the same ways by moral necessitation that they are in fact related.) If, then, we agree that transactions of this sort require theistic explanation, and of the immediate sort, then the appeal to divine responsibility for the relevant moral properties does not satisfy the desiderata that we have set for theistic explanation of moral law.

If one wishes to preserve theistic immediacy, then one will have to claim that properties are themselves divine entities—divine concepts, or something like that. This is progress. For there is on this formulation of the view no basis to question theistic immediacy, for even if we say that the properties themselves bear the power to morally necessitate, what bears the power to morally necessitate is *ex hypothesi* itself divine. Now there are multiple reasons to worry about views of this sort, but I will not consider here objections against the plausibility and even the very coherence of such a position. I have a distinct worry, one that does not trade on any general worry about theistic activism.

In the first chapter, I developed an account of moral law on an analogy with the laws of nature. (This is a comparison to which we'll return in Chapter 5.) Suppose that one were asking for a theistic explanation of some law of nature. What we are looking for is an account of the character of this law of nature *as law*—that is, an account of the governing (I called it "selecting": 1.4) relationship that holds between these properties. While it would be interesting to know that these properties are themselves theistically explained, in asking for an explanation of this *as a law* it is the *necessitation* between the properties that is at issue. And that is just what is not explained by an appeal to God simply as the explainer of the existence of the properties themselves. We would still want to know why it is the case that these properties physically select other properties, at least in a given context. After all, on this view, all properties' existence is theistically explained; what is the explanation for why some properties in particular physically select others?

Here is another way to approach the problem. Unless we say something more than this about the role that God has in explaining the moral law, we have not said anything about God's role with respect to that about these properties which is distinctively moral. The role of God in explaining moral law would be just the same as the role that God has in explaining any truth about what properties are exemplified by what things, or any generalization relating multiple properties. The way in which we can give a theistic explanation of *this dog is black* is the same as that to be given for *it is a moral law that one refrain from lying*; neither of those could be true unless the properties in question exist, and God is responsible for the existence of those properties.

Now, natural law theorists inclined to this divine-responsibility-for-properties response might say: "You are moving the goalposts on us. You wanted a theistic explanation of moral law, and we've given you one. If you are complaining that there is nothing *distinctive* about God's role here, then the complaint is misguided. The distinctiveness of moral properties does not come from God's explanatory role with respect to them, but from the basic character of the properties themselves—to put it crudely, not from the way that God's activity explains them, but from the way that they turn out given God's explanatory role with respect to them. It is the nature of those properties that we call 'moral properties' or 'morally relevant' that they effect the moral necessitation that they effect." I will offer a further objection to this view in a moment (3.7). But I deny that the objection I have been developing is an exercise in goalpost-moving. What I am pointing out is that the divine-responsibility-for-properties view is no explanation at all of the *power* of these properties to morally necessitate. And the response just offered on behalf of the defender of that view does not help; to appeal to the character of the properties is, so far, just to repeat the fact that some properties morally select others, and in a way that does not require any further theistic facts as part of the explanans. That is something for which we have not been given any accounting.

3.7 The natural law theorist's fifth reply: natural law as not explanation-eligible

The natural law theorist's last reply, which can be used to supplement the divine-responsibility-for-properties (3.6) view, is that the relationships of moral necessitation present in the moral law are not explanation-eligible— or, perhaps, even if they are in a way explanation-eligible, they are not *theistic*-explanation-eligible. The natural law theorist, as I have described the view, traces the explanation of the moral law back to certain fundamental human goods, and explains the character of those goods as such in terms of human nature; the natural law theorist traces the explanation of the rightness or wrongness of action in terms of what appropriately responds to those goods. I have denied that a "divine background" story succeeds in turning this account, which seems nontheistic, into a theistic explanation of moral law (3.5); and I have denied that the additional thesis that God is responsible for the existence of the properties at work in the natural law view suffices as an explanation for the moral necessitation in which we are interested (3.6). But the natural law theorist's last, and in my view best, reply is that there is simply *no room* here for the sort of further theistic explanation that I have been asking for.

Suppose, for example, that I asked for a theistic explanation for H_2O's being an ingredient of lemonade. If I were to ask for such an explanation, one might rightly retort that I am asking too much: "Perhaps we can give a theistic explanation for the existence of the properties *being lemonade*, *being water*, and *being H_2O* and of the relation's *being an ingredient of*, along the lines of the 'divine-responsibility-for-properties' theories discussed above

(3.6). And we can even give a sort of explanation—a *constitutive* explanation—for why H_2O is an ingredient of lemonade: it is that water just is H_2O, and lemonade just is a drink made up of ingredients one of which is water. So H_2O is an ingredient of lemonade. So while we can talk about God's role in seeing to the existence of these properties, there can be no further theistic role in explaining the status of H_2O as an ingredient of lemonade." This reply is very plausible. When we have an explanation that is produced by way of a string of necessary constitution and/or identity claims, there seems to be no additional room for theistic explanation. God's being responsible for the existence of the property *being lemonade* just is God's being responsible for the existence of a certain complex property one of the parts of which is *having water as an ingredient*.

So now the obvious comparison: one might make the same sort of claims on behalf of the explanation of the moral law offered by the natural law theorist—that the explanation of the moral law, like the explanation of water's being an ingredient in lemonade, is the sort of explanation that is too tightly-wrapped for theistic explanation to enter into. One might say: Moral facts can be informatively identified with, that is, reduced to, certain facts about human nature. Perhaps one might claim that the property *being morally necessary* just is the property *being backed by reasons for (human) action (of a certain kind)*, and *being a reason for (human) action* just is *being humanly good*, and *being humanly good* just is *being related (in a certain specific) way to human nature* (say, being its perfection). On this view, the questions about the modal relationships holding between these properties—properties that, we will allow, owe their existence to theistic activity—are answered by identification. And so there is no room for theistic explanation.

I think that this is the natural law theorist's best reply because, were this account correct, it would insulate the natural law theorist from further explanans-centered criticism. I agree that were the case of moral law and human nature precisely analogous to the case of H_2O and lemonade, then we would not have a case in which further theistic explanation is possible. But these cases are not thus analogous, and so we should reject the "tightly wrapped" account of the moral law suggested by this natural law response.

Recall the intuitive formulation of the norm for expecting theistic explanation: whenever there is a *transaction*, theistic explanation is called for, and I claim that the sort of theistic explanation of a transaction must be an explanation involving theistic immediacy (2.4). Now, it is clear that there is no further theistic explanation called for when asking why H_2O is an ingredient of lemonade. We can give a constitutive explanation that is as good an explanation as can be offered, on account of its being the case that to be lemonade just is to be a drink one of whose constituents is water (= H_2O). But as there is nothing here that can be called a further transaction between the properties in question, there is no basis for thinking that further theistic explanation is called for—nothing beyond what would be involved in the existence of the properties themselves. One way to bring this point home is to note that a theistic activist account of properties, one in which (say) properties just are divine ideas, can explain all that could possibly be theistically explained here just by accounting for the properties at issue. Any further explanatory questions—why does God's lemonade thought involve water rather than kerosene?—is out of place; that's just what that divine idea is, though perhaps there is some other divine idea of a lemony kerosene concoction that is less potable but just as much a divine idea, and thus just as much a property, as that of being lemonade.

But this is what seems implausible in the case of human beings and the moral law that expresses what properties morally necessitate our acting in various ways. Moral necessitation, first off, seems very much a *transaction*—that certain properties in the world make it the case that certain ways of acting are morally defective and others not. So it looks like further theistic explanation is called for here that would not be called for in the case of the H_2O/lemonade connection. And the range of explanatory issues that arise with respect to moral norms just seems obviously much more open here. We can ask ourselves: why is it that this particular range of properties contains the properties that morally necessitate human action rather than others? Why is it that this particular range of properties, which exemplified, counts as realizing the human good? Why is it that the range of properties that creatures can exemplify that count as their good fall into a recognizable pattern (for example, life, knowledge, sociability, agency, and so forth)? I think that these sorts of questions should not even make sense if the identification view were correct—what we would have here is just a set of identities for which further explanation seems unapt. (For an elaboration of this argument, see 6.2.)

I also think that becoming more explicit about the various notions of kind, perfection, reason, and necessitation to which this sort of natural law theorist will have to appeal makes clear that giving the outlines of the "tightly-wrapped" view does not decide the issue against the possibility of theistic explanation. Recall that the basic idea is that for x to be a human good is to stand in some relation to human nature, say, perfecting it; and to be a reason just is to be a human good; and for something to be morally required is for it be backed by sufficiently strong reasons. It is perfectly proper to ask for more explicitness from the natural law theorist who defends this view.

Here is what I mean. In defending a natural law account in earlier work, I argued—much as the defender of the "tightly-wrapped" response argued—that *being a human good* is to be identified with *being a perfection of human nature* (Murphy 2001, p. 19). But it seemed plain that we need some understanding of this talk of the perfection of human nature, and I suggested that the best way to do so would be Aristotelian: to say that x is a perfection of human nature is for it is belong to the human kind to have the function of x-ing such that x-ing is not merely instrumental to some other human function. But this invites further questions about functioning, and I argued, drawing on the work of Mark Bedau (1992a and 1992b), that for A to have the function of x-ing is for A's x-ing to serve some end of y-ing, for A's x-ing to be brought about because A's x-ing serves the end of y-ing, and A's y-ing is good in some relevant sense of goodness. (So a thermostat's function is to turn the heat on at a given set temperature; this is true because its turning the heat on at that temperature serves the end of the room's reaching and remaining at that temperature; its turning the heat on at that temperature occurs because turning the heat on at that temperature tends toward the room's reaching and remaining at that temperature; and the room's reaching a set temperature is a characteristic aim of designers/users of thermostats. A heart's function is to pump blood because pumping the blood serves the end of keeping the organism alive; it pumps blood because its pumping blood serves the end of keeping the organism alive; and staying alive is characteristically good for the organism. And so forth.)

Human flourishing is the limiting case, in which the human's x-ing is for the sake of its x-ing—that is, for its own sake—rather than for some distinct, further end. Notice, though, that once we engage in the sort of analysis required to get clear on the "perfection of human nature" talk, we have reintroduced into our analysis some variety of goodness, and we will want to know what variety of goodness that is, and whether it is somehow theistically explained.

Here is a straightforward argument that it is. It seems extremely plausible that what explains the transaction of morally necessitating will be something that is itself normatively loaded—something just like some variety of goodness involved in this analysis of "perfection of human nature." But we have agreed that whenever there is a transaction, there is reason for the theist to think that the transaction is theistically explained (2.4). So there is good reason to think that the variety of goodness that is essential to an account of what it is to be a perfection of human nature will be theistically explained. The result of this argument is that even if the tightly-wrapped natural law theorist claims to have a view involving identifications with nontheistic properties, there is room to doubt whether the tightly-wrapped natural law theorist has succeeded in making out this view.

Another way to see the point of this argument is to think of how a nontheistic Aristotelian might respond to it, and to see how this response is unavailable to theistic natural law theorist. A nontheistic Aristotelian might say: "No, we need to just drop that value condition, or simply hold that it is satisfied trivially when we get to the highest level of the activity of a kind: if there is some activity that belongs to a kind and is such that the other activities of the kind serve it and are explained by the fact that they serve it, then that just is the good of the kind. We should make no further appeal to a variety of goodness that is distinct from the activity of the thing." Two points. First, as I noted above, this view may well leave mystery intact that would not be present in a more theistic answer—we might from a theistic answer be able to get more informative accounts of why a certain range of properties is what constitutes the flourishing of all creatures for which flourishing is a possibility, whereas this sort of answer will necessarily be more limited. Second, and this is the more important point, the nontheistic Aristotelian makes this identification of the variety of goodness with the highest level activity of the kind *as a forced move*, a move that the theistic moral philosopher cannot treat as a forced move. And when the theistic moral philosopher cannot treat this as a forced move, then the explanans-centered considerations loom large. If we have reason to suppose that theistic explanation figures immediately in all transactions, and it is available to us to understand the flourishing of creatures that morally necessitates our action in a way that draws on theistic explanation, then we have good reason to understand the flourishing of creatures in that way. (For the working out of this idea in the context of the theistic explanation of moral law defended in this book, see 6.2.)

My view, then, is that while it is open to the theistic natural law theorist to claim that the properties involved in moral laws are so interconnected as to make further theistic explanation of moral necessitation impossible, I think that there are strong reasons against this route and that taking it requires the ignoring of the sort of explanans-centered considerations that have guided our argument thus far.

3.8 A theistic moral argument against standard natural law theory, partially developed

My argument in this chapter has focused on reasons to think that the standard natural law view, even accompanied by various supplements, is unable to meet the explanans-centered desiderata for a theistic account of moral law. I want now to offer a more direct criticism of standard natural law theory on explanans-centered grounds. The criticism that I offer is, I think, weighty, but conditional: it raises a severe difficulty for standard natural law theory, but it is not yet clear whether *any* plausible view will be able to avoid it, so one might wonder whether it constitutes a comparative disadvantage for the natural law view. I will thus present the initial difficulty here, and will complete the argument later (6.4) by showing that there is an otherwise plausible view that is able to avoid it.

It is a truism that, according to orthodox theism, God is a being to whom one should be loyal. Putting it this way is, indeed, far too weak. For theism requires *undivided* loyalty to God; we are to love God with all our hearts, all our souls, and all our strength. Now, there are ways that agents can exhibit a particular structure of appreciation of multiple goods that includes a decisive preference for one of these goods over the rest that would nevertheless not serve as an adequate specification of the sort of undivided loyalty that we are supposed to have to God. Consider, for example, undivided loyalty achieved simply by subordination. So consider the suggestion that for one to have undivided loyalty to good A vis-à-vis good B is for one to always prefer good A to good B in any cases in which serving A and serving B are incompatible; one subordinates one's service to good B to one's service for good A. But it is clear that while of course we must never prefer anything to God, it is insufficient for the proper undivided loyalty to God simply to subordinate one's service to other goods to one's service to God. For what is contrary to orthodox theism is not simply acting contrary to what service to God requires; what is contrary to theism is having any practical concerns the value of which floats free of, is independent of, the goodness of God to which one ought to exhibit loyalty.

I think that undivided loyalty understood as I am characterizing it is a truism of theism. But one can make the case for this position explicit by appeal to the sorts of considerations raised in defending divine sovereignty as a perfection (0.2). Divine sovereignty as I described it there concerns God's ultimacy as an explanatory principle: there is nothing that exists that is independent of God. The appeal to the appropriateness of undivided loyalty vis-à-vis God is an appeal to God's ultimacy in the practical order. God's being ultimate in the practical order is not satisfied simply by God's being the best thing in that order, able to win a loyalty contest with any created good. Rather, God's being ultimate here involves God's being the source of all created goodness in such a way that no goodness exhibits any independence of God.

But if this view is correct, then standard natural law theory seems on its face to be at odds with theism. For standard natural law theory holds that there are various goods the goodness of which is relevantly independent of God, our loyalty to which is thus independent of and to be contrasted with our loyalty to God. Whether the standard natural law theory can plausibly argue that we should subordinate all our concern to serve these created goods to our concern to serve God is beside the point. For what orthodox theism condemns is not simply loyalty to created goods that is not subordinated to loyalty to God; it condemns any loyalty to any good that can be properly contrasted with loyalty to God. Again, we are to love God with all our hearts, all our souls, and all our strength. If there is a love that we have for created goods that can be properly contrasted with our love of God, then it seems that we are not loving God with all our hearts, souls, and strength.

Now, however pious it may sound to say that with respect to God, our loyalty must not be divided, it may be objected that there must be a mistake in the argument somewhere. For one might argue that any plausible view is bound to have the result that our loyalty to God cannot be undivided in this sense. Any alternative position, on which our loyalty to God is undivided, would involve such a repugnant attitude toward our fellow human beings and indeed all of God's creatures that it would have to be rejected. It would have to involve, one might think, either a horrifying nihilism about the value of God's creatures or at best an instrumentalizing of their value in light of love of and service to God. And not only does that seem objectionable in itself; it seems to be contrary to what God has required of us, that is, that we not only love God with all our hearts, souls, and strength, but that we love and serve our fellow human beings as we love and serve ourselves.

The objection is too quick. My point is that standard natural law theory as I have described and criticized it *entails* divided loyalty—it just *follows* from this view that there are loyalties that one ought to have that are independent of, and to be contrasted with, the loyalty that one has to God. This looks bad, from a theistic point of view. The objector is right that if it turns out that every view that tries to avoid such divided loyalty has even more implausible implications, then we will have to revise our thoughts about the sort of loyalty that is owed to God (or have to revise our thoughts about whether there is such a being). But the objector is wrong that every view that tries to avoid such divided loyalty will have terribly implausible implications; the account of theistic explanation of moral law that I offer in Chapter 6 avoids divided loyalty without being nihilistic or instrumentalist about the creaturely good. I make the case, and thus complete this argument against standard natural law theory, in 6.4.

3.9 The explanans-centered argument against natural law theory extended

Natural law theory is a plausible moral theory. But its status in theistic ethics is, while prominent, not privileged. Thus one who is unimpressed by the credentials of natural law theory as a moral view might therefore also be unimpressed by the lengths to which this chapter has gone in showing that natural law theory is unacceptable as a theistic explanation of moral law. Why think that natural law theory deserves such pride of place? Why think that an argument that natural law theory is theistically unacceptable makes some deep and important point about current thought about theistic explanation of morality?

The answer is that natural law theory's failure to provide of itself a theistic explanation of moral law and its inability to be plausibly located in a wider view that meets our theistic desiderata is not unique to it, nor is it dependent on eccentric features of the natural law view. For it turns out that natural law theory's way of providing an account of right action—offering a theory of the good that fixes a theory of the right—is the standard way for broadly realist normative theories to formulate their views. So the argument against natural law theory as a theistic explanation of moral law generalizes to these other views. And if these broadly realist views are unsuitable as parts of a theistic explanation of moral law, then other sorts of moral view—say, more intuitionistic forms of realism, or some form of constructivism—will be a fortiori unacceptable as well.

Why do I say that the failures of standard natural law theory will be inherited by any standard realist view? The reason is that such views—whether utilitarian, Kantian[6], or virtue theoretic—have a common theoretical structure: each of them holds that what makes action right is that it responds to value appropriately, where the appropriateness of the response is fixed by the features of the relevant value and the character of the value as such is fixed independently of any theistic facts (Murphy 2001, pp. 157–71). So the utilitarian takes what is fundamentally of value to be certain states of affairs, which have their value either by exemplifying items on some objective list (perhaps as minimal as pleasure and the absence of pain; perhaps as robust as the catalogs of goods acknowledged by standard natural law theorists) or by being the objects of desire. In either case, these states of affairs bear value agent-neutrally, and are commensurable with each other as goods; thus, the appropriate response to them is to maximize overall goodness. Or: take the realist forms of Kantianism, on which what is fundamentally of value is not any states of affairs ("producible ends"), but rather persons ("ends-in-themselves"); the value of persons is the condition for anything else having value, and the fundamental moral norm is to respect persons as ends-in-themselves. Or: take the standard virtue theoretic approach to right action. Here one may have a variety of theories of the good, but the distinctive feature of the virtue theoretic approach is that we cannot fully capture what constitutes an appropriate response to these goods other than as the response that would be taken by the person of virtue.

[6] Here I am thinking of the sort of Kantian view defended by Donagan, in which at the foundation of the theory is a realist picture of humans as bearers of value as subsistent ends (1977), or more recently by Kain (2006).

In each of these views it appears that the explanation of moral facts, the moral necessities that are our explanandum, can proceed in a way that is independent of theistic facts. The theories of the good are not themselves theistic, and the proper response to these goods is not fixed by any theistic facts. Thus, these theories do not constitute theistic explanations of moral facts, and thus insofar as we should expect theistic explanations of such facts (0.2, 2.4), these views are condemned as defective from a theistic standpoint. And there is no reason to suppose that attempting to supplement these views with the sorts of responses considered in 3.3–3.7 will be any more successful when supplementing Kantianism or utilitarianism than they were when supplementing natural law theory.

It is also clear that the theistic moral argument against standard natural law theory (3.8) will have just as much force against these alternative moral theories as it has against the standard natural law view. For any of these views that acknowledges the existence of morally necessitating values distinct from God will call for divided loyalties; and this seems incompatible with the theistic requirement that the goodness of God is such as to call for undivided loyalty. Again, as I noted above, it is at present unclear whether any view can avoid an unpalatable set of implications here. But I will argue that the best account of the explanatory relationship between God and moral law avoids divided loyalty without accumulating other implausible commitments (6.4).

There are, no doubt, other types of moral theory besides the ones that I have considered, but these are obviously no more amenable to theistic explanation of moral law than the utilitarianism, Kantianism, and virtue theory discussed above. If we imagine a theory of the right in which actions have their rightness in a way that is not fixed by the character of the good—think of certain intuitionist positions—it seems we have even less room for theistic maneuvering. And if we move away from realism to some sort of constructivism about moral necessities, then it seems plain that we have given up on immediate theistic explanation (2.4): for it is essential to the constructivist view that moral norms are constructed by the agents whom those norms bind, and so the most that God could account for is the existence of beings who are capable of engaging in such construction. We will have to look elsewhere for an adequate theistic account of moral law.

4

Theological voluntarism

4.1 "Divine command theory" and "theological voluntarism"

There is a well-known and much-maligned moral theory commonly labeled "divine command theory," which holds that moral requirements are in some way the products of God's commanding acts. It is a commonplace within theistic ethics to contrast natural law theory, the subject of the previous chapter, with divine command theory. But the better contrast with natural law theory is *theological voluntarism*, a genus of moral theory of which divine command theory is but one species.

To be a theological voluntarist is to hold that there is some moral status M that stands in a dependence relationship D to some act of the divine will A. The distinct species of theological voluntarism differ in the range of moral statuses alleged to depend on the divine will, the sort of dependence relationship supposed to be present between the moral status and the divine will, and the particular act of divine will upon which moral statuses are held to depend. But we can add, in order both to ensure the contrast with natural law theory and to fit with actual theological voluntarist practice, that the dependence relationship is supposed to be *complete* and thus *unmediated*. Whatever the dependence relationship is held to be, it is not that moral statuses are explained by some third factor that is immediately or mediately explained by the divine will; the idea is that moral statuses depend directly and immediately on God's will, and that there is nothing else upon which moral statuses immediately depend.

While one might be a theological voluntarist about a variety of moral statuses, recent formulations of the view have moved toward a consensus that theological voluntarism is most plausible simply as an account of how deontic moral statuses—like *being morally required*, or *being morally obligatory*, or our *being morally necessary*—are to be explained (see, for example, Alston

1990, Adams 1999, Quinn 1999, Hare 2001, Evans 2004, Wainwright 2005). This consensus is primarily motivated by the aim of making theological voluntarism less vulnerable to standard objections to the more ambitious formulations of the view.

For example: it is sometimes claimed that theological voluntarism, because it grounds moral statuses in God's free will, is bound to make nonsensical or utterly contentless the claim that God is good. That God is good is both a fixed point concerning God's nature and a plausibility-making feature of theological voluntarism. If one were to deny that God is good (understood *de dicto*—that is, "if there is a being that qualifies as God, then that being is good"), one would call one's own competence in use of the term "God" into question. And even if it were allowed that one can employ the term "God" masterfully while denying that God is good, it would still be true that if one were to deny that God is good, then one would undercut one's capacity to defend theological voluntarism. For theological voluntarism is plausible only if God is an exalted being; but a being that is not good is not an exalted being.

The most straightforward formulation of the objection is as follows. For God to be good is for God to be morally good. But if moral goodness is to be understood in theological voluntarist terms, then God's goodness consists only in God's measuring up to a standard that is itself set by God. While this is perhaps an admirable resoluteness—it is, other things being equal, a good thing to live up to your own standards—it is hardly the sort of thing that provokes in us the admiration that God's goodness is supposed to provoke.

Now, one might dispute the claim that if God's goodness consists simply in God's living up to a standard that is itself set by God, then that goodness is far less admirable than we would have supposed. (See, for a nice discussion of this issue, Clark 1982, esp. pp. 341–3.) Suppose, though, that we grant this part of the argument. How powerful is the objection from God's goodness against theological voluntarism?

The power of the objection against some formulation of theological voluntarism varies directly with the range of normative properties that the formulation of theological voluntarism in question purports to explain. If one wishes to provide a sweeping account of normativity in theological voluntarist terms, then the objection is extremely strong. If, on the other hand, one wishes only to account for a proper subset of moral notions, such as obligation, with one's theological voluntarism, then the objection from God's goodness is much, much weaker. For if it is only moral obligation that is dependent on acts of the divine will, one can appeal to moral notions other than deontic ones in order to provide a substantive sense in which God is good. Granting to some extent the force of the objection, we can say, on this view, that God's moral goodness cannot consist in God's adhering to what is morally obligatory. But there are other ways to assess God morally than in terms of the morally obligatory. Adams, for example, holds that God should be understood as benevolent and as just, and indeed concedes that his theological voluntarist account of obligation as the divinely commanded is implausible unless God is thus understood (Adams 1999, pp. 253–5). The ascription to God of these moral virtues is entirely consistent with his theological voluntarism, for his theological voluntarism is not meant to provide any account of the moral virtues. One can hold, as Adams does, that God's moral goodness involves supereminent possession of the virtues, at least insofar as those virtues do not presuppose weakness and vulnerability (Adams 1999, p. 31). God is good because God is supremely just, loyal, faithful, benevolent, and so forth. It seems that ascribing to God supereminent possession of these virtues would be enough to account for God's supreme moral goodness: it is, after all, in such terms that God is praised in the Psalms.

It has been retorted that this appeal to God's justice is illegitimate within a theological voluntarist account, because what is just is a matter of moral requirement, and so to suppose that God's acting justly is metaphysically prior to God's imposing all moral requirements by way of commanding is incoherent (Hooker 2001, p. 334). But the theological voluntarist may deny that acting justly is morally required prior to God's commanding it, any more than acting courageously, temperately, or prudently are morally required prior to God's commanding us to act courageously, temperately, or prudently. Just as one can coherently acknowledge the excellence of temperance while wondering whether one is morally obligated to act temperately, one can coherently acknowledge the excellence of justice while wondering whether one is morally obligated to act justly. It thus seems an available strategy for the theological voluntarist who holds a restricted view of the range of moral properties explained by God's willings to appeal to justice in accounting for God's goodness. (See also Adams 1999, p. 234.)

Here is a second classic difficulty for theological voluntarism the force of which is avoided by the now standard restriction of its explanatory ambitions: that it entails that morality is objectionably arbitrary. There is, however, more than one objection here. One arbitrariness objection against theological voluntarism is that if theological voluntarism is true, then God's willings must be arbitrary; and it cannot be that morality could wholly depend on something arbitrary; and so theological voluntarism must be false. In favor of the claim that if theological voluntarism were true, then morality would be arbitrary: morality would be arbitrary, on theological voluntarism, if God lacks reasons for the divine willings on which morality depends; but because theological voluntarism holds that reasons depend on God's willings, it is clear that there could ultimately be no reason for God's willing one thing rather than another. In favor of the claim that morality could not wholly depend on something arbitrary: when we say that some moral state of affairs obtains, we take it that there is a reason for that moral state of affairs obtaining rather than another. Moral states of affairs do not just happen to obtain

Just as in the case of the objection from God's goodness, the strength of this version of the objection from arbitrariness depends on the formulation of theological voluntarism that is being attacked. The arbitrariness objection becomes more difficult to answer the stronger the relationship between God's willings and moral properties is held to be; and it becomes more difficult to answer the wider the range of normative properties for which one attempts to account by appeal to God's willings. The claim made by the objector is that morality is arbitrary on theological voluntarism, because God has no reason for having one set of willings rather than another. But this is so only if one appeals to a very strong form of theological voluntarism on which all normative states of affairs depend on God's will. If one holds that only the obtaining of deontic states of affairs are determined by God's will, then God might have moral reasons for willing one thing rather than another: that, for example, one set of willings is more benevolent, or just, or loyal, than another.

Now, one might respond on behalf of this version of the arbitrariness objection that even if it is true that there can be reasons for God to choose the willings that God chooses, it is unlikely that these reasons would wholly determine God's choice of willings, and so there would be some latitude for arbitrariness in God's willings. But of itself this is not nearly so pressing a worry. The initial claim leveled against theological voluntarism was that it made *all* of God's willings ultimately arbitrary, and morality could not depend on something so thoroughly arbitrary. But the chastened claim—that there is *some* arbitrariness in God's commands—is far less troubling on its own. We are already familiar with morality depending to some extent on arbitrary facts about the world: if one thinks about the particular requirements that he or she is under, one will note straightaway the extent to which these requirements have resulted from contingent and indeed fluky facts about oneself, one's relationships, and one's circumstances. It does not seem that allowing that God has some choices to make concerning what to will with respect to the conduct of created rational beings that are undetermined by reasons must introduce an intolerable arbitrariness into the total set of divine willings.

Allowing for such pockets of divine discretion does not provide backing for this version of the objection from arbitrariness, but rather offers a premise for another version of the objection from arbitrariness. This other version of the objection from arbitrariness holds that moral states of affairs exhibit a certain rational structure that they would not exhibit if theological voluntarism were true. Here is the idea, roughly formulated. Suppose that some deontic state of affairs obtains—say, that it is the case that murder is wrong. The idea is that for any such moral state of affairs, the following is true: either we can provide a *justification* for the obtaining of that moral state of affairs, or that moral state of affairs is *necessary*. Stipulatively, a justification of an obtaining moral state of affairs A is some obtaining moral state of affairs B (where A is not identical with B), which in conjunction with the other non-moral facts explains A's obtaining in some way that entails that the obtaining of B and the relevant non-moral facts entails the obtaining of A. So, for example: it may be the justification for murder's being pro tanto wrong that murder is an intentional harm (nonmoral fact) and intentionally harming is pro tanto wrong (obtaining moral state of affairs). (Such a view obviously has some affinities with what Schroeder calls the "Standard Model" for explaining normative reasons and moral requirements; see 2.2.) Now, presumably not all moral states of affairs can be justified: eventually there will be basic moral states of affairs, for which no justification can be given. But it would be very unsatisfactory, the objection goes, to say that these basic moral states of affairs just happen to obtain. So any basic moral states of affairs must obtain necessarily. Perhaps *unrelieved suffering's being bad* is a state of affairs of this sort, or perhaps *rational beings' being worthy of respect*.

The claim that the structure of morality is not arbitrary is the claim that there are no moral states of affairs that both lack a justification and are not necessary. The view that God's willings are not wholly determined by reasons, together with theological voluntarism, offer our basis for holding that there are some moral states of affairs that both lack a justification and are not necessary. For consider some act of φ-ing that is not subsumed under any other issued divine command and which is such that God lacks decisive reasons to command or not to command its performance. In the possible world in which God issues a command to φ, there is a moral state of affairs—*its being obligatory to φ*—which lacks a justification (for the action is subsumed under no other divine command) and is not necessary (for God might have failed to command the action).

Some theological voluntarists have responded to this sort of worry by claiming that whatever God wills with respect to the deontic status of human action, God wills necessarily. (More on this below; see 4.3.) I will not here complain if the theological voluntarist wants to say that there are *some* divine willings with respect to human action that are necessary, or necessary given God's creating embodied rational beings. But to say that *all* of the divine willings are necessary seems either to understate the divine freedom or to overstate the determination of God's commands by reasons. The more plausible theological voluntarist response denies the claim that morality must exhibit the particular structure presupposed in the objection, for its appeal to necessary moral states of affairs as the only proper starting point is dubious. It is not clear why the starting points for justification have to be necessary moral states of affairs. Surely if these moral states of affairs are basic, their moral status must not be explained by appeal to other moral states of affairs, but that does not mean they must be necessary; they might be contingent, and have their moral status explained in some way other than an appeal to another moral state of affairs. It could be, for example, that the explanation of them appeals to a contingent nonmoral state of affairs plus some necessary state of affairs involving a connection between that contingent nonmoral state of affairs and the moral state of affairs—perhaps a relationship of necessitation that necessarily holds between some contingent nonmoral state of affairs and a moral fact. Theological voluntarism would be an instance of this latter model. (For a discussion of a similar objection raised against theological voluntarism by Ralph Cudworth (*A Treatise Concerning Eternal and Immutable Morality*) and a similar response on behalf of theological voluntarism, see Schroeder 2005.)

So it seems to me that these classic arguments against theological voluntarism—that it strips of content the notion that God is good and that it condemns morality to objectionable arbitrariness—are failures when pressed against theological voluntarism as an account of moral necessities, though they find greater success when pressed against more ambitious versions of the view. This explains, I think, why theological voluntarism has moved to a consensus on the more restricted formulation. And since it is the explanation of moral necessities with which we are concerned in this book (2.1), the restrictedness of this formulation of theological voluntarism makes no trouble for theological voluntarism's case to provide an adequate theistic explanation of morality.

So we will concern ourselves only with theological voluntarisms that aim to explain moral necessities; and while we have not yet characterized the sort of dependence that moral necessities have on the divine will—I will focus on this in the next section—we know that such dependence will be immediate and complete. The other variable in formulations of theological voluntarism is the sort of act of divine will that is the explanans for moral necessities: some defend the divine command formulation (Adams 1999, pp. 258–62; Mann 2005b, pp. 286–91), while others appeal to other acts of divine will, like wanting, intending, or even generic willings (Murphy 1998; Quinn 1999; Miller 2009); and of those who appeal to divine will, different theological voluntarists appeal to different contents to those wills—some the content that the action be morally necessary, others the content that the action be performed. My argument will proceed largely without entering into this dispute among theological voluntarists, though it is clear that certain views of the dependence relationship naturally suggest certain views on how the act of divine will is to be understood.

My aim in this chapter is to make clear the unacceptability of theological voluntarism as a theistic explanation of moral law. My argument will begin by distinguishing two versions of theological voluntarism based on the way that the divine will is implicated in the moral necessities that it is invoked to explain: *causal* and *normative*. I will argue that theological voluntarisms that proceed by appealing to a causal connection between the divine will and moral necessities—I have in mind Quinn's view (1979, 1999) in particular here—are less plausible formulations of the theological voluntarist position: in one way of formulating that version of the view, theological voluntarism fails for explanans-centered reasons just as surely as natural law theory does; in another way, it offers an implausible view of what is involved in moral necessitation. The more plausible version of theological voluntarism appeals to God's will as normatively necessitating, not causally, but rationally (4.2). This more plausible version, of which I take Robert Adams's view to be exemplary, satisfies some of our explanans-centered desiderata extremely clearly, but nevertheless is deeply objectionable for explanandum-centered and even explanans-centered reasons (4.3). Adams may argue that the voluntarist view captures the social character of moral obligation in a way that my criticisms do not acknowledge, but I show both that Adams misconceives the way in which obligation is plausibly essentially social and that at any rate the theological voluntarist view itself fails to capture that character (4.4). Thus theological voluntarism turns out to be, like standard natural law theory, an unsuccessful theistic explanation of moral law.

4.2 Rival versions of theological voluntarism

How is the moral status *being morally necessary* supposed to depend on some act of divine will? There are two sorts of view in play, one on which the dependence in question is causal dependence, the other on which the dependence in question is rational dependence.

Begin with the former. Suppose that, following Philip Quinn, we take God's will to have the causal power to actualize—totally, immediately, completely, necessarily—moral requirements (Quinn 1999, pp. 54–5). On Quinn's view, the divine will's having that causal power explains, and explains necessarily, the holding of those moral requirements, for, necessarily, every moral requirement depends immediately and completely on God's will.[1] One can think about it this way. Orthodox theism holds that God has the power to act in an unmediated and complete way in the

---

[1] At different points in his career Quinn held different views on this nature of the divine willing that explains moral requirements. He originally held that the divine act that brings about the moral fact *A is morally required to ϕ* is God's willing that it be morally obligatory for A to ϕ (Quinn 1990); later (Quinn 1999), he held that it is God's intending (antecedently) that A ϕ that causes the resultant obligation. (For the idea of antecedent intention of which Quinn was making use, see Murphy 1998, pp. 17–19.) But Quinn nevertheless continued to hold that the "bringing about" relation between the theistic fact and the moral fact is an unmediated causal relationship. For an account of the difficulties with Quinn's appeal to the intention account in combination with a causal account of how the divine will brings about moral requirements, see Murphy 2002b.

created order. So God can cause, immediately and completely, for there to be an armadillo, and can cause, immediately and completely, the armadillo to be plaid-colored. On Quinn's theological voluntarism, what distinguishes these divine acts of bringing about an armadillo, or bringing about an armadillo of a certain color, from the divine act of bringing about the holding of a moral requirement is not the sort of causation involved but that in which the causation terminates.

Quinn offers an argument from divine sovereignty for this view (Quinn 1990 and Quinn 1999, pp. 63–5). Quinn's conception of divine sovereignty is not too different from the conception defended as an aspect of the divine perfection in 0.2: on Quinn's view, divine sovereignty combines divine aseity with the dependence of non-divine facts on God's agency, where a fact is non-divine if it neither involves nor logically entails God's existence. He thinks that from this notion of divine sovereignty, it follows that all moral facts are theistically explained—at least, it follows if we exclude from the scope of the moral facts to be explained all moral facts that involve or logically entail God's existence (Quinn 1990, pp. 293–5). It is plausible, though—this is related to the discussion above of God-involving goods (3.3)—that *no* moral facts involve or entail God's existence, at least not in virtue of their being about how one ought to respond to God. For a fact that involves or entails God's existence is one that an atheist must deny. But moral facts regarding how one ought to respond to God are not those that an atheist need deny. That God is to be obeyed entails that we are to render obedience to whatever being *qualifies as God*—to whatever being is the most perfect possible being. This moral fact could hold even without God's existing, and even though God does exist, that does not make this moral fact God's-existence-involving.[2] So if Quinn's argument from divine sovereignty to theological voluntarism is successful, then it shows not only that moral requirements regarding the non-divine are immediately and completely explained by God's will; it shows more broadly that all moral requirements are immediately and completely explained, and necessarily are thus explained, by God's will.

It is important to note that Quinn's view does not entail the necessity or the contingency of non-subsumed moral facts. It might be thought that since such moral facts are, on this view, the result of God's free creative

---

[2] Indeed, Rachels uses this alleged *de dicto* logical truth about God to argue that there is no such being as God (Rachels 1971).

choices, such moral facts must be contingent. But it may be that God, though free, has a character such that God necessarily causes non-subsumed moral facts to obtain (Quinn 1999, pp. 69–71). More plausible is the view that, even if non-subsumed moral facts are contingent, it is a necessary truth that if God creates human beings, then God causes certain moral facts to obtain. God's necessary love for the beings that He creates may well ensure that God freely wills the norms of morality to obtain that are the most loving. (For worries about this strategy, see Chandler 1985.) If one doubts this, the likely source of the doubt would be that there is no set of moral norms that counts as *the most loving* norms that God could bring about. (More on these possibilities below, 4.3.)

Now, of course I am sympathetic with Quinn's appeal to divine sovereignty in defense of a specific sort of moral theory. But I want to register two objections to Quinn's use of divine sovereignty here. The first is that even if Quinn is right about the centrality of divine sovereignty in the formulation of a proper moral theory, it does not follow that divine sovereignty favors a causal view of the relationship between God's will and moral requirements. As will become clear below, there are alternative understandings of the relationship between God's will and moral requirements that also affirm that facts about God are the immediate and complete explanation for the holding of moral requirements. The second is that Quinn has not given any good reason to suppose that divine sovereignty requires that God's will be the *complete* explanation for the holding of moral requirements. It is sufficient for dependence to hold that God is necessarily *part* of the immediate explanation for a moral requirement's holding. And it seems very strong to claim that divine sovereignty requires that the relationship between God's will and facts about physics, chemistry, and biology are all immediate and complete.[3] But since the argument from divine sovereignty offered by Quinn is not domain-specific, if the argument were to suffice to show that morality immediately and completely depends on God's will, then it would suffice to show that not only are the norms of morality immediately and completely dependent on

---

[3] One view of God's relationship to the natural order, occasionalism, affirms that God's complete sovereignty requires such control (5.2). But note that Quinn himself rejects occasionalism in other work, hoping to affirm a view of God's relationship to the created order that "can avoid being tarred with the ugly brush of occasionalism" (Quinn 1988, p. 73).

the divine will but also physical, chemical, and biological facts immediately and completely depend on the divine will as well.

But these criticisms of Quinn's use of divine sovereignty in defense of a causal version of theological voluntarism do not themselves go to the falsity of that view. I think, though, that we have good reason to think Quinn's view inadequate as a theistic explanation of morality.

Begin by noting an ambiguity in the view that God's will is the immediate and complete cause of the holding of moral requirements. We noticed above (2.2) that the claim that A is morally required to ϕ is ambiguous: it can be read as the claim that there is a moral requirement that A ϕ (that is, that it is a moral law that A ϕ), and it can be read as the claim that it is morally necessary that A ϕ. Quinn's causal formulation of theological voluntarism is ambiguous between these two readings: it can be read as the view that God's willing is the immediate and complete explanation for the holding of any moral law; and it is can be read as the view that God's willing is the immediate and complete explanation for the holding of any moral fact.

Suppose first that what the defender of the causal formulation of theological voluntarism has in mind is that the morally relevant state of affairs that God actualizes immediately and completely by an act of will is the holding of some moral law or laws. The idea would be, on this view, that God actualizes moral laws, which in turn explain the holding of various moral facts. Given our understanding of moral laws as relationships of moral necessitation between properties (1.4), we could understand God's bringing a moral law into existence through an act of will as God's conferring on various properties the normative power to make morally necessary certain performances, which then counts as a moral law's obtaining; or we could understand it as God's bringing into existence a moral law, which itself has the normative power to necessitate certain performances in the presence of certain properties.

But, perhaps surprisingly, on this way of understanding the causal formulation of theological voluntarism, theological voluntarism fails to satisfy the explanans-centered desideratum that all moral facts be immediately theistically explained (2.4). For while on this view God is causally relevant in bringing about moral laws, there is a further normative transaction that occurs that God has no part of. Theistic explanation of moral facts turns out to be fully mediated by the obtaining of some moral law. So while it is true that moral facts turn out to be theistically explained on this view, there is still the failure of immediacy that rendered even the most promising version of standard natural law theory objectionable (3.6).

Suppose that instead of holding that the divine will causes the existence of moral laws that then explain moral facts, the causal theological voluntarist has no interest in positing moral laws as a tertium quid in such explanations. It is the positing of moral laws as this tertium quid that eliminates theistic immediacy and makes the moral necessitation simply between creatures, without any divine presence involved. So instead this theological voluntarist will say just that the divine will causes it to be morally necessary that acts of certain types are performed. Some act-types have their status as moral necessary precisely because God wills that that type have the moral status *moral necessary*; any act-type that is moral necessary that is not such that God wills that that type have that moral status is morally necessary in virtue of being subsumed under an act-type that is morally necessary. Because subsumption preserves theistic immediacy, it follows that all moral necessities are immediately explained by the causal efficacy of God's willing. So if God wills that refraining from lying be morally necessary, my refraining from lying here and now being morally necessary is immediately explained by God's fiat, as *refraining from lying here and now* is included in the act-type *refraining from lying*.

Now, one might object that in the view that I have described, there are no moral laws at all, and as we argued earlier, moral law is a privileged explanans with respect to moral facts (2.2). The argument that there are no moral laws on this second formulation of the causal view is that, by contrast with the first formulation, God does not bring about moral laws, but only moral facts. But this is a mistake. It is true that on this second model, God does not by an exercise of causal power bring about moral laws. But in virtue of God's causal power a moral law holds. For a moral law's holding just is some property's morally necessitating—that is, making morally necessary—performance. But *being an action that God wills that it be morally necessary to perform* does make morally necessary *being performed*.[4] Indeed, this sort of theological voluntarist can claim an advantage for his or her position. As part of the challenge in defending a theory of moral law is providing glosses on the notions of "morally selects" and "morally necessitates" (1.4); we should evaluate theistic theories of moral

---

[4] Here I am assuming a certain view on the sort of divine volition at stake. But nothing in my argument will turn on the specific act of will one plugs in here.

law partly in terms of their ability to provide such glosses. And this sort of theological voluntarist can offer a gloss on "morally selects": moral selection is simply causation—the divine will selects certain moral necessities by causing those necessities to obtain.

But while it is indeed a point in favor of a theistic account of moral law to provide glosses of moral selection and moral necessitation, it is of course a point against such an account if the gloss it provides is an implausible one. And it does seem to me that this appeal to efficient causation as how to understand *makes* in *makes morally necessary* renders this version of theological voluntarism highly implausible. For it is hard to make any sense of the view that moral facts are made to obtain simply in virtue of an exercise of God's causal power. When we look at the specific ways in which changes in nonmoral facts can make a difference to the moral facts that hold, there is a pretty limited number of intelligible relationships that can hold between these nonmoral facts and the moral facts that supervene on them. A nonmoral fact can be part of what constitutes a reason to perform an action. (That you promised to φ can be cited in explaining why you have a reason to φ; your promising to φ constitutes, at least in part, the reason that you have to φ.) It can be part of an enabling condition for that reason. (The existence of a social practice of promising can be cited in explaining why you have a reason to φ; the existence of that practice might explain why your promise has the reason-giving force that it has.) It can be cited as a defeater-defeater for a reason. (While the fact the promisee told you that you need not fulfill your promise to φ typically releases you from your promise to φ, the fact that you threatened to beat up the promisee if he or she did not tell you that you need not fulfill your promise invalidates that release, and can be cited in explaining why you have a reason to φ.) Pretty obviously what all of these relationships have in common is that they are rational relationships, not causal ones. And this is the source of the implausibility of this version of the causal view: while theological voluntarists generally hold that a nonmoral fact—the fact that God wills something or other—explains why it is morally necessary that one ϕ, the causal formulation further holds that this fact falls into none of the familiar explanatory categories: it is not constitutive of the reason, it is not an enabling condition for the reason, it is not a defeater-defeater for the reason. The way that the fact is supposed to explain the reason is merely causal: it just brings the reason about, exclusively, totally, immediately. This is an entirely unfamiliar phenomenon: nowhere else do we encounter a merely causal connection between a nonnormative fact and a normative one. (The appeal to the very strangeness of divine causation itself is not sufficient to answer the objection. For there is an *extra* strangeness here: that the relationship between nonmoral and moral facts is in every case with which we are familiar a rational relationship, whereas on the causal formulation of theological voluntarism the relationship is merely causal. Creation ex nihilo does not constitute *carte blanche* to multiply strangenesses.)

So it seems to me that the formulation of theological voluntarism most worth taking seriously is a formulation that takes the dependence of moral necessities on the divine will to be not a causal but a rational relationship. I think that the view defended by Robert Adams, which is the best-developed version of theological voluntarism, is of this sort. There may be questions about whether Adams's view is correctly so represented. For Adams is well-known for his view that divine commands just are moral obligations, and even more strongly that the property *being divinely commanded* just is the property *being morally obligatory*. By contrast, the conception of theological voluntarism on which the dependence of moral necessities on the divine will is a rational dependence need not make that identity claim. My view, though, is that Adams's account on which *being morally obligatory* is to be identified with *being divinely commanded* is defended (and must be defended) by way of the view that the relationship between divine commands and moral necessities is a rational relationship, and thus Adams's view is a species of this broader type.

Here is what I mean. A perspicuous way of understanding Adams's methodology is that he starts by asking a sort of *functional* question—what is it to obligate?—and he proceeds by making explicit what it is to function in an obligating way (Adams 1999, p. 232). His way of spelling this out is to list a variety of platitudes that hold with respect to obligating—that one can be obligated only by what one can know about; that one can be obligated only to something that is good in some way; that to obligate includes to give reasons to do something; and so forth (Adams 1999, pp. 234–8). Once we have an adequately clear picture of what obligating is, it becomes clear that the only thing that is capable of morally obligating is divine commands (Adams 1999, pp. 252–8). That is why I think Adams's view fits this third formulation: his picture is one on which the most fundamental explainer of deontic moral facts is God's commands, for being commanded by God obligates, or I would say morally necessitates, one to performance. But the way God's commands make performance morally necessary is not a causal power; it is an essentially normative power.

What Adams adds to this view is an *identity* claim: because God's commanding is the only thing that can fill this role, and indeed (we can assume) is necessarily the only thing that can fill this role, then we should say not just that only God's commanding can and does morally obligate but also that *being morally obligatory* just is *being divinely commanded* (Adams 1999, p. 250). I need not take a firm stand on whether this move is justified, though I note that it seems generally a suspicious move to identify a functional property with a categorical one. When a property the analysis of which is under consideration is a purely functional property, it is unclear to me whether it is justified to identify the functional property with any structural or material properties, even when only things that exhibit certain structural or material properties could possibly carry out those functions. (Of course one should be willing to make such identifications if one has a strongly sparsist view of properties, but I don't think that this is Adams's position; he surely does not rely on a strongly sparsist view in defending his specific formulation of divine command theory.) But my criticisms of this third formulation of theological voluntarism do not turn on whether or not one is willing to identify the property *being morally necessary* or *being obligatory* with *being divinely commanded*.

So the view here is that what makes performances morally necessary is some act of divine will—whether it is a divine intention, perhaps, or a divine command. *Being divinely willed* (in the relevant sense) morally necessitates—and does so immediately, completely, necessarily, and totally—*being performed*. This is the most basic and explanatory moral law, on which the divine will is the bearer of normative power capable of explaining the holding of other moral laws and of morally necessitating performance.

How does this master moral law connecting the divine will and performance explain the holding of other moral laws? The idea is not going to be, as it was in the case of the formulation of theological voluntarism on which God causes moral laws with power to morally necessitate obtain, that God's willing somehow confers upon certain properties or norms some active power of moral necessitation. The idea is that certain properties become morally relevant because of their relationship to the intrinsically morally necessitating divine will. Because these properties occur in relevant acts of divine will—in Adams's preferred view, they occur in what is divinely commanded, whereas in other views, they occur in what is divinely wanted or intended—they become what one might call the *elements* of morally necessary action, the *occasions* by which one can act rightly or wrongly. Suppose, for example, that God wills that humans not tell lies. The view is not that *being lying* is a property that intrinsically bears the power to normatively necessitate, or that *being lying* stands in some privileged relationship to some creaturely property (*being human*) that ensures that a lie is a morally defective act (3.1). The view is, rather, that *being lying*, in virtue of occurring within an intrinsically normative relevant act of divine will, is such as to ensure that one who lies acts in a morally defective way. The proper way to conceive of the moral law that one not lie, on this view, is that *being lying* is relevant because it is an element—in this case, the sole element—of the offense.

Notice that moral laws thus explained do meet the criteria for a theory of moral law that we discussed in 1.4. What was essential to that view is that properties that are morally necessitating be intensionally relevant in the selection of an action-type as to be performed or not to be performed. *Being lying* is intensionally relevant, as *being lying*—not simply some property that happens to be extensionally equivalent to it, whether contingently or necessarily—is what occurs in the act of divine will that actively morally necessitates. And it is clear that *being lying* is morally selecting, on this account—it is not itself what bears active normative power (that would be the divine will) but it is a property the presence of which is itself relevant to actions' being to be or not to be performed.

Here is a comparison, useful for this limited point. Consider the notion of the *legally required*, in the familiar context of ordinary legal systems. There is no natural property of an action that is intrinsically able to legally necessitate; it is only by occurring in a legal rule of the relevant kind that such properties can legally necessitate. So *being the operating of a motor vehicle with a blood alcohol level of over 0.08* does not by its nature legally necessitate. But it does legally necessitate when brought under a rule of the right sort; what *being the operating of a motor vehicle with a blood alcohol level of over 0.08* gives is the elements of an offense, what counts as the breaking of this legal rule. What the theological voluntarist view I am considering holds is that the status of such natural properties in legal norms is closely analogous to the status of such natural properties in moral norms: they give the elements of offenses, the occasions of wrongdoing.

So the rational necessitation formulation of theological voluntarism is able to meet the minimal conditions on an adequate explanation of moral law. And whatever else we say about this formulation of theological voluntarism, we should first note its cardinal virtue from an explanans-centered standpoint. It is *undeniably theocentric*. In 2.4 I argued that an explanation of moral law requires not just that such laws be theistically explained but that such explanations exhibit theistic immediacy: facts about God must enter immediately into the explanation of the holding of such laws. Views like Adams's fully meet this condition of adequacy: with respect to every moral fact, the explanation of that fact's holding refers immediately to God, to God's will rationally necessitating the performance of the act-type in question. God is not pushed to the side, or given some background role. God is in the *center* of things. And this is where God must be, given God's character as sovereign (2.4), and this stands in stark contrast to the position taken by the natural law view (3.2, 3.8).

4.3 Explanandum- and explanans-centered objections to theological voluntarism

Theological voluntarism, even in the rational necessitation formulation (4.2), is nevertheless unacceptable as a theistic explanation of moral law. One very serious objection that I will press against the view is explanandum-centered, holding that theological voluntarism must make an unmotivated and implausible claim about the role of created natures in explaining moral law. It is perhaps unsurprising that theological voluntarism should be subject to such a criticism; one might think that its being open to such a criticism is simply an unfortunate consequence of theological voluntarism's satisfying the explanans-centered desiderata so plainly. But I will argue that there is a second, devastating objection to theological voluntarism that is not explanandum- but explanans-centered—that theological voluntarism is committed to making deeply implausible claims about how divine action is related to natural facts.

Begin with the explanandum-centered objection. I say that it is an extremely unfortunate consequence of theological voluntarism that it entails the normative impotence of natural facts, at least in relation to created agents. (More on this qualification below.) The normative powerlessness of features of the created world is objectionable, and the objectionableness of this implication of theological voluntarism is the truth behind many failed objections to theological voluntarism. Some have objected to theological voluntarism that it makes moral law contingent; but as we have seen, this objection is a failure, for it is open to theological voluntarists to respond that the moral law, or at least that part of it about the necessity of which we are confident, holds necessarily—the immediate and complete dependence of the moral law on the divine will does not entail the contingency of that law, as God might necessarily will certain things. Retrenching, objectors to theological voluntarism have held that even given this response, theological voluntarism still is objectionable, for it entails, counterpossibly, that if God *were* to command differently, then the moral law would be very different, and in objectionable ways (Wielenberg 2005, pp. 41–3, 48–9). Again: even granting that we are able to come to well-justified judgments on the nonvacuous truth of counterpossibles—no doubt itself a contentious supposition—the argument is flawed. The theological voluntarist in question holds that God necessarily wills certain things, and this on account of God's supereminent possession of the virtues; and this theological voluntarist also holds that God's being so great explains, in part, why theological voluntarism is the true account of moral necessity. Thus he or she is in a position to respond to the objection that in any (impossible!) world in which God lacks those qualities, theological voluntarism is not the true explanation of moral law. It seems to be not much of an objection to theological voluntarism to hold that in some impossible world in which God is other than God necessarily is, theological voluntarism is not the correct view of morality. (If I were a theological voluntarist, I would be happy to concede that theological voluntarism is true in all possible worlds, but perhaps only in the possible ones. See also Pruss 2009.)

Counterpossible thinking is typically just a way of trying to get at, or to exhibit, where the true dependencies lie. If one thinks that necessarily, there is a created world and necessarily, there is a God, we can use counterpossible thinking—if there were no God, then there would be no creation—to exhibit the dependence of the created world on God. And I think that this is the truth behind these objections to theological voluntarism, objections that as stated seem to be easily parried. The truth behind the objections is that the theological voluntarist account strips natural facts of any active normative power. On the theological voluntarist account, what bears normative power—the normative power to morally necessitate, at any rate—is God's will, and God's will alone. This follows from the voluntarist's view that God's will is the immediate and complete active explanation of the action's being required. Perhaps that does not sting when we think about the natural facts involved in promising. But if we turn our attention to, say, a small child, and the good of the child's life, and the way that *this being a harmless child's life* seems to necessitate my refraining from harming the child, the sting intensifies. The voluntarist view closes off the good of the child's life from being the, or even a, *wrongmaking* feature of the harming (see also Morriston 2009, pp. 258–9), relegating it simply to the *occasion* of wrongdoing.

That this is so is clear when we return to the apt comparison between the moral law and civil law (4.2). While it is of course true that good lawmakers have strong reason to make premeditated murder illegal, *being a premeditated killing* bears no power—none at all—to legally necessitate *being refrained from*. Once the relevant law has been enacted, *being premeditated* and *being a killing* are *elements* of an offense, so that it is true that by performing a premeditated killing one has by that very fact done something that it is legally necessary that one not do. This is what one has to say about the relationship between any such properties of actions and the property of being performed or refrained from: no such properties have of themselves any active power to contribute to the making morally necessary the performance or nonperformance of an action. In that respect, natural facts are idle from a moral point of view, just as such facts are idle from a legal point of view.

Now, one might object that the claim that theological voluntarism holds that natural facts lack the active power to make actions morally necessary must be mistaken. For, after all, on Adams's paradigmatic theological voluntarist view, facts about what is good, though not natural facts, supervene on natural facts, and Adams holds that facts about what is good *constrain* what can be morally obligatory. But I allow the truth of this reading of Adams's view while denying that it calls into question the criticism that I have leveled against theological voluntarism. That natural facts somehow impose a constraint on the *range* of action that God can make morally necessary does not call into question the claim that God's willing is the *sole active cause* of actions' being morally necessary. We properly distinguish between the features that determine the range within which an active cause can operate and the features that themselves actively cause an effect.

Here are two similar cases that should bring the point home. Consider first occasionalism, the view that God is the sole active cause of effects in the natural order. (I will consider occasionalism in much more detail below; see 5.2 and 5.4.) On this view, fire does not burn cotton; the effects of burning are caused directly by God when cotton is in the presence of fire. Water does not dissolve salt; the effects of dissolving are caused directly by God when salt is in the presence of water. Now, suppose for a moment that it is true that there are certain patterns of effects that are more aesthetically pleasing than others, and that God, being a lover of beauty, necessarily does not cause the more severely aesthetically displeasing patterns. No one would say that this supposition would render occasionalism false, appealing to the premise that, necessarily, the aesthetic features of patterns in the natural order constrain what laws of nature God might actualize. The aesthetic features of action remain just as idle with respect to causal necessitation in the natural order. But this is the sort of argument we would have to accept for the proposed defense of theological voluntarism to succeed: we would have to say that just because the range of actions that God could make obligatory is constrained by the good, God is not the sole active cause of moral necessity.

Or consider again legal obligation. Suppose we say that in some jurisdiction the rule of recognition—that is, that social rule that specifies what norms are law within that jurisdiction—specifies that only someone *humane* may serve as monarch, and that whatever the monarch lays down is law and therefore legally obligatory. In this jurisdiction the fact that, say, *gratuitously harming animals is not humane* constrains what can be the law in that jurisdiction: for no one who would require the gratuitous harming of animals could be humane, and thus no one who would require that could be monarch, and thus no one who attempted to make that the law in that jurisdiction would succeed. But we would still not say that the fact that *gratuitously harming animals is inhumane* is the active cause of any legal obligation. Similarly, even though facts about goodness have something to do with fixing who is the being that counts as God and thus qualified to give commands that constitute moral obligations, such facts themselves are not the active cause of any moral obligation.

That natural facts have no active normative power is on its face deeply objectionable. But as I allowed above (2.4) it makes perfect sense for our views on these matters to be adjusted in light of arguments that militate against them. If, for example, the considerations of divine sovereignty that we have used to guide our inquiries indicate that we must hold that God's will is the immediate *and complete* active explanation of the holding of moral facts, then we would have good reason to revise our assessment of the role of natural facts in moral necessitation. *But we have no such reasons.* Divine sovereignty, as I have argued (2.4), does militate in favor of an immediate active role for God in the explaining of moral facts, but it does not militate in favor of completeness. And it is only by appeal to completeness that we would have reason to deny that natural facts can play an immediate active role in the explanation of moral facts.

So the first objection to theological voluntarism is that, without adequate basis, it entails that natural facts are morally impotent—they are unable to play any active role in the moral necessitation of creaturely action. As I noted, it might be unsurprising that theological voluntarism is subject to the objection that it gives nature an inadequate role in the explanation of moral law. What is more surprising is that theological voluntarism is open to a very powerful *explanans*-centered objection—that it is committed to the view that God is morally necessitated by natural facts by which no creaturely agent could be morally necessitated.

The objection requires some setting up. While some writers in the theological voluntarist tradition have, as I noted above, emphasized the necessity of the moral law, others have wanted to emphasize its contingency. So John Hare, for example, has argued against the natural law theorists that they have failed to appreciate the contingency of the moral law. The natural law theorist's claim that the moral law forbids the slaying of humans does not adequately account for this contingency: "Perhaps ... God could have willed that we kill each other at the age of eighteen, at which point God would immediately bring us back to life" (Hare 2001, pp. 68–9). But it seems to me that the seeming strength of Hare's point is undercut by his adding the "at which point" qualification to the supposition. The natural law theorist's claim may well be just that, in our world, and with human life and death as it is, slaying is wrong; to add that it could fail to be wrong if the world were different is not to introduce an interesting point about the contingency of the moral law that bears on the dispute between natural law theorists and theological voluntarists. And it is not as if Hare has anything other than such examples by which to move us to accept wholesale contingency here. For Hare allows that there are moral laws that govern our relationship to God that are not contingent—that, say, God is to be loved and honored (Hare 2001, p. 67). So there is a distinction between the moral law regarding our treatment of God, some of which might hold necessarily, and the moral law regarding our treatment of each other, none of which hold necessarily. What would the principled basis be for affirming such a discontinuity? It cannot be that our relations to God can have their moral structure of necessity but our relations to each other cannot; for, after all, our relationships to each other are in one or another way relationships to God as well: I stand in relation to you as one creature of God to another, as one made in God's image to another, and so forth.[5]

The second objection that I want to raise against theological voluntarism is independent of any particular arguments in favor or against some account of the extent to which the moral law exhibits necessity or contingency. It takes as a premise only the rejection of what I will call, stipulatively, "wholesale moral contingency." I define wholesale moral contingency in terms of moral contingency *simpliciter*. Say that a set of facts exhibits *moral contingency* with respect to some moral fact if and only if it is metaphysically possible that that set of facts along with that moral fact holds and it is metaphysically possible that that set of facts along with that moral fact's complement[6] holds. Now suppose that all facts are either divine facts (facts about God) or nondivine facts, and that all facts are either moral facts or nonmoral facts. I will say that *wholesale moral contingency* holds if and only if every possible maximal set of nondivine, nonmoral facts exhibits moral contingency with respect to every moral fact. In other words, to believe in wholesale moral contingency is to believe that for every moral fact that holds or could hold, it could have failed to hold even given the same nondivine, nonmoral states of affairs obtaining.

---

[5] Hare attempts to emphasize the modesty of his claims by saying that "I am not claiming that we know that God could have willed these things, but that we do not know that God could not have" (Hare 2001, p. 69). But this is not to restate the claim with a quieter voice; it is to retreat past the claim that the moral law is contingent to the claim that we do not know that it holds necessarily. Well, perhaps we do not know. Perhaps we are viewing only through a glass darkly, speculating on the necessity or contingency of the moral law, and the precise way that God's will is related to it. But that point does not favor the defender of the contingency or the necessity of the moral law.

[6] A fact F's *complement* is the fact that holds just in case F does not hold. See Plantinga 1974, p. 36, which formulates this definition of a complement in terms of states of affairs; I understand facts to be simply the obtaining of states of affairs.

Two clarifications. First, note that to believe in wholesale moral contingency requires more than denying that the moral supervenes on those nonmoral facts that are nondivine. I have no objection to *that* denial; we may be under some moral requirements that hold in virtue of contingent divine commands.[7] The view under consideration requires a much more radical denial; it commits one to denying that *any particular moral fact* supervenes on the complete set of nonmoral facts that are nondivine. So one must hold, for example, that the fact that it is morally necessary not to torture this child might have failed to hold even if there were no benefits to this child or any other creature by so doing, if there were no difference in the effects of the torture on the child, and indeed even if the world is in every nonmoral, nondivine detail precisely the same. I have endorsed the voluntarist's claiming that there is *some* looseness between the set of nonmoral, nondivine facts and the moral law; it is a much more radical and implausible step to hold that there is looseness between *every* set of nonmoral, nondivine facts and *every* metaphysically possible moral necessity. Indeed, you can think of wholesale moral contingency as the limit of arbitrariness, at least with respect to the natural order (4.1)—wholesale moral contingency is as bad as such arbitrariness gets.

Second, note that this claim that it is implausible that the set of nondivine, nonmoral facts exhibits wholesale moral contingency is not, all by itself, the rejection of theological voluntarism. Many theological voluntarists, as I have acknowledged, reject this sort of moral contingency; their explanation for this is that the set of nonmoral, nondivine facts entails that God wills certain things, thus bringing about the relevant moral necessities. What explains this entailment is God's perfect goodness, on account of which God could not have a relevantly different will—at least in *some* cases—unless there were some difference in nonmoral, nondivine facts.

So I say that it is very hard to believe the view that the set of nonmoral, nondivine facts exhibits wholesale moral contingency, and no recent

---

[7] Brink (2007, p. 153) argues against certain voluntarist views by holding that they reject the supervenience of moral facts on natural facts, where natural facts do not include descriptive facts about God. But this is crudely question-begging. What is uncontroversial is, if anything, that moral facts supervene on *descriptive* facts, not that moral facts supervene on some proper subset of them, the *natural* ones. No theist or agnostic about theism, even those who reject theological voluntarism with extreme prejudice, should accept Brink's version. For it would entail that a divine command could never be the difference-maker with respect to the moral status of *any* action.

theological voluntarist that I know of has wanted to assert it. But if wholesale moral contingency is to be denied, which it should, then the voluntarist has a very nasty paradox on his or her hands. *For it looks all the world like these natural facts have a normative power with respect to God that they are, on the voluntarist view, not supposed to have with respect to created moral agents.* The voluntarist's view is that no set of nondivine facts has the active normative power to morally necessitate human performance of any action. Only divine facts, facts about what God wills, can do this. No set of nondivine facts alone can make it the case that a morally excellent human agent acts a certain way, and that the agent would be morally defective if he or she acted otherwise. But on the view proposed, sets of nondivine facts have the active normative power to morally necessitate divine action.[8]

We can make the argument more explicit. The denial of wholesale moral contingency together with the affirmation of theological voluntarism means that in some totality of nonmoral, nondivine circumstances, God must perform some particular act of will—that is, whatever act of will accounts for the relevant moral necessity holding. Now, God's willings are not brutely necessary—for one thing, we would not think of God as an excellent agent if what God willed were inexplicably necessary; and for another, we think that the moral necessities that must hold given a certain totality of nonmoral, nondivine facts are related to the relevant goods and evils at stake in that totality. Rather, it is God's being excellent as an agent that accounts for God's responding to, say, the harmless child's life (etc.) by performing the act of will that makes it true that the child is not to be murdered. But generally if an agent's excellences as an agent as such fully account for that agent's responding to a set of natural facts in a particular way, ruling out any other possible response by that agent, then it follows that those natural facts morally necessitate that agent's response. So the denial of wholesale moral contingency along with the affirmation of theological voluntarism entails that nonmoral, nondivine facts can of

---

[8] Note well: my argument does not depend on identifying some particular act-type that God is morally necessitated to perform that humans are not morally necessitated to perform. Indeed, it is compatible with my argument that there are no such (nontrivial) act-types. What is important is the role of natural facts in doing the moral necessitating: given the denial of wholesale moral contingency along with the affirmation of theological voluntarism, God is morally necessitated in some way by *some* set of natural facts, whereas humans cannot be morally necessitated by *any* set of natural facts.

themselves morally necessitate divine action. But it is essential to theological voluntarism that nonmoral, nondivine facts cannot of themselves morally necessitate human action.

This is a perverse result. The notion that while created nature can of itself morally necessitate *God's* action it cannot of itself morally necessitate *human* action is exceedingly paradoxical—that created nature has the power to bind God to action but lacks the power to bind us to action is a bizarre combination. The only way for the theological voluntarist to avoid that result is to affirm wholesale moral contingency. But wholesale moral contingency is also intolerable. So theological voluntarism is a false account of moral necessitation.

4.4 Theological voluntarism and the social character of obligation

The best version of theological voluntarism, one that appeals to a rational dependence of moral necessity on the divine will (4.2), is a failure: it produces an unacceptable account of the way that natural features are among the wrongmaking features of actions and seems to have the unhappy implication that natural features can have the power to morally necessitate divine action while lacking the power to morally necessitate creaturely action (4.3). Thus, as an account of moral law understood in terms of moral necessitation, theological voluntarism is an inadequate view.

There is, however, a line of thought within recent theological voluntarism that suggests that we could embrace this conclusion while denying that it makes difficulty for the voluntarist position. Adams has argued, for example, that while we ought to give a theological voluntarist account of moral obligation, we ought not give a theological voluntarist account of goodness; goodness is, on Adams's view, a theistic but not voluntaristic property. (I discuss Adams's theistic-but-not-voluntaristic account of goodness, from which I will draw a great deal, in Chapter 6; see 6.2.) But, surprisingly, Adams makes some remarks that suggest that he would think of moral necessitation as I have characterized it not along the lines by which he thinks about obligation but along the lines by which he thinks about goodness. Even if it is essential to obligation that obligations involve moral necessitation, that does not mean that there is nothing more to being a moral obligation than being morally necessitating. And it could well be that this something more is best captured in theological voluntarist terms. So Adams has argued in favor of his theological voluntarist account of obligation that obligation is an essentially *social* notion and that, therefore, an account of moral obligation must capture its social character; and on Adams's view the account that best captures this social character while satisfying other desiderata concerning obligation is a theological voluntarism that appeals to divine commands.

Now, I have taken as my explanandum *moral facts*, defined stipulatively to be moral necessities. It is thus open to me simply to say that Adams's appeal to obligation as distinctively social is beside the point; perhaps there is this distinct phenomenon of moral obligation that needs explaining, and which is best explained voluntaristically, though it is not the phenomenon that I am interested in explaining. But I favor a more confrontational route: I don't think that the antivoluntarist should make any concession that the voluntarist view has greater explanatory power with respect to any central ethical phenomenon than its nonvoluntarist rivals.

The first matter about which we should be clear is what the social character of obligation is supposed to amount to, and why it is the case that theological voluntarism is supposed to capture that character better than alternative views. What Adams claims is that, unlike goodness-concepts, deontic concepts make essential reference to the social: "If an action is wrong, . . . there must be a person or persons, distinct from the agent, who may appropriately have an adverse reaction to it. For the meaning of the obligation family of ethical terms is tied to such reactions to the wrong" (Adams 1999, p. 233). Adams is not claiming that for an action to be wrong it is sufficient that someone may appropriately have an adverse reaction to it; there are numerous other platitudes characterizing obligations—their being characteristically motivating, their being reason-giving, even typically decisively so, and so forth—that must be satisfied as well. (For a Kantian view of the right that makes similar claims, see Darwall 2006; I discuss Darwall's view below, in 6.5.)

The basic thrust of my reply is this. In order for Adams's argument to work, it is not sufficient that obligation be essentially social. It has to be essentially social in a way that can be explained by positing the divine will as the active cause of obligation, so that God is the source of the moral norms in such a way that renders them obligatory. But when we distinguish between the various ways that obligation can be held to be essentially social, we can see that theological voluntarism in some cases does not do the explanatory work and in others does not do the explanatory work in an interestingly distinctive way. So there is no sense in which obligation is both plausibly essentially social and best explained by theological voluntarism.

Here is one sense in which one might hold that obligation is essentially social. One might connect the normativity of obligation to a distinctive form of normativity to which Michael Thompson has called our attention (Thompson 2004). The idea is that the descriptors *monadic* and *bipolar* aptly characterize distinctive forms of normativity. In cases of monadic normativity, there is the agent and the action that the agent is to perform; and if the agent does not perform the action, that agent is defective as an agent. In cases of bipolar normativity, there is the agent and the potential victim; the agent owes it *to the potential victim* to perform the action, and if the agent fails he or she has not simply fallen short as an agent but has made the potential victim an actual victim. So, one might claim that obligation is essentially social in that obligations are invariably instances of bipolar normativity; obligations are always owed *to someone*, such that when one fails to act on that obligation one not only acts wrongly but wrongs someone, the victim of the violation.

I think it safe to say that this is not the sort of sociality that theological voluntarists should be relying on, for it is false that obligations are essentially instances of bipolar normativity and, even if they were, nothing about the theological voluntarist view would be particularly helpful in explaining this distinctive sort of normativity.

First: there is no reason to think that obligations should be thought of as invariably instances of bipolar normativity. Thompson himself sets out the intuitive distinction between monadic and bipolar normativity by noting the different sorts of normativity present in criminal law and in tort law (Thompson 2004, pp. 344). While tort law exhibits the bipolar structure— in torts there is always a tortfeasor and a victim, and it is central to tort law that a wrong is a violation of care owed to the victim, and thus to be answered by compensation to that victim—criminal law exhibits a monadic structure, in which there may be no victims at all, and when there are victims, they enter as elements of the offense rather than a party to whom a duty is owed. As Thompson notes, while it is of course possible for other legal actors to be the victims of a crime, they serve as "raw material" for the wrong action—even if the criminal act has as its direct object some legal actor, that place could equally well have been occupied by rare birds or old buildings (Thompson 2004, pp. 254). But it is obvious that we think of the requirements imposed by the criminal law as legal obligations just as surely as we think of the requirements imposed by tort law as legal obligations. So it seems wrong to think of obligations as essentially social in the sense of exhibiting bipolar normativity.

Second: even if obligations were essentially social in this sense, we have no reason to think that a voluntarist view would be sufficient or necessary to account for such obligations. A voluntarist view would not be sufficient. For we can imagine a legal system, headed by a monarch, in which there is no tort law, only criminal law; and this would be a system in which the only obligations exhibited monadic rather than bipolar normativity. Similarly, a moral system, headed by the divine sovereign, could consist of moral laws that are all matters of monadic rather than bipolar normativity. On the other hand, we can imagine a legal system in which there is no sovereign at all, just the general acceptance of a variety of norms of the proper form and content to be bipolar rather than monadic. So there seems to be nothing to the notion of bipolar normativity that would plausibly favor voluntarist over other accounts of moral norms.

So the sort of sociality to be interpreted as bipolar normativity is not essential to obligation, and even if it were, there is no advantage offered by appealing to a theological voluntarist account of obligation. Another sort of sociality that has been attributed to obligation as such is that of sanctioning; the idea is that sanctions are essential to obligation, and sanctioning (as opposed to other sorts of negative consequences befalling a violator for a violation) is necessarily an interpersonal matter (Mill, *Utilitarianism*, p. 47). But, one might say, there is obviously no sense to be made of the idea that everyone who is under the jurisdiction of the moral law is subject to sanctions for violations of it unless we appeal to God as punisher. It is important that holding this view does not require one to say that to be obligated *just is* to be subject to a sanction for an offense; at the very least, if one were to make this claim, then one should make clear that to sanction *presupposes* the existence of a norm, in that when one is sanctioned, one has an evil inflicted upon him or her *for* failing to act in accordance with the norm.

Still, this seems an implausible view of obligation; and again, to see why, go to the legal case. We can point out, as Hart pointed out (Hart 1994 [1961], pp. 217–18, 291–2; see also Shapiro 2010, p. 169), that there seems to be nothing incoherent about the existence of a legal system that has no machinery for the infliction of sanctions. To make matters more vivid, we might imagine a community in which wrongdoing is very rare and relatively inconsequential, and which has neither the inclination nor the expertise to support a regime of sanctions. Such a community might have a system of legal norms, including not only norms imposing duties but also norms concerning the adding, subtracting, and modifying of duties, along with the full range of procedures for authoritatively identifying wrongdoing. But no sanctions are imposed. If the members of the community describe the norms that they are under as obligatory, and specifically legally obligatory, they do not seem to be in error: they take themselves to be bound to adhere to these norms because they are the norms of that system.

Or, again: we can imagine a legal system that has a tort law regime but no criminal law regime. (Imagine that the members of this community are not so worried about punishing people, either to exact retributive justice or to discourage wrongdoers—they may not think retribution their job, and might think that extralegal means of discouraging wrongdoers is to be preferred—but they are worried about seeing that people are compensated for wrongs done to them, or about seeing to it that the party best positioned to prevent accidents prevents accidents, or whatever.) A tort law regime need not have sanctions. We could, to add realism, allow that it has recourse to unwelcome uses of force by agents of the law enforcing tort judgments, but unwelcome uses of force by agents of the law are not all sanctions, and an agent of the law taking possession of my car or garnishing my wages is not sanctioning me for my conduct. Nevertheless, it would be true in this regime that I have legal obligations to show due care with respect to others, obligations that are part and parcel of tort law. So it again it seems false that there is any essential connection between obligation and sanctions.

But there is a much more plausible nearby view with which it is hard not to feel some sympathy, and it is the view suggested by Adams when he writes that when there is a violation of an obligation, one "may appropriately have an adverse reaction to it" (Adams 1999, pp. 233). It is an error to connect obligation and sanction. But *sanctioning* is a species of a broader class of action, which is *holding responsible* (cf. MacNamara 2009). And so we might want to say that while being subject to sanctions may well be a contingent feature of being obligated, being subject to being held responsible for failures to adhere to the relevant norms is not a contingent feature. In the cases of legal obligation that I described, it is plausible to reply that while sanctioning is absent, being held responsible is not thus absent; we have in the former case official holdings not only that someone is a wrongdoer but a calling of him or her to account for it, and we have in the latter case parties being held responsible for their violation of duties in tort by making right their wrongs.

I am not entirely sure whether this view is correct in any way that does not trivialize the notion of "holding responsible." But this is not the issue that I aim to concern myself with here. The more important point for our purposes is that this appeal to holding responsible does not offer any benefit for the theological voluntarist who wants to claim that the social nature of obligation militates in favor of his or her view. Again, we can return to a paradigmatic set of obligations, legal obligations. The view under consideration holds that part of what makes it the case that legal obligations are correctly characterized as such is that the norms that are legally obligatory are those to which we can be appropriately held responsible for our failures of compliance. We can add to this: it is not merely that we are subject to being held responsible for adhering to these norms, but that we are subject to being held responsible *in some distinctively legal way* for adhering to them. By "in some distinctively legal way" I do not mean by some *technique* that is distinctive to law, but that it is a way of holding responsible that can only be done by legal actors—actors *authorized by the law* to engage in that response. So the law employs a variety of ways of holding responsible—authoritative court judgments, imposition of criminal sanctions, injunctions, orders to pay compensation, orders for specific performance, and so forth. The view, then, is that what makes it the case that these legal norms are correctly characterized as legal obligations is that there are parties legally authorized to hold others responsible for performance.

But one of the most striking things about the law is how *distributed* the authorization to hold responsible can be, and indeed how much more so it could be. As things stand, there are a variety of legal officials authorized to hold others responsible (and, indeed, to be held responsible in turn). And we can imagine legal systems where the holding responsible is much more widely distributed, where private citizens are typically deputized, say, to apprehend lawbreakers. The key point, though, is that there is nothing about legal obligation that so much as suggests that the party who is the source of authoritative legal norms is one and the same as the party who is legally authorized to hold persons responsible for adhering to those norms. Indeed, there is nothing about the nature of legal systems that requires that there be *any* party in charge of making law at all. At the foundation of a legal system might be a rule of recognition that specifies the criteria for a norm's being legal that does not include, and might even preclude, there being some party who has the power to make law. (This is just a commonplace of contemporary, Hart-inspired legal theory; there is nothing new, interesting, or original in any of this.)

The key point here is that if the social character of obligation is understood in this "holding responsible" sense, there is nothing that militates in favor of obligatory norms' originating in some authoritative party, whether an earthly sovereign (in the case of legal obligation) or a divine sovereign (in the case of moral obligation). What matters in either case is that there be some parties who have the standing to hold others responsible for their adherence to the relevant norms. But whether there are parties who are authorized to hold others responsible for adherence to the relevant norms is independent of whether the lawmaking source is in some sovereign, like God, or in some set of customary rules, or in some set of norms that hold independently of anyone's willing or commanding. We can allow for the sake of argument that obligation has this social character, and that it would be true that this sort of social character would be satisfied by the moral law's being given by a God who both lays down the law and holds us responsible for following it. (Note, though, that this is strictly speaking an addition to theological voluntarism; for one could imagine a theological voluntarist position that holds that God lays down the law but does not assume responsibility for holding us to adhering to it.) But it could also be true that this sort of social character would be satisfied by a set of moral laws, holding through sheer necessity, that necessitate acting in certain ways *and* authorize those under that law to hold each other (and themselves) responsible for acting in accordance with it (or authorize them to hold each other responsible for acting in accordance with some subset of it, if not all moral necessities are obligatory).

There might be some justification for theological voluntarism about moral obligation on the basis of this sort of sociality thesis if there were some reason to have a "trickle down" theory of authority to hold responsible—that the authority to hold people responsible for violating a norm must be in its origin held by the party with the power to lay down the norm, and this authority "trickles down" to other authorized parties. But to hold such a view is to be in the grip of something like an Austinian or Hobbesian theory of civil law, in which all legal authority originates in a single, legally unlimited sovereign, and from which all other legal authority flows (see, for example, Austin, *Province of Jurisprudence Determined*, lect. I, p. 21, and Hobbes, *Leviathan*, xxvi, [5]). But this is a theory of law that is wholly discredited (Hart 1994 [1961], pp. 26–49, 51–61) and it would be philosophical regress rather than progress if the theological voluntarists were to appeal to it in order to defend their essentially theistic account of obligation.[9]

So we have found thus far no refuge for theological voluntarism in the claim that it is meant to be only an account of moral obligation, where obligation has an essentially social character. Appeals to bipolar normativity, sanctions, and holding responsible gave no reason to accept a theological voluntarist view of moral obligation. One might think that the appeal to guilt is a distinct fourth option. As Adams suggests, it is a central platitude about obligation that failures to adhere to one's obligations are cases in which guilt characteristically results (Adams 1999, pp. 238–48). And guilt, on his view, is not a psychological state but an objective condition in which characteristically valuable social ties are ruptured. So we have another route to sociality, through the notion of guilt. And so the theological voluntarist can hold that what makes sense of guilt being the characteristic upshot of violations of moral obligation is that they rupture the valuable relationship with God, the giver of the commands in which morality consists.

This is of no use. The only sense in which this strong guilt-obligation tie can be made out is through a view in which guilt consists of the condition of being liable to being held responsible for a failure to adhere to the relevant norm. Again, think of legal obligation, say a legal obligation not to trespass on the nesting grounds of rare birds or not to alter the original architecture of an old building. That one can have such legal obligations is obvious. What is the condition of guilt in which one finds oneself by violating these norms? It may involve being at odds with nobody, at least in any normal sense of "being at odds with"; the most we can say is that if

---

[9] It is striking how similar divine command theory is to the old sovereign-subject legal theory defended by Austin. It seems to me that divine command theory needs reformulating in light of the criticisms of Austinian legal theory.

these are live laws, then I am subject to legal agents' acting against me to hold me responsible for my violations of the relevant norms.

None of this, of course, is meant to deny that social relationships can be valuable, and the source of obligations, conventional and moral. Nor do I mean to deny—indeed, I would affirm—the extreme value of relating socially to God, and that obligations can be explained by appeal to the value of that relationship. But this way of generating obligations is, I think, one among many, and does not belong to the nature of obligation as such.

The point of investigating the allegedly social character of obligation and the theological voluntarist's aim to defend the theological voluntarist view as best capturing that feature of obligation was to deal with the following retort: even if it is true that theological voluntarism is a bad theory of the explanation of moral necessities, there is nevertheless an important proper subset of moral necessities, *obligations*, the distinctive features of which call for theological voluntarist treatment. What I have shown is that this theological voluntarist response comes to nothing. Even if obligations do form an important proper subset of moral necessities, there is no reason to think that we should turn to theological voluntarism for a treatment of them. (I will consider this issue in more detail in 6.5.)

The recent history of theological voluntarism has been a history in which voluntarists have narrowed the range of moral statuses for which they claimed to provide an explanation. We have gone from moral statuses generally to deontic statuses more specifically, and from deontic statuses more specifically to obligations more specifically still. But theological voluntarism has been a failure at each point. Even when narrowing its ambitions, it has shown itself lacking. That should settle the theological voluntarists.

5

Theistic explanation of the laws of nature

5.1 Bad news and good news

In Chapters 1 and 2, I set a problem concerning the relationship between theism and morality: given theism, we should expect a theistic explanation of moral law; but what precise form ought that explanation to take? In Chapters 3 and 4, I delivered some bad news: both of the currently dominant views in theistic ethics fail to offer an acceptable theistic explanation of moral law. But there is good news. The good news is that the problem has been thought through before—or, at least, a problem that is structurally similar to this one has been thought through before, with the consequence that we can look to this debate for guidance in figuring out where we can go from here. (When I say that it has been thought through, I do not mean that resolution has been achieved; but we do have a much clearer picture of what the options are, and how they might be developed, than we have in the case of moral law.)

This similar problem is that of the relationship between God and the *laws of nature*—that is, those laws that express explanatory regularities and perhaps even governing relationships in the *natural* order. Recall that in Chapter 1 our account of moral law was developed on analogy with an account of the laws of nature. We have already, though, a history of working through the question of how we ought to understand the relationship between God and the laws of nature. And this is of course entirely unsurprising. If God is taken to be sovereign over everything else, then the question of how we ought to characterize God's role in the ordinary operations of nature is inescapable.

My argument is this. It is clear that two of the historically most important theories of God's relationship to the natural order, mere conservationism and occasionalism, correspond very precisely with natural law theory and theological voluntarism, respectively (5.2–5.4). This is so not only in terms of the structure of the views in question but also in terms of the arguments given in their support and the difficulties to which they are subject. So we can see the difficulties that we have discovered with extant theistic moral theories present in extant theistic philosophies of nature. But—and here, finally, is some good news—there is a third, well-developed view of God's relationship to the natural order that does not suffer from the difficulties that plague the other two views (5.5). This suggests a strategy: to formulate a theistic explanation of moral law along the lines of this third theory of the laws of nature. The working out of this strategy is the task of Chapter 6.

5.2 Mere conservationist and occasionalist accounts of the laws of nature

There is an account of the relationship between God and the ordinary course of nature that has been labeled "mere conservationism." Suppose that we distinguish between what we might call particular transactions in the natural order and the general laws of nature that express the governance relationship between the properties involved in those transactions. Mere conservationism is typically characterized in terms of its account of God's role in the particular causal transactions that take place in the natural order, though we can extend the view intuitively to an account of God's role in explaining the holding of the laws of nature. So let us first give an account of mere conservationism regarding the ordinary transactions in the natural order.

The mere conservationist affirms both a positive and a negative thesis (see, for example, van Inwagen 1995b). The positive thesis is that God conserves in existence all substances and their causal powers. The proper contrast here is with, say, *deist* views, on which God's creative act brings the universe into existence out of nothingness but the universe nevertheless requires no sustaining action by God to be held in existence from moment to moment. On the mere conservationist view, God is immediately involved in the *sustaining* of all substances. The negative thesis is that God does not ordinarily have any immediate role in the *transactions* between created substances (cf. van Inwagen 1995b, p. 44). When we want to explain why, given the existence of the fire and existence of the cotton, the fire burns the cotton, the explanation will not mention God at all; it will mention only the active and passive potentials of the fire and the cotton. It is of the nature of fire to have a range of causal powers, which involve the bringing about of certain effects in certain determinate conditions. It is of the nature of cotton to have a range of passive potentials, which involve a susceptibility to being changed in certain ways by substances acting in certain determinate conditions. Thus what happens between the fire and the cotton is, so to speak, entirely between the fire and the cotton. Theistic explanation of such transactions in the natural order will be ordinarily mediated explanations, that is, we can explain this fire's burning this cotton by appealing to God's sustaining in existence those substances and their causal powers, and it is in turn those substances and their causal powers that immediately and completely explain the transaction (the burning) that transpires between them.

What, then, do we want to say is the privileged account of the laws of nature for someone who affirms the mere conservationist picture? While this is not, I think, a requirement of the position, mere conservationists are typically necessitarians concerning the range of causal powers exhibited by given properties, that is, that to each property there is some range of active and passive potentials that belong essentially (see, for an example of this sort of necessitarianism, Harré and Madden 1975). It is not a contingent feature of water that it has the power to dissolve salt (as it is not a contingent feature of salt that it has the passive potential to be dissolved by water), and it is not a contingent feature of fire that it has the power to burn cotton (as it is not a contingent feature of cotton that it has the passive potential to be burned by fire). Rather, these causal powers belong to *being fire*, *being salt*, *being water*, *being cotton*.

With such a view in hand we can see how a defender of this sort of mere conservationist view would provide an account of the laws of nature. The laws of nature are to be understood along Armstrong/Dretske/Tooley lines, as relationships of physical necessitation between universals. As in any attempt to defend a theory of the laws of nature along Armstrong/Dretske/Tooley lines,[1] one must offer an account of how the selection of some properties by others occurs (1.4). On this mere conservationist view,

---

[1] Recall that I distinguish between what I take to be the central anti-Humean thrust of the Armstrong/Dretske/Tooley view—that the relevant relation in laws of nature is between

it will be in terms of the intrinsic causal powers belonging to the kinds in question that selection takes place: the universals involved in a law of nature will either be those kinds or will be properties that either trigger or are the outcome of the exercise of those causal powers.

With respect to particular transactions, the mere conservationist holds that God's role is only that of conserving in existence the substances that interact, and so the mere conservationist takes the role of God with respect to the obtaining of this law of nature to be very limited. Since there is no possibility that these properties could exist while failing to have the associated causal powers, God's role would have to be restricted either to that of seeing to it that there are beings to whom the relevant laws of nature can apply or to that of seeing to it that the relevant properties exist. So, on one hand, one might hold that the role of God in explaining the holding of the law of nature *fire burns cotton* is that for this law to be operative, or effective, there must be beings that can instantiate the relevant properties, so God's role as necessarily explaining the existence of every concrete being gives God some role in explaining the character of that law of nature as operative. On the other hand, the explanation might appeal to God's bringing about the existence of properties rather than beings that might exemplify those properties. One might have a theory of properties on which a property does not exist unless instanced, so God's role is to bring about the property's existence by seeing to it that that property is instanced. Or one might have a theory of properties on which properties are more directly brought about, say through divine intellection.

To summarize, then: With respect to particular transactions in the natural order, the mere conservationist holds that God's role in explaining those transactions is fully mediated; God's role is to hold the substances that exhibit the causally-relevant properties in existence so that they can exercise their own proper powers. With respect to the laws of nature, the mere conservationist holds that God's role in explaining those laws is that of explaining either the obtaining of their application conditions or the existing of the properties implicated in those laws.

It is clear—and I will discuss this in more detail below—that mere conservationism involves an account of God's relationship to the natural properties—and their particular readings of that relationship (that it is a causal relationship, that it is contingent, etc.).

order in which God's role is fully mediated with respect to necessitation relationships, both the particular necessitation relationships present in transactions in the natural order and the general necessitation relationships expressed in laws of nature. When a flame burns cotton, it is between the flame and the cotton; the making necessary the burning of the cotton resultant upon this being fire needs no further theistic story, given the existence of this fire and this cotton. And that *being fire* necessitates *burning cotton* requires no further theistic story, given the existence of the properties *being fire* and *being burnt* and *being cotton*.

The view of God's relationship to the natural order with which mere conservationism contrasts most sharply is a view on which God's relationship to events in the natural order is entirely unmediated, and is indeed complete. This is *occasionalism*. According to this view, every event in the natural order[2] has God as its immediate and total active cause: immediate, because there are no natural agents as intermediaries between God's will and the occurrence of the event; and total active, because there are no natural agents that make any active causal contribution to the event's occurrence. While some entities in the natural order might appear to exercise causal agency (the fire appears to actively cause cotton to burn), this is mere appearance. There are no efficient causes in nature; apparent efficient causes are but "occasional" causes, labeled as such because their presence is merely the occasion for God's causing a state of affairs to obtain (as the presence of the fire near cotton is an occasion for God's willing the cotton to burn). Regularities in nature that are commonly attributed to intercreature efficient causation are really nothing but manifestations of God's "abiding intention to act in certain fixed ways" (Freddoso 1988, p. 103).[3]

Freddoso has argued that the way in which natural substances and events can be the cause of other events in the natural order can be no more than causation as counterfactual dependence (Freddoso 1988, p. 85). But this is not quite right. The reason is that with counterfactual

---

[2] Except, perhaps, the free actions of created rational beings—occasionalists have strong reason to want to exempt rational beings from the occasionalist thesis, for otherwise God is the agent of sinful action—though I confess that I can't see a principled occasionalist rationale for making this sort of exception.

[3] Here and elsewhere in the text I am heavily indebted to Freddoso's work on rival views of God's activity in nature (Freddoso 1986, 1988, 1991, 1994) and also to the careful dissertation work by Louis Mancha (2003).

dependence states of affairs that are necessarily co-instantiated will be the causes of the same states of affairs in the counterfactual dependence sense. But to be an occasion for some divine willing is not closed under necessary co-extension—the occasion for fire's burning cotton is *fire's being near the cotton*, not *fire's being near the cotton and Fermat's last theorem's being true*. That is because the occasion for the cotton's burning is fixed by the divine mental state, what God wills to occur, and what God wills is burning in the presence of fire's being near the cotton, not fire's being near the cotton and Fermat's Last Theorem's being true.[4]

This point I think paves the way to respond to the objection to occasionalism that it cannot account for laws of nature, because in genuine laws of nature (for example, *fire burns cotton*) there is a *necessitation* relationship among the properties (for example, *being cotton, being placed in a flame, being burned*). For it is clear that there is more than just a regularity relationship, and indeed even more than counterfactual dependence. The cotton is burned *because* it is placed in the flame, as the divine decision that cotton burn when it is near to flame is what supports the truth of *if x were made of cotton and placed near flame, then x would burn*. The natural event—the cotton being placed in the flame—is what we can call the *occasion* for the *efficacy* of the divine intention. The natural event itself does not actively cause anything—it does not cause the cotton's burning, nor does it cause God to burn the cotton. But because the cotton's being placed in the flame has the role in the general divine intention that it has, the cotton's being placed in the flame makes necessary the cotton's being burned in that it (and nothing that is merely necessarily co-extensive with it) is the occasion for it. Thus *being cotton* and *being placed in flame* are, jointly, an *occasional* cause—not an active cause in any sense, but a cause at least insofar as it is non-accidental and genuinely explanatory.

To summarize, then: With respect to particular transactions in the natural order, the occasionalist holds that God's role in explaining those transactions is, as a matter of active causation, immediate and complete;

---

[4] As John Foster emphasizes in *The Divine Lawmaker*, it is important that, if God's causal contribution is to support the view that it is a law that fire burns cotton, it must be that God intends this *as a regularity*: it must not simply be true that, for each instance of cotton's being placed in fire, God wills that the cotton burn; it must be that God wills that, if the cotton is placed in the fire, then the cotton burns. Otherwise the bearing of the divine willing on the case will not validate the status of *fire burns cotton* as a law of nature as opposed to a mere regularity (Foster 2004, p. 157).

God's general intention that certain events obtain in the presence of other events is the complete active cause of the occurrence of particular events in the natural order. With respect to the laws of nature, the occasionalist holds that those familiar statements of laws of nature which mention only natural properties can nevertheless be correct; what is important is that natural properties make necessary other properties only in the sense of occasioning them, and that this occasioning relationship is explaining by a divine general willing.

5.3 Mere conservationism and natural law theory

Standard natural law theory is, *mutatis mutandis*, mere conservationism.

The mere conservationist holds that various properties intrinsically have causal powers, which powers can be exercised independently of further theistic involvement. Thus the transactions in the natural order are characteristically entirely between creatures, some properties of which physically necessitate other properties of which. The standard natural law theorist holds that various properties intrinsically have normative powers, which powers can be exercised independently of further theistic involvement. Thus the transactions in the normative order are characteristically entirely between creatures, some properties of which normatively necessitate other properties of which. The way that God can enter into the explanation of laws of nature on the mere conservationist view are as limited as the way that God can enter into the explanation of moral law on the standard natural law view: God can be invoked to explain the presence of beings the properties of which can be governed by the laws, whether laws of nature or moral laws, or God can be invoked to explain the existence of the relevant properties involved in those laws.

Now it is also plain that mere conservationism and standard natural law theory share not only their strengths but also their weaknesses. The strengths of mere conservationism are clearest in terms of explanandum-centered (0.1) considerations. It seems obvious that the features of objects in the natural and moral orders actively make a difference with respect to what is necessitated—this seems a matter of common sense—and it is this capacity to make a difference that accounts for the fact that we can gain scientific/moral knowledge by investigation of those properties. But when we turn to explanans-centered considerations, it is clear that mere conservationism shares the liabilities with which standard natural law theory is burdened. If God's status as ultimate, omnipresent explainer gives us reason to think that all transactions involve God, and involve God immediately (2.4), then we should have our doubts about both of these views, for both views require that characteristically such transactions occur without immediate theistic involvement.

5.4 Occasionalism and theological voluntarism

Theological voluntarism is, *mutatis mutandis*, occasionalism.

What theological voluntarisms have in common is that they hold that some act that is itself or is partially constituted by a divine willing is the sole active normative source of moral necessity—the divine will alone (actively) morally necessitates performance. (It may well be true that God's willings are in some way themselves explained by something else—it may be, for example, that God wills that I not kill my neighbors because part of my neighbors' good consists in their remaining alive. But this something-else does not have, of itself, *moral* power—it does not itself actively contribute to moral necessitation, to binding me to action. As I noted above (4.3), this is not a disanalogy between occasionalism and theological voluntarism. For it could be that there are features of natural properties (e.g. *being fire* and *being cotton*) that somehow explain why God link them together in laws of nature—aesthetic features, perhaps. But that would not in the least suggest that these properties themselves have or confer causal powers.) Similarly, the occasionalists hold that some act that is itself or is partially constituted by a divine willing is the sole active cause of physical necessity—the divine will alone (actively) physically necessitates any event. So, on theological voluntarism, the existence of a moral law such as *promisors are to keep their promises* is to be understood in the following way. It is true in an important sense that being the object of a promise that one has made necessitates one's performing, just as on the occasionalist view the salt's being placed in water necessitates the salt's dissolving. But in both cases the real active cause is God, not the creature, whether we have in mind the features of the promise or the features of the water. Theological voluntarists hold that the features of the promise are as morally inert as the occasionalists hold that the features of the water are causally inert.

Theological voluntarism is occasionalistic in its *structure*. It is also occasionalistic in its *rationale*. Occasionalists have offered both explanans- and explanandum-centered considerations in favor of the view. It is plain what explanans-centered grounds can be offered for occasionalism and theological voluntarism: whatever else one wishes to say against these views, it cannot be denied that they satisfy the desideratum that an adequate philosophy of nature or moral theory must respect God's sovereignty over the nondivine. As I noted above (4.2), Quinn defends theological voluntarism in part by appeal to considerations of divine sovereignty. And occasionalists have often defended their view in precisely those terms: only a view in which God is the complete active explanation of the transactions in the natural order adequately honors God's sovereignty over creation.

It is unsurprising that theological voluntarists and occasionalists would both appeal to explanans-centered considerations regarding divine sovereignty in support of their views. They also have appealed to similar *explanandum*-based considerations to defend their positions. Occasionalists preceded Hume in pointing out that it seems possible to imagine very different effects following from cotton's being placed in fire or salt's being placed in water; and so we must think that what events follow these are a contingent matter, the sort of thing that is fixed by the divine will rather than inherent in these creaturely natures. These occasionalists pointed out that such a view also provides an interpretation of what is happening in *contra naturam* miracles: we can explain without strain the failure of the fire to burn Shadrach, Meschach, and Abednego (Daniel 3:1–97); because the fire has of itself no tendency to burn, its failure to burn the three due to God's decision is not especially problematic. So what one would expect, given what I have said so far, is that some theological voluntarists would make similar appeals to the contingency of the moral law, and to the possibility of moral miracles, in defending that view. As we have seen (4.3), Hare, following his reading of Duns Scotus, argues for the contingency of the moral law; and again following Scotus, he employs his voluntarist conception to offer an account of what we might call "moral miracles"—cases in which, by divine will, the moral order becomes quite other than what it seems to naturally tend to be (Hare 2001, pp. 68–9). (The premier example of this is God's command making it morally licit, even required, that Abraham intend to sacrifice Isaac.) Quinn has also taken this feature on board in his theological voluntarism, holding that it is one of the main supports for theological voluntarism from the perspective of traditional monotheism that it allows a satisfying explanation for these disruptions in the moral order (Quinn 1992).

I have already criticized the appeal to contingency in defense of theological voluntarism (4.3), and it should be noted that there are serious doubts about the contingency of the laws of nature on which some occasionalists have relied (see, e.g. Bird 2001, 2002, 2005, and 2007). (I will say something about miracles, natural and moral, in Chapter 6; see 6.6.) But what seems to be most troubling, I say, about the occasionalist and theological voluntarist views is that in neither case do natural features of the world function as active causes in the natural or moral orders. On the occasionalist view, the natures of created things are idle; they have no natural power to bring about any effects. Creatures do not do anything, though they are the occasion of God's doing something. On the theological voluntarist view, the natures of created things are morally idle; they have no moral power to necessitate action.

So far, then, it seems that I have simply continued to deliver bad news. In Chapters 3 and 4, we saw two important theistic moral theories, both of which seem inadequate from a theistic perspective. And in this chapter I have argued that corresponding to these two theories are two theistic theories of nature, each of which corresponds to one of our failed moral theories both in its merits and in its ultimate unacceptability. But, finally, the good news: the discussion of the relationship between God and the laws of nature is much further advanced than the discussion of the relationship between God and the moral law. For we have in the discussion of the relationship between God and the laws of nature a well-worked-out third view that claims to be able to capture the immediate presence of divine action in every causal transaction that occurs in nature but without precluding a genuine, ineliminable role for creaturely natures in those transactions.

5.5 A third way: concurrentism and the laws of nature

The occasionalist says that God's role in necessitating events in the natural order is *immediate* and *complete*. The mere conservationist says that God's role is *incomplete* because *mediated*, with the result that the transactions between creatures are entirely between those creatures; what happens between the fire and the cotton is between the fire and cotton, and divine action is not implicated in that transaction. One who is dissatisfied with both of these yet who is also concerned to preserve the immediacy of theistic explanation in the natural order will notice right away that one can consistently reject both views while preserving the immediacy of theistic explanation: the key is to affirm that theistic explanation both of particular transactions and of general laws can be *immediate* but *incomplete*. On this alternative view, the occurring of particular transactions and the holding of general laws results immediately from both divine and creaturely contributions. So there is hope to meet the objection to mere conservationism that it makes God explanatorily superfluous and the objection to occasionalism that it makes creaturely natures explanatorily superfluous.

The view is called *concurrentism*, and it is disputed among concurrentists how, in formulating the position, best to characterize the respective contributions of God and creatures. But we do need to have a tolerably clear notion of the general concurrentist strategy and some sense of how this general strategy might be specified promisingly in order to see how it might be transformed in a way that can serve our search for an adequate theistic explanation of moral law.

Begin with particular transactions in the natural order. To put the concurrentist view broadly, with regard to each natural effect, God's contribution to the bringing about of that effect is *general* while the creature's contribution is *specific*. As Aquinas puts it, creaturely causes are "like particularizers and determinants of the primary agent's [that is, God's] action" (Aquinas, *Summa Contra Gentiles*, III, 66, [6]). But it is crucial that it is not merely that God's contribution is general and the creature's specific; it is also that the divine cause's contribution to the produced effect is no less immediate than the creaturely cause's. As Leibniz writes, God's contribution is immediate in that "God concurs no less nor more indirectly in producing this effect than in producing its cause" ("Vindication," §11).

This is what concurrentists want to say about the relationship between divine and creaturely causes in the production of effects in the natural order. But it is difficult to assess the promise of concurrentism so long as we remain at that level of abstraction. So we might consider a couple of models of how this general concurrentist picture might itself be specified, not for the sake of ultimately evaluating natural concurrentism—this is not our goal—but for the sake of having a clearer idea of how natural concurrentism might be transformed into a theory of God's relationship to the moral order.

On one view, which we might call the "instrumentalist" reading of natural concurrentism, we should think of effects in the natural order as proceeding entirely from God and entirely from creatures, though in different "orders" of causation. As Aquinas writes,

> The same effect is ascribed to a natural cause and to God . . . : . . . the whole effect proceeds from each, yet in different ways: just as the whole of the one same effect is ascribed to the instrument, and again the whole is ascribed to the principal agent. (*Summa Contra Gentiles*, III, 70)

This specification of the concurrentist view takes it that we can reasonably ascribe the effect of a principal and the principal's instrument entirely to each, so long as we distinguish the orders of explanation. So if I use a bat to hit a ball over a fence, the ball's going over the fence is wholly explained by me and wholly explained by the bat; but since the order of causation in which I am acting as agent is distinct from that in which the bat is acting, there is neither causal exclusion nor causal overdetermination.

Now, I take it that the instrumentalist reading will be insufficiently specified unless we can say what is involved in there being two distinct orders of causation, with respect to which it is true both that the causal relationship between God and the effect and the creaturely cause and the effect are immediate and that the sort of causation at stake in both cases is efficient causation. One cannot say, for example, that God's relationship to the effect is immediate in that God immediately *intends* the effect—the way that I intend to hit the ball over the fence—while the creaturely cause's relationship to the effect is immediate in that it is the proximate means by which God's intention is effected—the way that the motion of the bat is itself all that is needed to explain the change in velocity of the baseball so that it goes over the fence. For thus characterized the view might be indistinguishable from a minor emendation on mere conservationism, differing only by its making explicit that the conservation of creatures and their causal powers is an instance of God's exercise of rational providence over creation. But it seems to me that meeting both of these conditions, that the relationship of God's causing to the effect is immediate and that it is a kind of efficient causing—cannot be satisfied wholly by reference to an appeal to the instrumental character of the relationship between God and creaturely cause. One will have to say something about the character of the creaturely causing itself, about its internal character, in order to make clear how divine causing could be related to effects in the natural order in the way that concurrentism requires.

An alternative model, which we might call the "complementarity" model, offers such an account. On this view, God and creature are complementary causes: in each instance of efficient causation in the natural order, God contributes general, undifferentiated power, while the creaturely agent contributes the specific way that this power will affect other objects; together, these constitute the causing of the unified effect. Consider, for example, an overhead projector, on whose surface is placed a clear plastic sheet on which a variety of colored shapes have been drawn. When the overhead projector is turned on, there will appear on the wall a number of images: a red triangle, a blue square, a green octagon, etc. We might refer to both the overhead and the ink shapes in even the most immediate explanation of the presence of the images on the wall: the overhead projector's contribution is to produce the light that beamed the images, and the ink shapes determined (along with the nature of the wall) the particular images that would appear on the wall. This case seems to be a close analogy to the complementarity view of how God and creatures cooperate in causation within the natural order. Just as the overhead is a generic cause in virtue of its producing an undifferentiated beam of light, God is the general cause of all events in the natural order; and just as the particular ink shapes on the transparency determine the particular effects that would result, the natures of individual creatures determine what particular effects will be produced by them.[5] Or consider the toaster analogy (McDonough 2007, p. 43). Of itself, the toaster is unable to cause anything. But powered by an electrical current—a current that is of itself indifferent with respect to the causing of heating and cooling—the toaster brings about a *specific* effect, toasting, when situated properly with respect to a suitable object.

On this concurrentist view, the transactions that take place in the ordinary course of nature are characteristically instances of joint action, carried out by both God and creatures, which terminate in a single effect. It is important for the concurrentist view that we cannot divide this joint action into two independent actions, one by God, one by the creature,

---

[5] Free agents differ from other natural agents in that their natures do not specify a determinate set of effects.

which somehow together combine to produce a particular effect. If this were the way to characterize the position, then the concurrentist would have failed to provide a theory on which no creaturely action can take place without immediate theistic involvement, for there would still be a creaturely action that is independent of divine action, even if always accompanied by it. What's more, such a view would be incoherent, for it would portray God as causing something general, but every effect is particular. Rather, the concurrentist view holds that the jointness of the action between God and creatures is not divisible into really distinct actions; God and creatures cooperate in bringing about a given effect, though some features of that effect are more properly attributable to God and some are more properly attributable to creatures.

We can think of this phenomenon using the commonplace idea of contrastive explanation. If the fire burns cotton, this effect (the burning of the cotton) is jointly attributable to God and the fire. If we ask why something happened rather than nothing at all, this can be primarily traced to God, for it is God's active causation that is responsible for there being an exercise of causal agency. If we ask why this in particular happened—why what happened was a burning rather than a chilling or freezing—this can be primarily traced to the fire, as it is the specific character of the creaturely causes that determines the specific effects brought about.

This gives us some idea of how the concurrentist can specify the roles of God and creature in transactions in the natural order. So how, then, does concurrentism give an account of the laws of nature, and God's role with respect to them? I think that there are multiple options here for formulating a concurrentist account of the laws of nature, but here is the view that I think most clearly brings out the divine and creaturely contributions. We begin by noting that the specific effects that creatures can cause *are* fixed by the nature of those creatures. It is just false to say that the creatures make no real difference to the effects that are brought about, just as it would be just false to say that the color and shape of the ink figures on the transparency sheet make no real difference to what is projected on the screen, or that the configuration of the toaster makes no difference as to whether toast or frozen bread pops out at the end of the power cycle. Insofar as creatures of these kinds are acting in the natural order, they will bring about these ranges of effects; it is not a contingent fact that fire, if acting, burns.

What raises questions in formulating the concurrentist view is the role in which to cast the divine general contribution. I suggest that the best way to cast the divine general contribution is as part of the standard conditions in which creatures are acting in nature. For we allowed that the way in which properties necessitate other properties in laws of nature is *defeasibly* (1.4); in *standard* conditions, fire burns cotton, water dissolves salt, and so forth. The framework in which nature characteristically operates—call these "ordinary worlds"—is with divine concurrence, and given such concurrence, *being placed in fire* and *being cotton* necessitates *being burned*. But because God's contribution to this sort of causation is free, though, God might choose to withhold God's contribution in extraordinary worlds, and in those worlds flame might fail to burn the cotton—much less Shadrach, Meschach, and Abednego.

The concurrentist claims to capture the explanans-centered and explanandum-centered features of occasionalism and mere conservationism, respectively. With the occasionalists, the concurrentist rightly claims to satisfy the theistic desideratum that there be no particular transaction in nature and no holding of a general law that does not have God as part of the immediate explanation. With the mere conservationists, the concurrentist rightly claims that his or her view gives creatures an active, rather merely an occasional, role in determining the course of nature.

Now, we should no doubt be interested in pursuing further how exactly the concurrentist should understand the divine contribution, and so forth. But my interest in pursuing this investigation of various theories of God's relationship to the laws of nature is not for its own sake but for the sake of our moral inquiry. There is a third view of God's relationship to the laws of nature that holds out some hope in avoiding the difficulties of occasionalism and mere conservationism, appropriating their strengths and avoiding their weaknesses. But there is no third view of God's relationship to moral law extant. Thus we should want to know: Is it possible to provide an analog to concurrentism for the moral order, a view on which moral law is fixed by God and creaturely nature in a way that avoids the difficulties of both theological voluntarism and standard natural law theory?

The answer is Yes. The working out of moral concurrentism is the task of Chapter 6.

6
Moral concurrentism

6.1 The basic idea of moral concurrentism

The basic idea of moral concurrentism is that moral necessitation, and thus moral law, is immediately explained both by God and by creaturely natures. This is not overdetermination, but cooperation; they somehow jointly morally necessitate. But to state the basic idea of moral concurrentism is not to show that moral concurrentism can be sensibly worked out. While in this inquiry we can rightly beg off the challenge of formulating natural concurrentism (5.5) in a sufficiently complete way, we cannot have justifiable confidence in the prospects of a moral concurrentism without seeing how the details of such a view can be plausibly worked out. And so my aim in this final chapter is to work out a particular moral concurrentism.

The particular moral concurrentism that I will deliver is obviously aiming to fit with the sort of natural law view I favor (Murphy 2001)—of course, not the standard natural law view criticized in Chapter 3, in which theistic explanation is entirely mediated, but nevertheless a recognizably natural law position. In 3.9 above I noted that while natural law theory has a sort of prominence among theistic moral theories that endorse mediated theistic explanation, one might nevertheless defend a mediated theistic view that is not of the natural law sort—some sort of consequentialism, Kantianism, or virtue theory, perhaps. In offering a particular moral concurrentism formulated in natural law terms, I am not suggesting that this is the only way that moral concurrentism can be worked out, for one might attempt to transform these other unsatisfactory-because-mediated views into versions of moral concurrentism. I do think that there are distinctive advantages to working out the view in a natural law way, even putting to the side the attractiveness of natural law theory generally. But my focus here will be on showing how a moral concurrentism can be plausibly worked out, not on showing that this is the uniquely best way to work it out. After all, my argument here is for the superiority of moral concurrentism over standard natural law theory and theological voluntarism as theistic explanations of moral law, not for the superiority of natural law ethics over Kantianism, utilitarianism, etc. as substantive views within moral theory.

For the purposes of this inquiry I accept the general correctness of the natural law theorist's strategy of explaining the moral law in terms of the good's morally necessitating certain forms of response. (I return to some characteristic voluntarist worries about this approach below.) What I aim to do is to show that this way of explaining moral law can meet both the explanans- and explanandum-focused desiderata (0.1, 2.4) so long as we have in place an adequately theistic account of the good that does the moral necessitating. What is objectionable about the standard natural law views criticized in Chapter 3 is not, I say, the structure of their explanation of moral laws but their substantive account of the goods that do the moral necessitating; on these views, facts about goodness are not themselves theistic facts, and thus the moral necessitation of action by goods is either not theistically explained at all or only mediately theistically explained. If, however, facts about goodness were themselves theistic facts, then theistic immediacy would be preserved, for theistic facts would enter immediately into the explanation of all moral necessitation. So what needs to be defended is an account of the good that is still recognizably a natural law view—that is, one in which the goodness of a creature is fixed by the kind to which that creature belongs—but which is also immediately theistic. Or, to put it in more obviously concurrentist terms, it would be an account of the good in which facts about God and facts about the creaturely nature cooperate in fixing the character of creaturely goodness.

I begin by turning to the theory of the good offered by Robert Adams. Adams's view, it is plain, meets immediacy conditions on theistic explanation, but we have good reasons to supplement that view in a way that makes it less Platonist and more Aristotelian, though Aristotelian in an essentially theistic way (6.2). This view can then be put to work in a recognizably natural law account of moral law that, unlike the views considered in Chapter 3, satisfies the constraint of theistic immediacy (6.3) and answers the objection from divided loyalty (6.4). I conclude by answering in a more tentative way a couple of objections from defenders of more voluntarist accounts of theistic explanation of moral law: first, that this moral concurrentist view must lack an adequate account of moral obligation (6.5), and second, that moral concurrentism lacks any way to deal with the problem of the "immoralities of the patriarchs" (6.6).

6.2 Concurrentist goodness

In Chapter 4 I argued against theological voluntarist accounts of moral law, paying particular attention to the theological voluntarist account offered by Adams; I argued there that theological voluntarism is a very implausible account of moral necessities and moral necessitation (4.3) and that there is no reason to think that there is a special sort of moral status, the morally obligatory, that we have distinctive reason to capture in voluntarist terms (4.4). This is a thoroughgoing rejection of Adams's account of the right. But we have not considered Adams's account of the good. The sort of goodness that Adams takes to be central to ethical inquiry is goodness as excellence, and on this point I will follow Adams, though I would disagree with some of the ways that he characterizes other notions of goodness in relation to it.[1] While I think that as it stands Adams's account of goodness as excellence lacks some of the support that he claims for it, and that it ultimately requires revision in order to be plausible, its central distinctive feature—the goodness of creaturely goods consists in their resemblance to God—should be preserved within any theistic account of the good and provides a basis for an adequate theistic explanation of moral law.

We have distinguished between two sets of argumentative considerations that underwrite the explanation of moral matters in theistic terms: *explanandum*-focused and *explanans*-focused (0.1). Adams relies, I think, on both sorts of considerations. To begin with his appeal to explanandum-focused considerations: to give an account what the nature of something is is to explain it, to give a constitutive explanation (Schroeder 2008, p. 63), and Adams offers a procedure of a sort to pursue this kind of inquiry:

It is possible, I think, to indicate a general pattern for the relation of natures to meanings where the nature is not given by the meaning. What is given by the meaning, or perhaps more broadly by the use of the words, is a role that the nature

---

[1] For example, I reject Adams's account of well-being as enjoyment of goodness as excellence (Adams 1999, pp. 93–101), holding that well-being is just perfection of subjects or those subjects' lives; see Murphy 2001, pp. 46–95.

is to play. If there is a single candidate that best fills the role, that will be the nature of the thing. (Adams 1999, p 16)

(While there is some ambiguity here, it is clear from Adams's later argument that he is allowing that what fixes the role of goodness is not simply what is true conceptually of goodness, but also what is commonsensically taken to be true of goodness, even if held a posteriori rather than a priori.) Adams's view is that the most straightforward way to give an argument for an informative property identification is to hold that there is some property that uniquely, and necessarily uniquely, plays that role.[2] And so Adams argues that once we are clear on the role that the notion of goodness plays, it is clear that it could be played by a theistic property but could not be played by any nontheistic property.[3]

Here is Adams's basic argument. Consider the candidate theistic identification of *being good* with *resembling God*. (This is approximately the truth, on Adams's view; Adams 1999, p. 28. We will consider qualifications to this in a moment.) The property *resembling God* can play the role of goodness: for *resembling God* is, like *being good*, something that is objective, knowable, motivating, reason-giving, supervenient on natural features, and so forth. Now we can assume for the sake of argument that there is some naturalistic account that also satisfies these features. But the theistic account will satisfy these criteria, *and more*: for the theistic account, unlike these naturalistic accounts, can satisfy the criterion that goodness is *transcendent*. The transcendence of the good is that feature of it, whatever it is, that ensures that we are always able to take a critical stance with respect to anything characterized solely in terms of its natural properties. So with respect to anything naturalistically characterized, we can ask "Is that really good?", withholding attitudes of respect and admiration until we are satisfied of its genuine goodness.

---

[2] I do find this a little dubious, not because of any scruples about property identifications, but because it is not at all obvious to me that one should ever identify what seems clearly to be a functional property (which is what "playing the role" is, at least in the case of normative properties like *being good*) with what seems clearly to be a nonfunctional property. Even if there is necessarily only one kind of thing that can do a certain job, it seems mistaken to identify the property *being that kind of thing* with *being able to do that job*. This point also applies to his account of rightness as being commanded by God, as I noted above (4.2).

[3] Adams qualifies here: it could not be played *as well*. But his own view commits him to the position that any nontheistic account would be revisionist of the role of the good.

On Adams's view, though, the transcendence of the good ensures that goodness must forever resist capture by any set of natural properties. For if one puts forward some naturalistic identification of the property *being good*, then one commits oneself to no longer taking a critical stance with respect to the goodness of whatever satisfies that naturalistic identification. But it is essential to the role of goodness that it enable one to adopt this critical standpoint. So any naturalistic identification of goodness will be self-defeating (Adams 1999, pp. 77–82). (This is, on Adams's view, the true lesson of Moore's Open Question argument (Adams 1999, p. 78); contra Smith (1994, pp. 35–9), it is not simply an instance of the paradox of analysis, but arises from the specific character of the role of normative properties like goodness.[4])

Now, I find Adams's argument for the superiority of the divine resemblance account of goodness over any naturalistic account on the basis of the critical character of the good to be dubious—I think that any attraction that we might have for Adams's view is drawn from the specific naturalistic view with which he contrasts his own position rather than with naturalistic accounts generally. Adams uses Boyd's naturalistic account of the good as his foil; on Boyd's view, "A term *t* refers to a kind (property, relation, etc.) *k* just in case there exist causal mechanisms whose tendency is to bring it about, over time, that what is predicated of the term *t* will be approximately true of *k*" (Boyd 1988, p. 195). Approximately, then, "good" refers to whatever property is responsible for applications of the term "good." Now it surely does seem plausible that we should be dissatisfied with empirical investigation of the explanation of our use of the term "good" as what would close investigation; with whatever property one determines to be the cause of the use of the term "good," one might well ask whether that property is really good, even while conceding that the investigation has shown that property to be what causes the use of the term. But all that would show is that this is too thin an account of the nature of goodness, that, after all, we should require an account of the nature of the good to satisfy the various other features of the role of goodness—that it be itself

---

[4] Does Adams have an argument against Moorean non-naturalism—that *being good* is a sui generis nonnatural property that fills this complex role? Yes: first, Adams's view explains why the various aspects of this role cluster as they do (see below in this section); second, there are specific aspects of the goodness role—in particular, supervenience and knowledge—that seem to work better on a theistic reduction than on a nonnaturalist account.

motivating, reason-giving, objective in the right ways, available to be known, fitting with our considered judgments about its extension, and so forth. So, that we should hold that Boyd's method of fixing a naturalistic account of the good fails to preserve the critical character of goodness does not seem to count in favor of Adams's view of goodness over and against any eligible naturalistic account.

The Adamsian response to this criticism would of course be to hold that the loss of *good*'s adequately critical function is not just an artifact of the particular view, Boyd's, that Adams took as his foil, but a more general phenomenon. But this seems to me false. Suppose that we lay out a rich account of the role of the good, including both its causal responsibility for our use of the language of goodness and its satisfaction of the various roles of objectivity, reason-givingness,[5] etc. And we come to the conclusion that naturalistic property N plays that role brilliantly. It is true that as things stand, for those of us who continue to hold this view on the brilliance of N in satisfying the role of the good, we cannot intelligibly take a critical stance toward N. But all that means is that so long as we remain convinced that N plays that role brilliantly, we must hold that to be N is to be good. On the other hand, nothing prevents our reconsidering the identification of N with goodness. After all, since our judgments of the goodness of particular created things is typically relatively spontaneous, it is always possible that we could come to the considered judgment that some object o is good, even though o does not exhibit N, or that o is not good, even though o does exhibit N. The fact that any naturalistic identification of goodness can be held subject to reversal in the light of contrary evidence is all that the naturalist needs in order to rebut Adams's claim that naturalistic accounts of the good are incompatible with the preservation of *good*'s critical function.

So while Adams's account of goodness does plausibly meet the explanandum-focused considerations at issue—he has plausible arguments that his thesis that goodness is resemblance to God satisfies the role of the good—I doubt that Adams's view can claim for itself *superiority* over any naturalistic rival simply as such with respect to the explanandum-focused

---

[5] If one is worried about whether a naturalistic account could coherently put itself forward as satisfying the reason-givingness platitude, note that one might take reason-givingness to itself be subject to naturalistic property identification using Adamsian techniques. See, for example, Smith 1994, pp. 151–77 and Schroeder 2008, pp. 56–60.

consideration regarding transcendence. For our purposes, though, it is worthwhile to dwell on the explanans-focused considerations in favor of Adams's account. It is not just that by assuming God's existence we have available to us some being that can be put to use in our theory of the good at no extra cost. Rather, the idea is that it is part of our understanding of God that God enters into the explanation of whatever is explanation-eligible (0.2, 2.4). And this consideration seems particularly pressing when we are dealing with normative matters. For it is central to theism that God is not merely the cause of all else that exists but the ultimate proper object of admiration and devotion and commitment (3.8). As Adams writes, echoing Buber, from a theistic perspective it is wrong to think of God as a mere competitor for our practical attention, even an overwhelmingly successful competitor (Adams 1999, p. 202); rather, the idea is that God is that in terms of which our practical attentions ought to be regulated. So from a theistic perspective we have strong reason to affirm an account of the good in which God somehow determines the character of the good. This desideratum Adams fulfills by characterizing goodness as resemblance to God.

My view is that any account of the good to be articulated within a theistic perspective should incorporate this sort of theistic determination. Nevertheless I think that Adams's view is unacceptable as it stands and would be improved by becoming less Platonist and more Aristotelian—that is, by moving from a view in which excellence of a thing is solely fixed by its resembling God, the form of the good, toward a view in which the excellence of a thing is jointly fixed by its resemblance to God and the kind to which the thing belongs.[6] Adams's identification of the property *being good* with *being Godlike* is hedged in various ways by him—I will discuss some of these ways below—but in order to make the case for a more Aristotelian formulation of Adams's view of goodness as excellence, I want to begin with a criticism of the straightforward, unadorned version.

Consider the goodness of a perfectly prepared chicken fried steak, covered with cream gravy. My objection is *not* that Adams's view implies that the goodness of this chicken fried steak, such as it is, consists in its Godlikeness. Adams has anticipated this objection—actually, he mentions a "gourmet dinner"—and has answered it. "Well, why not?" Adams asks.

---

[6] I don't mean that this theistic Aristotelian view will be merely a conjunction; as I suggest below, it is more plausible that it belongs to a thing's kind to resemble God in particular ways.

"'Taste and see that the LORD is good,' says the Psalmist (Psalm 34:8), seeming to find at least enough resemblance for a metaphor here" (Adams 1999, p. 30). Expanded a touch, the goodness of a chicken fried steak is a particular and distinctive aesthetic goodness, and it is not at all surprising to think of all that is excellent in this aesthetic way being but a reflection of God's goodness.

No, my objection is this. Suppose that I come down with a rare disease. Interestingly, the symptoms of this disease include my muscles taking on the taste and consistency of a piece of deep-fried tenderized round steak, my epidermis becoming crisp, like buttermilk-and-egg-saturated flour dipped into hot oil, and my pores oozing a whitish substance that is peppery and creamy. *I begin to share the properties that make a properly-prepared chicken fried steak good.* But this does not make me better, not in the least, or in any way. It is not that I become better in one way (I taste great!) but there are negative effects of other sorts (I'm really, really sick!). No: tasting like a properly-prepared chicken fried steak just isn't the sort of thing that makes me good, though it surely is what makes a chicken fried steak good.

I take it that what we should want from defenders of an Adamsian account of the good is an explanation as to why the chicken fried steak is made good by these features but I am not. But I should acknowledge that in discussing this example it has sometimes been replied that coming to resemble chicken fried steak in these ways does indeed make me good. I am surprised to discover that when one makes a long list of the ways in which Mark Murphy could be made better in one or another way— *intellectually, morally, creatively, relationally*, and so forth—*culinarily* is on the list as well. Indeed, one would have to include all of the different taste sensations that I might be made to exhibit on the now-lengthening list. Who would have thought that I could be made in some way more lovable, more worthy of admiration, by coming to taste not only like a chicken fried steak, but also were I to become the taste and consistency of chocolate pudding, cheese enchiladas, creamed spinach, and so forth? And of course the examples should not be restricted to culinary ways of being good. If I were to become diseased and to have my tendons shrink or stretch and my skin grow taut and discolored so that I resemble Rodin's *The Thinker*, I would on this view become more excellent—at least in that way—and thus merit admiration that I did not previously merit.

I think that we have prima facie evidence against this reply from the fact that, prior to being presented Adams's account of the good in terms of resemblance to God, no one would be at all tempted by such claims. If I put forward a group of objects—a human, a kudzu vine, a sculpture, a chicken fried steak—and asked a reflective person with a reflective grasp of the good to make a list of the properties that would make each of these things excellent, the lists would differ, and would differ strikingly. But the retort from those who take it that I would be made good by exhibiting chicken fried steak features seems to presuppose that the lists would in fact be the same—what differs among kinds of things is not what makes them excellent, but only their readiness to exhibit those properties.

Suppose, though, that one agrees that I do not become better, in the least or in any way, simply by coming to have these resemblances to a chicken fried steak. One might note, properly, that Adams is not committed to the view that I am made better by coming to be so like a chicken fried steak. Adams clarifies or qualifies this *goodness* = *Godlikeness* thesis in various ways, in part to avoid various worries about resemblance. But it seems to me that the addenda to his view do not help us to see why I am not made good by becoming crisp, juicy, peppery, etc. whereas it is through having these very properties that the chicken fried steak becomes good.

One qualification that Adams allows early on in his discussion is that we cannot take being Godlike to be sufficient for being good; it is only certain resemblances to God that make for goodness. He toys with the idea of connecting goodness to God's actual attitudes of love before settling on a view that has the benefits of keeping facts about what is good-making free of contingency while also retaining a tie to divine attitudes: to be good, Adams suggests, is to be like God in a way that could serve as a reason for God to love it (Adams 1999, pp. 34–6). Now, this qualification may be an extensionally correct account of what resemblances to God count as good, but it is hardly informative as to why my coming to taste like a chicken fried steak does not make me good in a brand new way. One would hope for a somewhat more illuminating account. One might reply: Surely the notion of resembling God has some haziness about it anyway, and is not tremendously informative if one is looking for new facts about what is good; adding this condition about what might be a reason for God to love it does not make matters appreciably more hazy. But this seems wrong to me. We *know* that what makes the chicken fried steak good is its crisp exterior, its juicy interior, the peppery flavor and creamy consistency of its gravy. So on Adams's qualified view, it is just those features of it that make it true that it resembles God in such a way that could be a reason for God to love it. But I've got those features, too. So why doesn't my exhibiting those features give God reasons for God to love me?

One might think that Adams precludes the worry about my coming to taste like a chicken fried steak by his appeal to a sort of *holism* about resemblances. He thinks that not just any sharing of properties is sufficient to make for resemblance; that I have the same number of hairs as that squirrel over there does not, Adams says, typically constitute a basis for a claim that I resemble the squirrel (Adams 1999, p. 32). Let us distinguish between the claims that resemblance is characteristically holistic from the claim that it is only resemblances that have a holistic character that are relevant to the *goodness is Godlikeness* thesis. Adams appeals to the former, which seems just false to me. We understand fully well claims of resemblance that are not holistic, given proper context. We understand fully well denials of resemblance, even with a lot of "holistic likeness," given proper context.[7] The trouble here may be just that Adams is looking for some notion of resemblance that he can put to work independently of such contextual considerations, which seems a chimera. On the other hand, it may well be that the way to preserve the goodness is Godlikeness thesis is to just make the second point: that the sort of Godlikeness that matters has a holistic character. But it had better be a specific sort of holistic character. I don't become better just by becoming holistically more like a chicken fried steak!

I do not think Adams's explicit qualification of the goodness is Godlikeness thesis in terms of what can be a divine reason or his explication of resemblance in terms of holism are persuasive ways of dealing with the chicken fried steak objection. I take a clue as to a better way to solve the problem from Adams's discussion of badness. Badness is not, on Adams's view, to be explained in the same way that goodness is—we are not to look for a supreme Bad, likeness to which constitutes being bad (Adams 1999, p. 102). Rather, bad is defined in relation to good—as being in some way deficient or defective with respect to it. One way of being bad is being opposed to the good, being against it—more on this below—

---

[7] You are the bouncer at the All Mammal 115 000–120,000 Hairs Club. My identical twin and I show up; I have 117,298 hairs and my twin 121,298 hairs. The squirrel waiting patiently in line behind us has 117,298 hairs. You rightly take the squirrel to resemble me more closely than I resemble my brother.

but this sort of badness is pretty clearly restricted to those things that can be responsive to goodness and badness. A more general sort of badness involves a lack of goodness, and it is instructive what Adams has to say about this:

> Historically the most important attempt to explain the bad in terms of a single relation to the good has identified badness with a privation of goodness—that is to say, with an absence of goodness that ought to be there. The qualification 'that ought to be there' may not be easy to explain, but it is not dispensable, for the absence of an excellence does not always cast badness as its shadow. It would be odd to call it something bad in a rhinoceros that it cannot play the oboe; I even doubt that it is something bad in me that I cannot. (Adams 1999, p. 103)

There is a great deal of interest here. Adams is endorsing the privation view as part of the best account of badness, but we cannot identify privation simply with failing to resemble God; it can, at best, be said that it involves failing to resemble God in ways that something ought to resemble God.

My suggestion is that we can appeal to the same thing in order to solve the chicken fried steak problem that we can appeal to in order to provide an account of the "ought" that Adams needs here in order to give an account of privation. Indeed, even those who are unmoved by the chicken fried steak example have some reason to be sympathetic with the suggestion that I am offering. For it seems plausible that we should appeal to the same sorts of considerations to explain why something is good that we use to explain why something is bad. So if there is some sort of factor to which we ought to appeal in explaining why some condition contributes to a thing's badness, we should have to appeal to that sort of factor to explain why some condition contributes to a thing's goodness.

Adams's own example suggests the type of factor to which we should appeal. If playing the oboe is the sort of excellent skillful activity that resembles God, why does the failure to play, and even the failure to be able to play, not render the rhino bad? Because *the rhinoceros* isn't supposed to be able to do that; it does not belong to its *kind*. The "ought" that can help Adams here is the ought of kind-membership, in which humans ought to be able to speak and rhinos ought to have one tail, four feet, twelve toes.[8] But while Adams acknowledges only the need for an *ought* of this sort in accounting for privation, we can add that this is what solves the chicken

---

[8] "The Rhino Song," from The Big Green Rabbit, <http://www.youtube.com/watch?v=QOvIot-i6rY>.

fried steak problem: it does not belong to my kind, *human*, to resemble God by tasting like a well-prepared chicken fried steak.[9]

It is, I think, an improvement on Adams's axiology to hold that no created thing is simply good; it is always X-ly good (or bad), where the X is filled in by the kind to which the thing belongs. While this view of course will remind of Geach's view in "Good and Evil" (1956) that good is always attributive and not predicative, I do not mean to affirm so strong a view. My view is that whenever a being belongs to some kind, then the standards for excellence for that thing are fixed in part by its kind. But it is possible to be beyond all kinds; and this is what is the case with God. So while we can say truly that God is simply good, for anything distinct from God its goodness will consist in its resembling God in a way that belongs to its kind.

Now, one might wonder why we should want to persist in the view that goodness involves resemblance to God once we appeal to the oughts of kind-membership. Why should we not at this point entirely abandon Adamsian axiology in favor of some form of nontheistic Aristotelianism, in which goodness is defined wholly by reference to the perfection of a thing in accordance with its kind? I think we should not, in part for the reason just given: this view does not provide a plausible account of God's goodness, for God is beyond all kinds. But there are further reasons as well.

On the explanandum-focused side of things, it is noteworthy that there is a limited range of properties that can figure in the excellence of a thing, but we can have no explanation of why this is so wholly in terms of the idea the conditions of goodness are set by the kind. Here is an example. I do not think that it belongs to the excellence of anything simply that it dies. Death is not an excellence of anything; it is paradigmatically the sort of thing to be abhorred and despised rather than loved and admired. When a thing's dying is admired, it is not admired as such, but as something that is accepted as just necessary, or as for the sake of something better or avoidance of something worse. One might say similar things about ignorance, sterility, philistinism, antisociality, and so forth. But there is nothing in the notion of a kind that precludes the ought of kind-membership from evaluating a thing in terms of these sorts of worthless conditions. I can make a machine the very point of which is to cease to exist. A lesser god

---

[9] For a discussion of the *ought* of kind-membership, see Thompson's discussion of Aristotelian categoricals in Thompson 2008, pp. 63–84.

might fashion a being that ought not to—that is, it would be defective with respect to its design plan if it came to—know things, or to make a friend, or to appreciate something beautiful. But we would resist the view that these things are admirable or lovable just by exhibiting the features *being dead* or *being ignorant* or *being friendless*. So it is plausible to argue that the modified Adamsian view has the advantage of explaining why there is a limited range of properties that can be objects of rightful admiration when exhibited by a member of some kind. What is more, the range of properties that can be the objects of rightful admiration are unified by being features of the one God (cf. 3.7).

This explanandum-focused consideration is, I think, a strong one in favor of theistic rather than nontheistic Aristotelianism about the excellence of created things. But the more important consideration is the explanans-focused. No argument that I've offered has given any reason to reassess the point that theism seems committed to the view that God is at the center of the normative world, not just one object of love among others, but both object of, and standard for, admiration. This view would not be satisfied by the sort of nontheistic Aristotelianism contemplated here, but it is satisfied by this theistic formulation of the view.

So I say that the best theistic account of the good will take what constitutes a thing's goodness to be *jointly* fixed by Godlikeness and by its kind—*being like God in ways that belong to the kind to be like God*. It is the kind that fixes the context for determining what counts as a relevant resemblance, or failure to resemble, God. Every good, then, is a divine likeness, but those that make a thing good are those divine likenesses such that members of the kind ought to exhibit them. This is a theistic Aristotelianism, and I think that the considerations raised by Adams himself indicate that it is a preferable theistic account of the good. For while Adams himself qualified the goodness is Godlikeness thesis so that things are good only if they are like God in a way that can give God reason to love them, this qualification is explanatorily pretty useless; but if we fix what gives God reason to love them as what these things need in order to become what they ought to become, this does at least have some content, and content that is plausible. And while Adams appeals to considerations involving holism of resemblance to make plausible his case for goodness as resemblance to God, we can specify at least that the way in which resemblance is relevant is in terms of the creature as a whole, the kind to which it belongs.

6.3 Concurrentist moral necessitation

A theistic account of the humanly good, then, should appeal both to human goods' being ways in which humans are made like to God and its belonging to our kind to be like God in these ways. If this is correct, then we can sketch an account of what it would be for human agency to be good—how certain instances of it can be good or less good, and how indeed certain kinds of agency are invariably defective and deficient.

God is a perfectly excellent agent, and it belongs to our kind to be like God in being agents, though in a way that is appropriate to our kind (6.2). It seems plausible enough that good agency always involves a response to what is valuable, good or bad, in some way—Adams affirms this—though the sorts of goods and bads to which we are appropriately responsive and the sorts of responses which are appropriate are fixed by the kind to which we belong. This seems simply to fall out of the general account of goodness; I am not here offering a specific account of the range of goods to which humans are rightly responsive and how far the character of appropriate human responsiveness is due to eccentric features of our kind.

Even without providing an account of the specific range of goods to which humans are properly responsive and how far the character of that proper responsiveness is due to eccentric features of our kind, we may be inclined to say, with Adams, that good agency is agency that is *for the good*. And so we can criticize action as bad insofar as that action fails to be adequately for the good: either by failing to be sufficiently sensitive to all of the goods that bear on one's action; or by opposing what is good, when, say, one takes as one's object the destruction or impeding of what is good (Adams 1999, pp. 103–4).

Considerations of this sort—all premised, note, on this modified Adamsian account of goodness—are the basis for standard, Thomistic natural law accounts of right action. Human action is humanly good if and only if it constitutes a nondefective response to the goods and bads that bear on that action; otherwise it is bad (3.1). A type of action is wrong if and only if to be an action of that type is to be a bad human action (3.1).

For an action to be bad is for it in some way to be a flawed response to the good. Which such responses are themselves *morally* flawed? Here we need an account of what demarcates the sphere of the moral, and I have no interesting story to offer. (Neither does Aquinas, who doesn't make these distinctions. Adams doesn't have much to say on this demarcation question either.) As I noted above (1.6), I am happy to say that an action is morally wrong if it is practically defective in a distinctively moral way. And I am happy to give what one might call the central case of being defective in the distinctively moral way: the paradigm of going morally wrong is responding in a defective way to those goods the existence and character of which make no essential reference to the agent. (This is not necessarily coextensive with the other-regarding; there may be goods that involve me but the character of the goodness of which does not follow upon their involving me.) When the goods that bear on action do make essential reference to the agent—bearing, say, on the agent's interests, aspirations, relations to others, and so forth—it becomes less than clear whether action that is defective in response to them counts as morally defective. But it is also unclear whether we have any reason to make a sharper demarcation than this between moral and nonmoral considerations.

The moral concurrentist claims that moral necessitation, whether in particular transactions or in moral laws, is immediately explained by both God and creaturely natures. It is not unnatural to think of particular goods as distinct, partial, diverse exemplifications of goodness, different guises under which the good can appear. But if nothing is good but God alone, if God is alone good without qualification, we can see all of the distinct and incommensurable goods that demand a response as participations in the divine goodness; indeed, they demand a response—they morally necessitate our action—just because they are participations in the divine goodness. What makes them distinct is the particular nature of that good. Just as on natural concurrentism all natural necessitation is the push of divine power specified by the nature of the creaturely causal agent, on moral concurrentism all moral necessity is the pull of divine goodness specified by the nature of creatures involved. Above we saw that on Aquinas's concurrentism, the natural order involves both God as universal efficient cause and creatures as "particularizers and determinants" (*Summa Contra Gentiles*, III, 66, [6]); what necessitates an effect in the natural order is this cooperation between God as general efficient cause and the specific character of the creaturely nature (5.5). Aquinas also writes that all creatures have God as their end, but that the manner in which they enjoy that good is diversified by their diverse natures (*Summa Theologiae* IaIIae 1, 8); what necessitates action in the moral order is this cooperation between God as general final cause and the specific character of our creaturely nature.

Now I have made the case for a moral concurrentism by incorporating a theistic account of the good—a modified Adamsian view—with the characteristic natural law account of right action. But, as is clear from above (4.4), Adams rejects this account of right action. He allows that something like this may be the correct account of the goodness or badness of action. To take one extreme example, we can give an account of moral horrors in terms of those actions that are opposed to the good in a certain radical way, what he calls "violating" the good (Adams 1999, p. 107). But he does not take the further step of holding that something's being a moral horror is itself sufficient to make it morally wrong to perform that action, not even pro tanto morally wrong. Why?

There are two distinct reasons that Adams offers for denying that the status of an action as a moral horror is not sufficient to make that action morally wrong. The first is that he thinks simply that the entailment doesn't hold: there are some actions that are morally horrible yet are not themselves morally wrong. I confess to finding Adams's view obscure here. Adams takes a moral horror to be a violation of the image of God, where what bears the image of God is a person. Such violating acts are "attacks" on the person, and they constitute horrors when such attacks are serious and direct (Adams 1999, p. 108). Again, to violate a person is not simply to cross his or her will, however clearly; indeed, in some cases even with another's consent it is possible to violate him or her. There are ways of proceeding against a human person such that they bear—or at least would bear, if the agent were fully aware and intending the action—*hostility* toward the party.

Now, there are disagreements between Adams and standard natural law accounts of the right on a number of points. But here I want to focus on Adams's claim that "More important for excluding the classification of the morally horrible as a species of the wrong is that one can reasonably find an action morally horrible even when one does not believe it to be wrong" (Adams 1999, p. 105). It may be as a matter of conceptual analysis right to hold that the moral horribleness of an action does not entail its moral wrongness—Adams is not, I allow, conceptually confused in holding that the former does not entail the latter. But that is a bad reason for denying the morally horrible is a species of the morally wrong, as whether the morally horrible is a species of the morally wrong depends on (to use Adams's language) what the *nature* of the morally wrong and morally horrible are, as opposed to what the *concepts* of the morally wrong and morally horrible are. The way that Adams characterizes the morally horrible is just the sort of action that fits within standard natural law theory as a clear case of morally wrong action, at least when such action proceeds with full awareness and intention.[10]

Even if the class of morally horrible actions were not wholly included within the class of morally wrong actions, that would not be sufficient to rebut the view that morally horrible actions are pro tanto morally wrong. But Adams offers a second reason to think that the status of an action as a moral horror is not sufficient to make it a moral wrong. It is that a clearer understanding of the nature of deontic properties—properties in the rightness and wrongness family—will enable us to see that there is a gap between an action's being morally horrible and an action's being morally wrong: all such properties in the wrongness family are irreducibly social (Adams 1999, p. 233). As I argued above (4.4), there are some senses in which deontic properties might be thought to be irreducibly social that do not bear scrutiny, and of those that do bear scrutiny, Adams's theological voluntarism is no better equipped to make a start on dealing with them than nonvoluntarist views. But even were one to concede these criticisms of Adams's sociality thesis, one might have doubts as to whether the concurrentist who explains moral necessitation in this natural law way can capture some distinctive features of moral obligation—in particular, that when an action is morally obligatory there is someone who can call for performance (4.4). I make a start on dealing with this objection in 6.5.

What I claim on behalf of this concurrentist account of moral necessitation is that it avoids the explanans- and explanandum-centered objections leveled against standard natural law theories in Chapter 3 and theological voluntarist views in Chapter 4. The explanans-centered objection leveled against natural law theory is that God is not an immediate explainer of moral necessitation. But on this moral concurrentist view, what morally necessitates are goods, and to be good just is (in part) to be a resemblance to God. The explanandum-centered objection leveled against theological voluntarism is that theological voluntarism excludes creaturely natures from having an immediate explanatory role in moral necessitation. But on this moral concurrentist view, what morally necessitates are goods, and to be good just is (in part) to belong to the nondefectiveness conditions for

---

[10] Adams's view could be helped out by the offering of persuasive examples of moral horrors that are not moral wrongs. But I do not see that he gives any.

members of the kind. If, then, this concurrentist account of goodness and its capacity to morally necessitate is defensible, then there is a view that avoids the explanans- and explanandum-focused criticisms of the more traditional moral theories in theistic ethics.

6.4 A theistic moral argument against standard natural law theory, completed

In Chapter 3 (3.8) I began a distinctively theistic moral argument against standard natural law theory that could not be completed until it could be shown that the difficulty I described there could be avoided by some otherwise defensible moral theory. The argument was from divided loyalties: if orthodox theism is true, then one should not divide one's loyalties between God and anything else; if standard natural law theory is true, then one should divide one's loyalties between God and something else; therefore, if orthodox theism is true, then standard natural law theory is false. The idea here is that theism requires not just that God be the being to whom one is most loyal; rather, one should not have any loyalties that can be properly contrasted with loyalty to God. But if there are a variety of goods in the explanation of which God's role is fully mediated, then there will be goods one's loyalty to which can be properly contrasted with loyalty to God.

I hesitated to treat this as a complete argument against standard natural law theory because if no plausible moral theory, theistic or not, avoided the unhappy implication of proper divided loyalties, then we might have good reason to reconsider whether theism really precludes divided loyalty in this sense. But with a concurrentist account of moral necessitation on the table, it is clear that we have a plausible account of the way that created goods can morally necessitate that nevertheless does not hold that the goodness of created goods can be properly contrasted to the divine goodness. For on this concurrentist view, all created goodness is merely a participation in, a resemblance to, God's goodness. One cannot properly contrast the love appropriately given to God and the love appropriately given to created goods if the goodness of created goods is thus derivative of the divine goodness; all love of created goods is, in a way, a love of the divine goodness. This does not entail horrifying instrumentalization or nihilism with respect to created goods, as we worried in 3.8; it does, rather, acknowledge that created goods have their goodness through another.

6.5 Concurrentist moral necessitation and moral obligation

I have held that we can get an account of God's role in the explanation of moral law that honors the explanans-focused constraints by employing the standard natural law defense of moral norms (3.1, 6.3) together with the view that the goodness that morally necessitates is itself a theistic property (6.2). One might object to this natural law account of moral norms in a retail way, arguing that it is unable to provide a defensible account of this or that moral norm; this sort of objection, I think, is best dealt with by presenting a more systematic defense of natural law theory, and I will not undertake that task here. (See Murphy 2001 for one natural law account of practical rationality and natural morality, still undoubtedly underdeveloped.) One might, on the other hand, argue against this view in a wholesale way, claiming that there is something about the structure of natural law explanations of moral law that precludes such views at the outset from having any hope of adequacy. And since I offer a moral concurrentism constructed along natural law lines in order to exhibit the viability of moral concurrentism, marking out a natural law view as in principle hopeless would make trouble for my defense of moral concurrentism.

The first of these objections revisits the discussion of theological voluntarism in Chapter 4. In 4.4 I considered the claim on behalf of theological voluntarism that it has a distinctive advantage: because obligation is an essentially social notion, and moral obligation is just obligation of a moral sort, an account of moral obligation that is built around a social relationship between a God who lays down norms and the people on whom those norms are laid has a leg up from the start. My response was that we need to get clear on what this allegedly social character of obligation amounts to, and that when we get clear on the plausible ways in which obligation is social, theological voluntarism lacks a clear advantage over other views in explaining obligation. But note that I did not there offer any account of moral obligation, whether to deny that it is anything over and above moral necessity, or to affirm that it is something over and above moral necessity, but that it could be explained in the nonvoluntarist terms that I favor. So

I want to turn here to a brief and no doubt inconclusive treatment of the question.

What I conceded in my treatment of Adams's defense of theological voluntarism in 4.4 is that there is some plausibility to the notion that obligation is social in one sense: it may well be that for adherence to some norm to be obligatory, it must be true that there is, at least characteristically, someone who can hold one responsible for adhering to that norm. Adams is not alone in thinking that this is a key point about moral obligation; Stephen Darwall has recently built a Kantian account of moral obligation around it (Darwall 2006). Darwall's discussion bears directly on the sort of natural law account at issue here, and so it is worth inquiring into the strength of that critique and the capacity of a natural law view to answer it.

Darwall allows that it is essential to moral obligation that the action that is morally obligatory be morally necessary—that the agent bound by the moral obligation has decisive reason to perform the action, such that he or she would be rationally deficient by failing to perform it (Darwall 2006, p. 28). But he rejects the view that to show that some way of acting is necessary to properly respond to value, even morally relevant value, is to show that this way of acting is morally obligatory (Darwall 2006, p. 13). To employ Darwall's favorite example—drawn from Hume—what makes it the case that you are violating a moral obligation by standing on my gouty toes (Darwall 2006, p. 5) is not merely that there is impersonal disvalue to the pain caused to me, nor even that I am valuable from some suitably impartial point of view, and thus my foot is a sort of "sacred ground" (Darwall 2006, p. 9) on which others have strong and even decisive reason not to tread. It is crucial that I have a certain sort of standing to hold you responsible for failing to avoid my gouty toes.

I am going to grant all this. It is plausible that there are moral necessities that are not morally obligatory, and it is plausible that the difference-maker is or is somehow related to the existence of someone with standing to hold one responsible for failing to do what is morally necessary. The question is whether there is some obstacle to a moral concurrentist view's providing a route to an account of how one could have the right sort of standing to hold others responsible.

What gives Darwall confidence that a responsiveness-to-value account of moral norms, like the one that I am employing, will fail to do the right work is that he takes the sort of standing to hold others responsible to be the authority to demand that others act a certain way (Darwall 2006, p. 14)—he thinks that this authority is what provides the decisive reason for compliance characteristic of moral obligation—and he thinks that responsiveness-to-value accounts cannot by themselves provide any account of practical authority (Darwall 2006, pp. 11–15). Now, Darwall's defense of the second point is very thin, but I will not dwell on this. I will focus on the former point: it is very implausible to think either that moral obligation is tied to authority to demand or that this authority to demand explains the decisive reason to comply with the morally obligatory norm. Once one thinks of the sort of status connected to moral obligation in more modest terms, we can see how progress could be made on it even in terms of the responsiveness-to-value view of moral norms.

It cannot be that in moral obligations it is the authority of some party to demand that one perform the required action that explains the decisive reason to perform that action (see also Murphy 2011). The presence of my authority to demand that you not ϕ does not, all by itself, establish any such reason for you not to ϕ. That's not the way that authority works. Authority is a *power*, a power to generate new reasons for action by performing the relevant speech acts (Raz 1984, p. 24; Murphy 2002a, pp. 10–12). The mere fact that I have the authority to demand that you not step on my gouty toes does not give you any reason not to step on my gouty toes, any more than the mere fact that the state has the authority to require you not to drive more than 50 miles per hour on the highway gives you a reason not to drive more than 50 miles per hour on the highway. It is not until the state *uses* this authority by promulgating a new traffic law that you have the relevant reason, and on Darwall's view as stated you would not have the relevant reason not to step on my gouty toes until and unless I (or someone else) demand that you not do so. Which would be an absurd view.

Darwall's attempt to explain the reason to conform one's conduct to one's moral obligations in terms of someone's authority to demand a certain sort of treatment is doomed to founder on the plain fact that agents can violate their moral obligations even without anyone's issuing any demands that they act in certain ways.[11] It thus seems to me that what

---

[11] Darwall suggests that we might understand the relevant demands as those made by "the moral community" "implicitly" (Darwall 2006, p. 290 n. 22). I have no sense of how to evaluate the notion that "the moral community"—a community massively extended in space and time, regulated by neither custom nor constitution—demands anything, explicitly or not.

we should say about moral obligation is that there is a norm of conduct to which agents have decisive reason to conform their conduct and to which someone has the standing to *insist* that they do conform. Unlike demanding, insisting presupposes the existence of such a prior norm. (Compare to Kukla and Lance's discussion of the distinction between "alethic" and "constative" holdings; see their 2009, p. 127; see also Little and Macnamara, manuscript.)

Suppose, then, that we take moral obligation to differ from moral necessities more broadly in that when an action is morally obligatory for one to perform, then someone can insist that one perform that action. It is plausible that in explaining why this someone can insist that one perform that action one will advert to the character of the prior norm compliance with which this someone may insist upon. How might such an explanation go?

I suggest that we interpret the "can insist" as the "can, compatibly with the moral necessities bearing on the case." It is not, as Darwall would understand it, that one is somehow normatively empowered, so that one is able to give new reasons for action constituted by one's say-so. It is, rather, that one is practically free to direct others to act in certain ways. One can insist that another act in accordance with some moral necessity if there is reason to do so and no reasons preclude one from doing so. If we are to provide a plausible sketch of those moral necessities that are obligatory and which are not, then, we need some account of the reasons that would enable one to insist on another's acting on a moral necessity and those reasons that might preclude such insisting.

Here is a general reason to insist that others act in accordance with the relevant moral necessities: Insisting that someone do something is a way of seeing to it that he or she do it, and it is good to see to it that what it is morally necessary to do is done, and if something is good to do, then the default setting is that everyone is free to do it. But, of course, there are lots of ways to switch the default setting. There is also general reason not to insist on others' acting in certain ways: it is not an ideal of human relations to be related to one another as insister to insistee. In particular types of case, some actions are so much better to be done without being told to do them that one should not insist. In particular types of case, not being free to insist on some action makes possible a valuable sort of social relationship. Some types of morally necessary actions are so hard for humans to do that insisting that they act upon them would be no more than haranguing to no good end. And so forth. (Such cases are insightfully described and diagnosed in Little and Macnamara, manuscript.)

The idea would be, then, that while it is presumptively good to insist that others act on their moral necessities, there are a number of ways to defeat this presumption in favor of freedom to insist. And without attempting a solution here, one can say that what will determine the shape of what our moral *obligations* are, as opposed to simply the moral *necessities* that we are under, is how likely insisting is to be effective, how difficult the action is, how important it is to the value of the action that it not be subject to insistence, and so forth. Indeed, in thinking from a Darwallian perspective as to how far one's authority to hold others responsible for conduct extends, these are the sorts of considerations that one would appeal to.[12]

One might object to this sketch of an account that it does not capture the *reason-giving* force of insistence. On the view that I have described, insisting that others perform some action need not give new normative reasons to comply with the moral law; what it gives may be simply new motivation to act on prior moral necessities, or clearer awareness of what moral necessities there are. But, one might object, when another insists that one perform some action, even if there is a prior binding norm of action, the fact of insistence is itself a reason for compliance. I simply deny this. In some cases the insistence will be a new reason, in some cases not; this is a contingent matter. When I drive down the highway and I see a billboard from Mothers Against Drunk Driving that insists that I not drink and drive, I may gain new resolution not to drive while drinking. But I would not say that I have a new good reason for not drinking and driving. On the other hand, I may inhabit a community in which there are fairly clear and well-structured norms regarding who is entitled to insist on compliance with moral norms from whomever else, and it may be that

---

[12] Here I am indebted to Coleen Macnamara's dissertation work (Macnamara 2006) on holding responsible (some of which can be found in Macnamara 2009), where she discusses helpfully what she calls "legitimacy" and "permissibility" conditions on holdings, Michael Ferry's dissertation work on supererogation (Ferry 2007), where he puts a much more sophisticated version of these very crude thoughts to work to give an account of the supererogatory in terms of what is morally necessary but not morally obligatory, and Macnamara's work with Margaret Little describing the space within the deontic occupied by the obligatory in great detail but in an "ecumenical" way distinct from an account of how the normative statuses involved in these descriptions are to be justified. I think that these writers would reject my suggestion that the standing to insist can be understood in terms of responsiveness-to-value considerations.

those norms themselves bear the sort of authority that make the facts of insistence new good reasons for acting. Or I may inhabit a special relationship within which some party's insistence counts as a good reason to perform the action insisted upon. But this would be a contingent matter.

One might claim, alternatively, that even if insisting might well fail to give rise to new reasons for action, what that shows is that explaining moral obligation in terms of standing to insist is not the right way to go. But I reject the view that being able to make new reasons through one's insisting is some sort of adequacy condition to serve as part of a theory of moral obligation. Here is a way to think about this. To be a moral obligation, I am willing to allow, is to be something that it is morally necessary that one do and, as a result of this necessity, others are justified in insisting that one do. Suppose that we consider three groups of moral necessities: those that others are not justified in insisting that I perform; those that others are justified in insisting that I perform but do not have the normative power to give me new reasons for performing; and those that others are justified in insisting that I perform and have the normative power to give me new reasons for performing. There is no dispute between Darwall and me about refraining from labeling as moral obligations norms in the first group; the disagreement is that he is committed to denying, and I am committed to affirming, that those in the second group constitute obligations. But what reasons could one have for treating norms in the third group, but not the second, as instances of "moral necessities that others may hold one responsible for complying with"? I have interpreted the "may" as the may of practical permissibility, and that view allows for a coherent account of moral obligation in terms of what one may do to respond properly to value. I do not see what nonarbitrary basis one has to hold to a conception in which the standing to insist that is essential to moral obligation involves a normative power rather than a permission.

One might also object that there is far too much vagueness here: given the various sorts and strengths of the reasons involved, even if this sketch of how one has standing to insist were on the right track, it is pretty clear that there would be a great deal of indeterminacy as to when parties may insist on compliance. And that is not all. What do we want to say about who, precisely, must have the standing to insist on compliance in order for the norm to be morally obligatory? Again, I deny that this is an objection; what it brings out is the extent to which moral obligation exhibits the sort of vagueness that calls for social specification. Natural law theorists have made a big deal out of this sort of specification in civil law (Finnis 1980, pp. 284–90, and Murphy 2006, pp. 112–20), but of course specification of natural norms is not restricted to that which takes place in and through legal institutions; it can be a matter of custom, or social norms more generally (Richardson 1999).

This is of course far too sketchy to be taken as anything close to the final word on what a defender of a responsiveness-to-value theorist like the moral concurrentist would want to say about the character of moral obligation. The point of going into even this level of detail is to answer the objection that these sorts of views must be at best radically incomplete or at worst just wrongheaded because they are unable to make progress toward an adequate account of moral obligation. I say that the considerations that I have raised put the lie to that charge: there is no basis for claiming that no progress can be made toward an account of moral obligation, even if we accept these particular Adams/Darwall points about obligation's not being simply moral necessity and its involving a certain kind of sociality.

6.6 Concurrentist moral necessitation and the "immoralities of the patriarchs"

The second wholesale objection to the approach to theistic explanation of moral law defended in this book appeals to certain highly unusual putative moral facts and the sort of theoretical machinery that must be put into place in order to explain them.

It is useful to begin with a comparison case. In considering the various accounts of God's relationship to the laws of nature, we noted that one of the considerations central in shaping and evaluating such accounts is the treatments of miracles that they are capable of providing. While it does seem that adherence to mere theism does obviously commit one to the possibility of divine action in the natural world in the interstices of the laws of nature, it does not seem that such adherence on its own straightforwardly[13] commits one to the possibility of contrary-to-nature

---

[13] If theism does commit one to the possibility of miracles in this strong sense, it is only by way of considerations of the sort raised in 0.2 and 2.4—that God's sovereignty precludes an inability to exercise that sort of control over the natural operations of creatures.

MORAL CONCURRENTISM 173

miracles—e.g. Shadrach, Meschach, and Abednego being placed in the fiery furnace while failing to be burned (Daniel 3:1–97). One might hold that given a strongly necessitarian view of the causal powers of created things and the conditions in which those powers are exercised, the correct view of the relation of God to those natures entails that contrary-to-nature miracles are metaphysically impossible (Harré and Madden 1975, pp. 45–6) and so outside the scope of divine power.

Nevertheless, orthodox theists coming of the Abrahamic faiths have typically been concerned to exhibit the possibility of contrary-to-nature miracles, given that the possibility, and indeed the actuality, of such miracles is part and parcel of their religious traditions. And as we saw the occasionalists have something to say on this issue. For the most straightforward account of the possibility of the miraculous is occasionalism. The argument is obvious. On the occasionalist view, the active cause of anything's happening in the natural order—say, Shadrach's, Meschach's, and Abednego's flesh undergoing a certain chemical change—is the divine will; God wills generally that, in the presence of fire, flesh undergo that change. There is nothing native to the fire that God has to somehow short-circuit or undercut or thwart in order to ensure the non-burning of the three in the fiery furnace. Instead, we can say that God's policy regarding fire and changes in flesh is God's standard policy, but subject to overriding at the divine pleasure, just as my habit of having coffee first thing in the morning is standard but subject to overriding at my will. And so the occasionalist holds that this view has an extremely plausible account of how the possibility of miracles is to be explained, and it seems implausible that any view that places some such native power in (e.g.) the fire and the flesh will be able to give as satisfactory an account.

The reason that we return to this issue when one might have thought that we had left matters regarding God and the laws of nature safely behind is that just as there is a tight structural similarity between issues regarding God's relationship to the laws of nature and God's relationship to the moral law, there is a tight similarity between this occasionalist argument for its view in terms of miracles and a theological voluntarist argument for its view in terms of what we might call *moral* miracles. Consider in this regard an unadorned, unqualified interpretation of the story of Abraham and Isaac. God commands Abraham to take Isaac to the land of Moriah and there to make a burnt offering of him. Abraham does as the Lord commands: he has Isaac accompany him to Moriah; he binds him; and he raises his knife to slay his son. At this point in the story, Abraham seems clearly to have the intention to place the knife into his son in order to kill him; it seems that if he lacked that intention, he would not be carrying out the command that God had given him. It thus appears that Abraham has violated the natural law prohibition on murder, and thus has done that which he ought not to have done. But Abraham was not guilty of a foul moral crime; he was guiltless and upright. How is this remarkable fact to be explained?

Quinn has called cases of this sort that appear in scripture instances of the "immoralities of the patriarchs" (Quinn 1992)—a label offered tongue-in-cheek, for on Quinn's view, the actions performed in these cases are not immoralities at all, properly speaking. A situation is a case of the immoralities of the patriarchs, or, as I shall say, an IP case, if the following holds: (1) God commands agent S to perform an act of ϕ-ing; (2) in ϕ-ing, S does not act wrongly; and (3) had God not commanded S to perform an act of ϕ-ing, S would have acted wrongly, even extremely wrongly, had S performed an act of ϕ-ing.[14]

Now, it is clear how theological voluntarism could offer an explanation of the possibility of IP cases along the lines of the occasionalist explanation of the possibility of contrary-to-nature miracles. According to that theological voluntarism, the active cause of the wrongfulness of killing is the divine will. Since this is the case, there is nothing in the way of God's will regarding the moral status of acts of killing being different on a particular occasion—that while God's typical will brings about the moral necessity of refraining from killing, God might freely will on some given occasion in a way that not only fails to result in the moral necessity of refraining from killing but even results in the moral necessity of killing. Thus, on theological voluntarism, it is possible for killing to be generally wrong yet in Abraham's case the killing of Isaac was not wrong—indeed, it was right.

I think that the appeal to IP cases should have very little clout as a reason to reject moral concurrentism. Here is what I do allow: it does seem to me that it is harder to provide an adequate account of IP cases within moral concurrentism than it is to provide an adequate account of miracles within natural concurrentism. The occasionalist provides a very strong accommodation of the miraculous; but the natural concurrentist provides just as

---

[14] Other often-cited instances of IP cases include the cases of Hosea's marrying "a wife of fornications" (Hosea 1:2) and the Israelites' despoiling the Egyptians (Exodus 12:35).

strong an accommodation of the miraculous. By contrast, the moral concurrentist has to make some trickier, less obviously plausible moves in order to fend off the IP cases. But this is not an objection to moral concurrentism, because all plausible views, even voluntarist ones, have trouble with IP cases. So there is no clear basis for rejecting moral concurrentism on account of the possibility of IP cases.

Suppose we were to follow the most obvious strategy and just try to adapt the concurrentist account of miracles, which I have claimed to be adequate, into a moral concurrentist account of IP cases. The concurrentist account of miracles trades on the fact that necessitation in the natural order is always a matter of cooperation between God's general causal power and the particular creaturely dispositions. Now, the concurrentist can hold that God's efficient causation is typically free: it is up to the divine discretion whether to cooperate with any given creature in any given transaction in the natural order, and it seems that there might be good reason to refrain from cooperating with some such transactions and not decisive reason not to so refrain. The result is that, even if the natures of creatures have their causal dispositions essentially, the activities of those dispositions can fail to be elicited so long as God refrains from making God's contribution to the typical effect. Without ceasing to be fire, fire can fail to burn, if God withholds God's general concurrence. So it can be simply literally true that Shadrach, Meschach, and Abednego were placed in the fire in the furnace, and yet the fire failed to burn them.

Attractive as this strategy is, we cannot appeal to it in order to provide a moral concurrentist account of IP cases. The explanation of miracles that is specific to concurrentism is that God withholds in a particular case the general causal contribution necessary for the production of any effect by a natural agent. Now, moral concurrentism holds that particular goods are such in virtue of the general goodness of God and the particular nature of the good that specifies God's goodness (6.1). If moral concurrentism is to provide an account of IP cases analogous to concurrentism's treatment of the miraculous, one must hold that in particular cases God's general contribution to the goodness of a particular good is withheld. In the case of Abraham and Isaac, what this would amount to is that Isaac's living, a good against which Abraham intended to act, was not good in that case because God withdrew His general contribution to its goodness. But (putting to the side for the moment the fact that this view seems, in the concrete case of Abraham and Isaac, terrifically implausible), it cannot be the correct explanation due to a disanalogy between natural concurrentism and moral concurrentism. Natural concurrentism is a doctrine about efficient causation. The miraculous is explicable in concurrentist terms because whether God causes anything efficiently is supposed to be a matter for God's free choice. But moral concurrentism is not framed in terms of God's *efficient* causation but rather in terms of God's *final* causation. And this is not a matter about which God is free: God is Goodness, God has no choice about whether God is the ultimate end of all things; God's nature sets, of necessity, the measure for goodness, and it is not up to divine discretion whether God contributes to the being good of some particular being (so long as that being exists and bears that nature).

So one might think that there is an important difference here. One might think that while natural concurrentism bears no interesting disadvantage vis-à-vis occasionalism in the explaining of miracles, this disanalogy between natural and moral concurrentism results in moral concurrentism's bearing an interesting disadvantage vis-à-vis theological voluntarism in the explaining of IP cases. But this turns out not to be the case.

There is, I allow, a sort of theological voluntarism that would have no difficulty with IP cases. If a theological voluntarist held that, say, God's conduct were not necessarily regulated by God in light of the value of the created things to which His commands bore relevance, or that the value of created things were fixed by God's arbitrary will, then IP cases would be easy to handle. For there would be nothing that would call into question the genuine possibility of God's having the relevant will that makes morally necessary something contrary to the ordinary course of moral matters. If the value of created things were simply an issue for created agents, and not for God, or if the value of created things were logically posterior to the arbitrary divine will, then we would accept without cavil that God could indeed make right, via a difference in the divine will from what is usual, the killing of Isaac.

But as was made clear in Chapter 4, theological voluntarism has, in its most plausible forms, rejected both of these theses, holding that God's will is responsive to the goodness of created things, which in turn can result in the impossibility of God's commanding certain actions in certain circumstances (4.3). Indeed, many theological voluntarists, in order to avoid worries about the contingency of morality, have held that God *necessarily* wills into being a variety of moral necessities (necessarily, that is, given the existence of created beings of particular kinds). Theological voluntarists of this stripe cannot affirm without difficulty the standard theological voluntarist appeal to the immoralities of the patriarchs.

Further evidence for this conclusion comes from an examination of Adams's treatment of IP cases. Adams himself comes to the conclusion that we have strong reason to believe that Abraham received no such command, and that we should reject the literal truth of the depiction of the sacrifice of Isaac as a result (Adams 1999, pp. 284–91). Adams's assessment is based on the evils that are involved in such a command, and how the command seems to fit badly with God's role as a perfectly loving and wise authority over us. There is, then, no easy route to the exhibition of the possibility of IP cases just from the affirmation of a voluntarist account of moral necessitation.[15]

Suppose, though, that, unlike Adams, one takes this sort of IP case to be something to be acknowledged and explained rather than to be, upon reflection, rejected as false. I say that at this point there is no longer a dialectical advantage held by the theological voluntarist over the moral concurrentist; what we have is a case in which the voluntarist, concurrentist, and indeed standard natural law theorist have a common interest in exhibiting the possibility of IP cases. So what resources are there to exhibit such possibility?

Recall that moral necessitation can be defeasible (1.5). So while it is possible that some good morally necessitates in standard circumstances, that good fails to morally necessitate in nonstandard circumstances. Of course these nonstandard circumstances cannot include God's withholding normative concurrence from some good. But there are other sorts of circumstances in which goods may fail to morally necessitate.

I am going to mention only two here. Any plausible condition that precludes a good that typically morally necessitates from morally necessitating will have to be something that makes it the case that a different agential response to that good is called for. This will be something that bears on the relevant features of action: intention, motive, and so forth.

---

[15] As I noted above, Hare makes such an appeal (2001, pp. 68–9), but he also alters the circumstances causally through divine power rather simply normatively via the giving of the command. The moral concurrentist might well agree that were the circumstances so changed, then the action would not even be seriously wrong in the absence of a divine command, and thus we lack a true IP case.

Now, here is one straightforward way that one might argue for the defeasibility of some particular moral necessitation: if some greater good morally necessitates an action incompatible with it. So suppose that obedience to God is a greater good than, say, remaining alive; obedience to God might be a good that morally necessitates compliance and defeats any incompatible instance of would-be moral necessitation. This is a solution that is available to concurrentist, voluntarist, or standard natural law theorist. If obedience to God is a great good, then God in making an occasion of action one on which action can satisfy that description can defeat any moral necessitation that would make ineligible rival possibilities for action. (See also Wainwright 2005, pp. 131–2.)

I put forward this solution not because I am happy with it, but because it is obvious. I am not happy with it because I reject the structure of moral necessitation that it presupposes (in which putatively greater goods can simply defeat erstwhile moral necessitation). Here is an alternative. Suppose that one holds that, say, it is typically morally necessary that a human not kill an innocent human; that this necessitation occurs via the character of the good of human life, and is not subject to defeat from rival goods. One might nevertheless hold that this moral necessity is defeasible, not by transforming the act of a human's killing of an innocent into something morally licit, but by transforming the circumstances so that it is improper simply to characterize the action as *a human's* doing the killing.

The basic idea is due to Aquinas's account of IP cases (here I closely follow Lee 1981). On this view, the moral absolutes implied by his natural law theory are not in any way suspended by the divine will in IP cases; rather, the divine command presents a circumstance capable of changing the nature of the act so that it does not run afoul of the absolute. The relevant change in circumstance is that the fact of divine command enables one to act as God's *agent*.

The idea is familiar. Suppose that I have a prima facie obligation not to discipline other people's children. On some occasion, though, I might be authorized to discipline some other person's child, and in disciplining that child I would be violating no obligation. It is not that I am released from my obligation not to discipline the child: the parent that authorizes my disciplining his or her child has no control over whether I am bound by that obligation. It is not that some other obligation overrides the prima facie obligation not to discipline the child: for authorization need not place me under any obligation at all. Rather, my being authorized involves my acting *in the place of another*, so that I am no longer under the normative constraint that I would be under were I to act on my own behalf.

The general solution to IP cases, on this view, is the following: that certain actions are not morally out of bounds for God; that God can make an individual human His agent for the performance of some of these actions; and that when one makes another his or her agent in the performance of an act that one is morally permitted to perform, then one's agent is morally permitted to perform that action.[16] This is, on one highly plausible interpretation, the sort of account that Aquinas puts forward to explain the case of Abraham and Isaac.

> All men alike, both guilty and innocent, die the death of nature, which death of nature is inflicted by the power of God on account of original sin.... Consequently, by the command of God, death can be inflicted on any man, guilty or innocent, without any injustice whatever. (*Summa Theologiae* IaIIae 94, 5 ad 2)

Given that God would act justly in putting Isaac to death on account of original sin, and that Abraham was made God's agent in this case by God's command, then if Abraham performed that act under the description "carrying out God's plan in His stead" then Abraham would have been morally blameless. For the act that he performed differed from an act of murder in the same way that a public executioner's act differs from an act of murder. In both cases, the person performing the act is authorized by an entity that is (by hypothesis) morally permitted to perform that act.

To this point, then, I have simply followed Aquinas. Now, I don't know what to think about the morally permissible purpose—the punishment of Isaac—that Aquinas ascribes to God in these cases. But it seems to me that we need not settle on any particular account of God's purposes in order to see the force of this sort of solution. So long as we are convinced of God's perfect goodness, we can be confident that there is some such purpose; and if there is some such purpose, then we can explain how IP cases could be explained within a moral concurrentist account of moral necessitation. Indeed, we may wonder whether there is any good reason to suppose that we can grasp the value of the divine purposes and the content

---

[16] I of course am not claiming that one can make another his or her agent with regard to every action that one is morally permitted to perform. I do think, though, that when one cannot make another his or her agent there is a special reason why this is true, that there is a reason for a person to perform that action one his or her own, or that there is a reason why the would-be agent should not be authorized to perform that action.

of the norms applying to God's conduct that justify our actions in certain IP cases (see, for example, Bergmann 2009). At the very least, it is clear that we now lack any adequate theory of divine ethics that would enable us to form much in the way of justified judgments in these cases.

As with the discussion of moral obligation above (6.5), the point of giving this account is not to give the last word on the best way to deal with a difficulty for moral concurrentism. The aim is to deal with the objection that there is no room within this view to accommodate a certain moral phenomenon. But the existence of live strategies shows that this objection is mistaken.

6.7 Explanans- and explanandum-centered success

Standard natural law theory is correct to claim that the goods that fulfill human persons specify the moral requirements that bind us, and that the goods that require of me responses of promotion and respect are fixed by the kind of being that you are. That your good includes life explains why I must not kill or assault you; that it includes knowledge explains why I must not lie to you; and so forth. But that your good morally necessitates a certain response from me does not mean that this normative transaction is entirely between us. For your good has its goodness as a participation in the divine goodness. And theological voluntarism is correct that no normative necessitation occurs without divine involvement. But that divine involvement need not be an act of divine will, but rather the participation in the divine goodness in which all human goodness consists. Moral concurrentism, unlike its rivals, can claim both explanans-centered and explanandum-centered success. It thus has the best claim to be the true theistic explanation of moral law.

References

Citations in the text are to author and date of publication except in the case of pre 20th-century works, which are cited by title.

Adams, Robert M. 1973. "A Modified Divine Command Conception of Ethical Wrongness." Reprinted in Adams 1987a, pp. 97–122.
Adams, Robert M. 1979a. "Divine Command Metaethics Modified Again." Reprinted in Adams 1987a, pp. 128–43.
Adams, Robert M. 1979b. "Moral Arguments for Theistic Belief." Reprinted in Adams 1987a, pp. 144–63.
Adams, Robert M. 1987a. *The Virtue of Faith and Other Essays in Philosophical Theology.* Oxford University Press.
Adams, Robert M. 1987b. "Divine Commands and the Social Nature of Obligation." *Faith and Philosophy* 4, pp. 262–75.
Adams, Robert M. 1999. *Finite and Infinite Goods: A Framework for Ethics.* Oxford University Press.
Alston, William P. 1990. "Some Suggestions for Divine Command Theorists." In Beaty 1990, pp. 303–26.
Alston, William P. 1999. *Illocutionary Acts and Sentence Meaning.* Cornell University Press.
Anscombe, G. E. M. 1958. "Modern Moral Philosophy." *Philosophy* 33, pp. 1–19. Cited to the version reprinted in Anscombe 1981, pp. 26–42.
Anscombe, G. E. M. 1981. *Ethics, Religion, and Politics.* University of Minnesota Press.
Antony, Louise. 2008. "Atheism as Perfect Piety." In Garcia and King 2008, pp. 67–84.
Aquinas, Thomas. 1975 [composed c. 1261–1264]. *Summa Contra Gentiles.* Trans. Anton Pegis. University of Notre Dame Press. References given by book, chapter, and section number.
Aquinas, Thomas. 1981 [composed c. 1265–1274]. *Summa Theologiae.* Trans. Fathers of the English Dominican Province. Christian Classics. References given by part, question, and article number.
Aquinas, Thomas. 2009 [composed c. 1273]. *Compendium of Theology.* Trans. Richard Regan. Oxford University Press. References given by chapter number.
Armstrong, David M. 1983. *What is a Law of Nature?* Cambridge University Press.
Armstrong, David M. 1993. "The Identification Problem and the Inference Problem." *Philosophy and Phenomenological Research* 53, pp. 421–2.

Audi, Robert and Wainwright, William, eds. 1986. *Rationality, Religious Belief, and Moral Commitment*. Cornell University Press.

Austin, John. 1995 [first published 1832]. *Province of Jurisprudence Determined*. Ed. Wilfrid Rumble. Cambridge University Press.

Avicenna. 2005 [first published 1027]. *The Metaphysics of the Healing*. Trans. Michael Marmura. Brigham Young University Press.

Beaty, Michael, ed. 1990. *Christian Theism and the Problems of Philosophy*. University of Notre Dame Press.

Bedau, Mark. 1992a. "Goal-Directed Systems and the Good." *The Monist* 75, pp. 34–49.

Bedau, Mark. 1992b. "Where's the Good in Teleology?" *Philosophy and Phenomenological Research* 52, pp. 781–806.

Beebee, Helen. 2000. "The Non-Governing Conception of Laws of Nature." In Carroll 2004, pp. 250–76.

Bergmann, Michael. 2009. "Skeptical Theism and the Problem of Evil." In Flint and Rea 2009, pp. 374–99.

Bergmann, Michael, Murray, Michael, and Rea, Michael, eds. 2011. *Divine Evil?* Oxford University Press.

Bird, Alexander. 2001. "Necessarily, Salt Dissolves in Water." *Analysis* 61, pp. 267–74.

Bird, Alexander. 2002. "On Whether Some Laws are Necessary." *Analysis* 62, pp. 257–70.

Bird, Alexander. 2005. "The Dispositionalist Conception of Laws." *Foundations of Science* 10, pp. 353–70.

Bird, Alexander. 2007. *Nature's Metaphysics: Laws and Properties*. Oxford University Press.

Boyd, Richard. 1988. "How to Be a Moral Realist." In Sayre-McCord 1988, pp. 185–228.

Brink, David O. 2007. "The Autonomy of Ethics." In Martin 2007, pp. 149–65.

Carroll, John W., ed. 2004. *Readings on Laws of Nature*. University of Pittsburgh Press.

Chandler, John. 1985. "Divine Command Theories and the Appeal to Love." *American Philosophical Quarterly* 22, pp. 231–9.

Chappell, T. D. J. 1995. *Understanding Human Goods*. Edinburgh University Press.

Clark, Stephen R. L. 1982. "God's Law and Morality." *Philosophical Quarterly* 32, pp. 339–47.

Cohen, Jonathan and Callendar, Craig. 2009. "A Better Best System Account of Lawhood." *Philosophical Studies* 145, pp. 1–34.

Crisp, Oliver D., and Rea, Michael C., eds. 2009. *Analytic Theology: New Essays in the Philosophy of Theology*. Oxford University Press.

Cudworth, Ralph. 1996 [first published 1731]. *A Treatise Concerning Eternal and Immutable Morality*. Cambridge University Press.

Darwall, Stephen L. 2006. *The Second-Person Standpoint: Morality, Respect, and Accountability*. Harvard University Press.

Dawes, Gregory. 2009. *Theism and Explanation*. Routledge.

Diamond, Cora. 1988. "The Dog That Gave Himself the Moral Law." *Midwest Studies in Philosophy* 13, pp. 161–79.

Donagan, Alan. 1977. *The Theory of Morality*. University of Chicago Press.

Dretske, Fred I. 1977. "Laws of Nature." Reprinted in Carroll 2004, pp. 16–37.

Evans, C. Stephen. 2004. *Kierkegaard's Ethic of Love: Divine Commands and Moral Obligations*. Oxford University Press.

Ferry, Michael. 2007. *Beyond Obligation: Reasons, Demands and the Problem of Supererogation*. Dissertation at Georgetown University.

Fine, Kit. 2002. "The Varieties of Necessity." In Fine 2005, pp. 235–60.

Fine, Kit. 2005. *Modality and Tense*. Oxford University Press.

Finnis, John. 1980. *Natural Law and Natural Rights*. Oxford University Press.

Flint, Thomas P. and Rea, Michael C. 2009. *Oxford Handbook of Philosophical Theology*. Oxford University Press.

Foot, Philippa. 2001. *Natural Goodness*. Oxford University Press.

Foster, John. 2004. *The Divine Lawmaker*. Oxford University Press.

Freddoso, Alfred. 1986. "The Necessity of Nature." *Midwest Studies in Philosophy* 11, pp. 215–42.

Freddoso, Alfred. 1988. "Medieval Aristotelianism and the Case against Secondary Causation in Nature." In Morris 1988, pp. 74–118.

Freddoso, Alfred. 1991. "God's General Concurrence with Secondary Causes: Why Conservation is Not Enough." *Philosophical Perspectives* 5, pp. 553–85.

Freddoso, Alfred. 1994. "God's General Concurrence with Secondary Causes: Pitfalls and Prospects." *American Catholic Philosophical Quarterly* 67, pp. 131–56.

Garcia, Robert and King, Nathan, eds. 2008. *Is Goodness without God Good Enough?* Rowman and Littlefield.

Geach, P. T. 1956. "Good and Evil." *Analysis* 17, pp. 32–42.

Gert, Joshua. 2008. "Smith on the Rationality of Immoral Action." *Journal of Ethics* 12, pp. 1–23.

Gomez-Lobo, Alfonso. 2002. *Morality and the Human Goods: An Introduction to Natural Law Ethics*. Georgetown University Press.

Grisez, Germain. 1983. *The Way of the Lord Jesus, Volume 1: Christian Moral Principles*. Franciscan Herald Press.

Grisez, Germain. 1993. *The Way of the Lord Jesus, Volume 2: Living a Christian Life*. Franciscan Herald Press.

Hare, John. 2001. *God's Call*. Eerdmans.

Harré, R. and Madden, E. H. 1975. *Causal Powers: A Theory of Natural Necessity*. Blackwell.
Hart, H. L. A. 1994 [first published 1961]. *The Concept of Law*, 2nd ed. Oxford University Press.
Helm, Paul, ed. 1981. *Divine Commands and Morality*. Oxford University Press.
Hobbes, Thomas. 1994 [first published 1651]. *Leviathan*. Ed. Edwin Curley. Hackett.
Hooker, Brad. 2001. "Cudworth and Quinn." *Analysis* 61, pp. 333–5.
Hubin, Donald. 2008. "Empty and Ultimately Meaningless Gestures?" In Garcia and King 2008, pp. 133–66.
Idziak, Janine Marie, ed. 1979. *Divine Command Morality*. Edwin Mellen.
Jackson, Frank. 1998. *From Metaphysics to Ethics: A Defence of Conceptual Analysis*. Oxford University Press.
Kain, Patrick. 2006. "Realism and Anti-Realism in Kant's Second Critique." *Philosophy Compass* 1, pp. 449–65.
Keller, Simon. 2007. "Virtue Ethics is Self-Effacing." *Australasian Journal of Philosophy* 85, pp. 221–31.
Kim, Jaegwon. 1993a. *Supervenience and Mind*. Cambridge University Press.
Kim, Jaegwon. 1993b. "Concepts of Supervenience." In Kim 1993a, pp. 53–78.
Kretzmann, Norman. 1991. "A General Problem of Creation: Why Would God Create Anything at All?" In MacDonald 1991, pp. 208–28.
Kukla, Rebecca and Lance, Mark. 2009. *"Yo!" and "Lo!": The Pragmatic Topography of the Space of Reasons*. Harvard University Press.
Kvanvig, Jonathan and McCann, Hugh. 1988. "Divine Conservation and the Persistence of the World." In Morris 1988, pp 13–49.
LaFollette, Hugh, ed. 1999. *Guide to Ethical Theory*. Blackwell.
Lance, Mark N. and Little, Margaret Olivia. 2006. "Where the Laws Are." *Oxford Studies in Metaethics* 2, pp. 149–71.
Lange, Marc. 2000. *Natural Laws in Scientific Practice*. Oxford University Press.
Layman, C. Stephen. 2002. "God and the Moral Order." *Faith and Philosophy* 19, pp. 304–16.
Lee, Patrick. 1981. "The Permanence of the Ten Commandments: St. Thomas and His Modern Commentators." *Theological Studies* 42, pp. 422–43.
Leftow, Brian. 1990. "Is God an Abstract Object?" *Nous* 24, pp. 581–98.
Leftow, Brian. 2006. "God and the Problem of Universals." *Oxford Studies in Metaphysics* 2, pp. 325–56.
Leibniz, Gottfried Wilhelm von. 1965a. *Monadology and Other Philosophical Essays*, trans. Paul Schrecker and Anne Martin Schrecker. Library of Liberal Arts.
Leibniz, Gottfried Wilhelm von. 1965b [first published 1710]. "A Vindication of God's Justice Reconciled with His Other Perfections and All his Actions." In Leibniz 1965a, pp. 114–47.

Lewis, David. 1973. *Counterfactuals*. Harvard University Press.
Lewis, David. 1983. "New Work for a Theory of Universals." *Australasian Journal of Philosophy* 61, pp. 343–77.
Lewis, David. 1994. "Humean Supervenience Debugged." *Mind* 103, pp. 473–90.
Lisska, Anthony J. 1996. *Aquinas's Theory of Natural Law: An Analytic Reconstruction*. Oxford University Press.
Little, Margaret O. and Macnamara, Coleen. Manuscript. "Between the Obligatory and the Optional."
Loewer, Barry. 1996. "Humean Supervenience." In Carroll 2004, pp. 176–206.
MacDonald, Scott, ed. 1991. *Being and Goodness*. Cornell University Press.
McDonough, Jeffrey. 2007. "Leibniz: Creation and Conservation and Concurrence." *Leibniz Review* 17, pp. 31–60.
MacIntyre, Alasdair. 1999. *Dependent Rational Animals*. Open Court.
Mackie, J. L. 1977. *Ethics: Inventing Right and Wrong*. Penguin.
Macnamara, Coleen. 2006. *Beyond Praise and Blame: Toward a Theory of Holding Others Responsible*. Dissertation at Georgetown University.
Macnamara, Coleen. 2009. "Holding Others Responsible." *Philosophical Studies* 152, pp. 81–102.
Maitzen, Stephen. 2009. "Ordinary Morality Implies Atheism." *European Journal of Philosophy of Religion* 1, pp. 107–26.
Mancha, Louis. 2003. *Concurrentism: A Philosophical Explanation*. Dissertation at the Purdue University Department of Philosophy.
Mann, William. 2005a. *Blackwell Guide to the Philosophy of Religion*. Blackwell.
Mann, William. 2005b. "Theism and the Foundations of Ethics." In Mann 2005a, pp. 283–304.
Martin, Michael, ed. 2007. *Cambridge Companion to Atheism*. Cambridge University Press.
Mavrodes, George. 1986. "Religion and the Queerness of Morality." In Audi and Wainwright 1986, pp. 213–26.
Merricks, Trenton. 2007. *Truth and Ontology*. Oxford University Press.
Mill, John Stuart. 1979 [first published 1861]. *Utilitarianism*. Ed. George Sher. Hackett.
Miller, Christian B. 2009. "Divine Desire Theory and Obligation." In Nagasawa and Wielenberg 2009, pp. 105–24.
Moore, G. E. 1903. *Principia Ethica*. Cambridge University Press.
Morris, Thomas V. 1987a. *Anselmian Explorations: Essays in Philosophical Theology*. University of Notre Dame Press.
Morris, Thomas V. 1987b. "The God of Abraham, Isaac, and Anselm." In Morris 1987a, pp. 10–25.
Morris, Thomas V. 1987c. "Perfect Being Theology." *Nous* 21, pp. 19–30.
Morris, Thomas V., ed. 1988. *Divine and Human Action*. Cornell University Press.

Morriston, Wes. 2009. "What if God Commanded Something Terrible? A Worry for Divine-Command Meta-ethics." *Religious Studies* 45, pp. 249–67.
Murphy, Mark C. 1998. "Divine Command, Divine Will, and Moral Obligation." *Faith and Philosophy* 15, pp. 3–27.
Murphy, Mark C. 2001. *Natural Law and Practical Rationality*. Cambridge University Press.
Murphy, Mark C. 2002a. *An Essay on Divine Authority*. Cornell University Press.
Murphy, Mark C. 2002b. "Theological Voluntarism." *Stanford Enyclopedia of Philosophy*. URL=<http://plato.stanford.edu/entries/voluntarism-theological/>.
Murphy, Mark C. 2002c. "The Natural Law Tradition in Ethics." *The Stanford Encyclopedia of Philosophy*, URL=<http://plato.stanford.edu/archives/win2002/entries/natural-law-ethics/>
Murphy, Mark C. 2006. *Natural Law in Jurisprudence and Politics*. Cambridge University Press.
Murphy, Mark C. 2007. "Finnis on Nature, Reason, God." *Legal Theory* 13, pp. 187–209.
Murphy, Mark C. 2009. "Morality and Divine Authority." In Flint and Rea 2009, pp. 306–31.
Murphy, Mark C. 2011. "God Beyond Justice." In Bergmann, Murray, and Rea 2011, pp. 150–67.
Nagasawa, Yujin, and Wielenberg, Erik J., eds. 2009. *New Waves in Philosophy of Religion*. Palgrave Macmillan.
Plantinga, Alvin. 1974. *God, Freedom, and Evil*. Eerdmans.
Plantinga, Alvin. 1980. *Does God Have a Nature?* Marquette University Press.
Plantinga, Alvin. 1984. "Advice to Christian Philosophers." *Faith and Philosophy* 1, pp. 253–71.
Pruss, Alexander R. 2009. "Another Step in Divine Command Dialectics." *Faith and Philosophy* 26, pp. 432–9.
Quinn, Philip. 1978. *Divine Commands and Moral Requirements*. Oxford University Press.
Quinn, Philip. 1979. "Divine Command Ethics: A Causal Theory." In Idziak 1979, pp. 305–25. Also reprinted in Quinn 2006, pp. 37–52.
Quinn, Philip. 1988. "Divine Conservation, Secondary Causes, and Occasionalism." In Morris 1988, pp. 50–73.
Quinn, Philip. 1990. "An Argument for Divine Command Ethics." In Beaty 1990, pp. 289–302.
Quinn, Philip. 1992. "The Primacy of God's Will in Christian Ethics." *Philosophical Perspectives* 6, pp. 493–513. Also reprinted in Quinn 2006, pp. 53–76.
Quinn, Philip. 1999. "Divine Command Theory." In LaFollette 1999, pp. 53–73.
Quinn, Philip. 2006. *Essays in the Philosophy of Religion*. Oxford University Press.
Rachels, James. 1971. "God and Human Attitudes." In Helm 1981, pp. 34–48.

Raz, Joseph. 1979. *The Authority of Law*. Oxford University Press.
Raz, Joseph. 1984. *The Morality of Freedom*. Oxford University Press.
Richardson, Henry S. 1999. "Institutionally Divided Moral Responsibility." *Social Philosophy and Policy* 16, pp. 218–49.
Rogers, Katherin A. 2000. *Perfect Being Theology*. Edinburgh University Press.
Sayre-McCord, Geoffrey, ed. 1988. *Essays on Moral Realism*. Cornell University Press.
Schroeder, Mark. 2005. "Cudworth and Normative Explanations." *Journal of Ethics and Social Philosophy* 1, pp. 1–27.
Schroeder, Mark. 2008. *Slaves of the Passions*. Oxford University Press.
Searle, John and Vanderveken, Daniel. 1985. *Foundations of Illocutionary Logic*. Cambridge University Press.
Shafer-Landau, Russ. 2003. *Moral Realism: A Defence*. Oxford University Press.
Shapiro, Scott J. 2010. *Legality*. Harvard University Press.
Sidgwick, Henry. 1907. *The Methods of Ethics*, 7th edition. Hackett.
Sinnott-Armstrong, Walter. 2009. *Morality Without God?* Oxford University Press.
Smith, Michael. 1994. *The Moral Problem*. Blackwell.
Suarez, Francisco. 2002 [first published 1597]. *Disputationes Metaphysicae 20–22*. Trans. Alfred Freddoso as *On Creation, Conservation, and Concurrence*. St. Augustine's Press.
Thompson, Michael. 2004. "What is it to Wrong Someone? A Puzzle about Justice." In Wallace, Pettit, Scheffler, and Smith 2004, pp. 333–84.
Thompson, Michael. 2008. *Life and Action: Elementary Structures of Practice and Practical Thought*. Harvard University Press.
Tooley, Michael. 1977. "The Nature of Laws." Reprinted in Carroll 2004, pp. 38–70.
Van Inwagen, Peter. 1995a. *God, Knowledge, and Mystery: Essays in Philosophical Theology*. Cornell University Press.
Van Inwagen, Peter. 1995b. "The Place of Chance in a World Sustained by God." In Van Inwagen 1995a, pp. 42–65.
Van Inwagen, Peter. 2006. *The Problem of Evil*. Oxford University Press.
Wainwright, William J. 2005. *Religion and Morality*. Ashgate.
Wallace, R. Jay, Philip Pettit, Samuel Scheffler, and Michael Smith, eds. 2004. *Reason and Value*. Oxford University Press.
Wielenberg, Erik. 2005. *Virtue and Value in a Godless Universe*. Cambridge University Press.
Wolterstorff, Nicholas. 2009. "How Philosophical Theology Became Possible within the Analytic Tradition of Philosophy." In Crisp and Rea 2009, pp. 155–68.

Index

Adams, Robert M. 3, 100–101, 102, 106
  on goodness 150–64
  on the 'immoralities of the patriarchs' 177
  on the normative formulation of theological voluntarism 113–16
  on obligation 124–32
Alston, William P. 79, 100–101
Anscombe, G. E. M. 14–16, 42
Antony, Louise 2–3
Aquinas, Thomas 5, 64, 67 n. 10, 162
  on concurrence 143–5
  on the 'immoralities of the patriarchs' 178–9
  on natural law as law 77–80
  and standard natural law theory 69–73
Armstrong, David M. 30–5, 39–41, 86, 135–6
Austin, John 131
authority 167–9
Avicenna 48
axiology, *see* goodness

Bedau, Mark 93
Beebee, Helen 23–4
Bergmann, Michael 180
bipolar normativity 126–7
Bird, Alexander 33 n. 11, 142
Boyd, Richard 152–3
Brink, David O. 5–6, 122 n. 7

Callendar, Craig 23
Chandler, John 109
Chappell, T. D. J. 74
Clark, Stephen R. L. 101
Cohen, Jonathan 23
concurrence, moral 148–80
  account of goodness 154–60
  defined 149
  and obligation 166–72
concurrence, natural 142–7
  complementarity model of 145
  instrumentalist model of 144–5
  and miracles 175
conservation 9, 134–7, 139–40
creation ex nihilo 8–10
Cudworth, Ralph 105

Darwall, Stephen L. 37, 125, 167–72
Dawes, Gregory 3 n. 2
defeasibility, *see* laws of nature, defeasibility of
Diamond, Cora 15
divided loyalty argument
  against nontheistic moral theories generally 99
  against standard natural law theory 95–7, 165–6
divine command theory, *see* theological voluntarism
Donagan, Alan 98 n. 6
Dretske, Fred I. 20 n. 2, 30–5, 40, 86, 135–6

ethics, law conception of 15–16
explanation 45–46
  explanandum-driven 1–3, 180
  explanans-driven 3–6, 180
  Standard Model of, *see* Standard Model explanation of moral facts
  theistic, *see* theistic explanation
explanatory completeness 62–3
explanatory immediacy 61–3
Evans, C. Stephen 100–101

facts, moral, *see* moral facts
Ferry, Michael 170 n. 12
Fine, Kit 32, 49
Finnis, John 80–4, 172
Foot, Philippa 71 n. 2
Foster, John 33 n. 8, 138 n. 4
Freddoso, Alfred 62 n. 6, 137–8, 137 n. 2

Geach, P. T. 159
Gert, Joshua 37
God
  as conserver 9
  as creator 8–10
  in moral concurrentism 158–66
  in natural law theory 74
  as perfect being 7–12
  in theological voluntarism 116
  as ultimate explainer 6–12
Gomez-Lobo, Alfonso 74
goodness
  Adams's account of 150–4
  and kind-membership 158–9
  moral concurrentist account of 154–60
  standard natural law account of 71–2, 93–5
Grisez, Germain 73, 74
guilt 131–2

Hare, John 101, 120–1, 141, 177 n. 15
Harré, R. 135, 173
Hart, H. L. A. 127–8, 130–1
Hobbes, Thomas 131
holding responsible 128–31
Hooker, Brad 102
Hubin, Donald 2–3

'immoralities of the patriarchs' cases 141–2, 172–80
  moral concurrentist account of 175–80
  natural law account of 177
  theological voluntarist account of 176–7
intuitionism 98–9

Jackson, Frank 24, 50–1

Kain, Patrick 98 n. 6
Kantianism 98–9
Keller, Simon 17–18
Kim, Jaegwon 50–1
Kretzmann, Norman 48
Kukla, Rebecca 169
Kvanvig, Jonathan 9

Lance, Mark 39–42, 169
Lange, Marc 39

law, moral, *see* moral law
law, natural, *see* natural law theory
laws of nature
  Armstrong-Dretske-Tooley account of 30–5
  concurrentist account of 146–7
  governing accounts of 34
  Lewis's account of 22–7
  mere conservationist account of 134–7, 139–40
  'metaphysical' approach to 39–40
  and necessitation 30–4
  nongoverning accounts of 29–30
  occasionalist account of 119, 137–9, 140–2
  'pragmatic' approach to 39–40
Layman, C. Stephen 2
Lee, Patrick 178
Leftow, Brian 11, 97
Leibniz, Gottfried Wilhelm von 143
Lewis, David 22–7, 30
Lisska, Anthony J. 74, 80, 84–5
Little, Margaret O. 21 n. 3, 39–42, 169–70
Loewer, Barry 23–5, 34, 40 n. 16
loyalty (to God), *see* divided loyalty argument

MacIntyre, Alasdair 72, 74
Mackie, J. L. 21
Macnamara, Coleen 128–9, 169–70
Madden, E. H. 135, 173
Maitzen, Stephen 2–3
Mancha, Louis 137 n. 3
Mann, William 106
Mavrodes, George 2
McCann, Hugh 9
McDonough, Jeffrey 145
mere conservationism 134–7, 139–40
Merricks, Trenton 31
Mill, John Stuart 127
Miller, Christian B. 106
miracles, moral, *see* 'immoralities of the patriarchs' cases
miracles, natural 141, 172–5
monadic normativity 126–7
Moore, G. E. 2, 152
moral concurrentism, *see* concurrentism, moral

INDEX 191

moral contingency 121–4
moral facts 46–7
   as explained by moral laws, 50–1
   as explained only by moral laws, 51–9
   as explanation-eligible 47–9
moral horrors 163–4
moral law
   Anscombe's view of 14–18
   Armstrong/Dretske/Tooley-style theory of 35–8
   as defeasible 39–42
   Lance and Little's theory of 39–41
   Lewis-style theory of 27–30
   and moral generalizations 18–21
moral necessity 36–8, 42–4
   and moral facts 46–7
   and practical necessity 36–7
Morris, Thomas V. 7–9
Morriston, Wes 118

natural law theory 69–99
   defined 70–74
   and divided loyalty argument 95–7
   and divine law 76–80
   as insusceptible to further explanation 90–95
   and mere conservationism 139–40
   on the nature of the good 71–2, 93–5
   as a nontheistic theory 74, 97–99
   and obligation 77–8
   and theism in the explanatory background 80–5
   and theistic immediacy 88–90
necessitarianism (about creation) 47–8
necessitation
   in laws of nature 30–4
   in moral law 35–38, 71, 110–12, 114, 161–2

obligation
   in moral concurrentism 166–72
   in natural law theory 77–78
   in theological voluntarism 124–132
occasionalism 119, 137–9, 140–2
Open Question argument 152

perfect being theology 7–12
   and conservation 9
   and creation ex nihilo 8–10

   and God's explanatory role 7–12, 108–10
   and divine sovereignty 10–12
Plantinga, Alvin 2 n. 1, 10, 121 n. 6
Pruss, Alexander R. 117

Quinn, Philip 100–101, 106–13, 131, 141–2, 174

Rachels, James 108 n. 2
Raz, Joseph 17, 168
reasons
   content-independent 15–17
   Standard Model explanation of 51–4, 58
Richardson, Henry S. 172
Rogers, Katherin A. 7
rule-utilitarianism 17
rules of thumb 28

sanctions 127–8
Schroeder, Mark 3 n. 2, 51–8, 104–105, 150, 153 n. 5
Searle, John 79
selection, *see* necessitation
Shafer-Landau, Russ 19
Shapiro, Scott J. 127–8
Sidgwick, Henry 2, 28 n. 6
Sinnott-Armstrong, Walter 5–6
Smith, Michael 37, 50, 152, 153 n. 5
sovereignty 10–12, 108–10
specification (of moral norms) 171–2
Standard Model explanation of moral facts 51–9, 104
   criticized 54–6
Suarez, Francisco 63 n. 7
supervenience 50–1
systems account of laws of nature, *see* laws of nature, Lewis account of

theistic explanation 60–8
   and sovereignty 64–8
   and theistic completeness 62–3
   and theistic immediacy 61–8
theological voluntarism 100–132
   arbitrariness argument against 102–05
   causal version of (Quinn's view) 107–13

theological voluntarism (*Continued*)
  defined 100
  divine goodness argument
    against 101–02
  explanandum-centered objections
    to 116–21
  explanans-centered objections
    to 121–4
  as an explanation of moral facts 100–101
  as an explanation of obligation 124–32
  normative version of (Adams's
    view) 113–116
  and occasionalism 140–2
Thompson, Michael 116–17, 159 n. 9

Tooley, Michael 30–5, 86, 135–6

universals account of laws of nature, *see*
  laws of nature, Armstrong/
  Dretske/Tooley account of
utilitarianism 98–9

Vanderveken, Daniel 79
Van Inwagen, Peter 8–9, 134–6
virtue theory 98–9

Wainwright, William J. 47, 100–101
Wielenberg, Erik 47, 117
Wolterstorff, Nicholas 2 n. 1